Daughters of Courage

Kathryn

DONNA FLETCHER CROW

MOODY PRESS
CHICAGO

ISBN: 0-8024-4527-6

3 5 7 9 10 8 6 4

Printed in the United States of America

To the memory of my grandparents,
Esther and Clarence Fletcher,
and
Tennie and John Book
and all the hardy Kuna pioneers

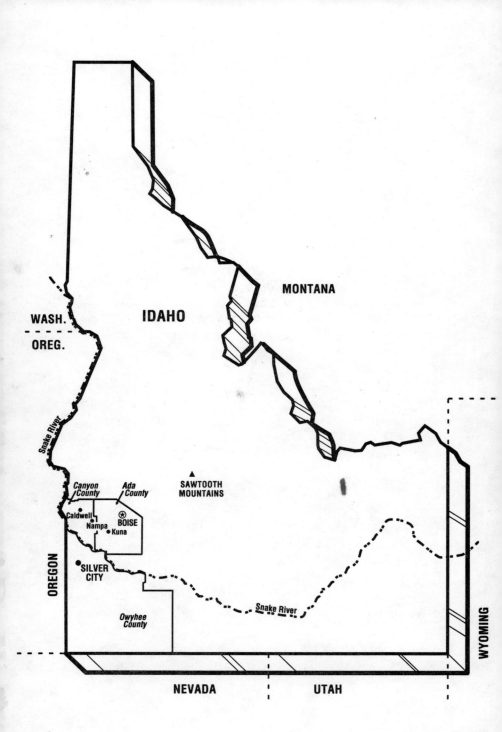

1

"But Papa, it's all brown!"

Seventeen-year-old Kathryn Esther Jayne stepped off the train and looked around her at the desolate, flat land covered with scrubby, knee-high bushes the color of greasy dishwater.

Adam Jayne flicked the dust off his almost-black mustache, which contrasted oddly with his brown hair. "That's why we've come here, my girl. Your Uncle Isaiah says this is the land of opportunity. With this new Reclamation Act Congress just passed they'll be building dams and canals all over. In no time at all the desert will be blossoming like a rose—just like it says in the Good Book."

The train blew a great cloud of steam and chugged noisily on down the track, leaving Kathryn and her papa deserted beside the unpainted wooden shack that served as a station and storage shed. It was the only building in sight.

When the Oregon Shortline train was far enough down the track that she could be heard, Kathryn shook her head. "Blossom as a rose? Those aren't rose bushes. What is that awful stuff?"

Adam Jayne swept the desert with his arm. "Sagebrush. You've just come through about a thousand miles of it on the train."

"Yes, but I didn't think I'd have to *live* in it." She stared at the empty sweep of land. There was nothing but sagebrush as far as she could see until a line of blue mountains broke the skyline about twenty miles away. Kathryn sighed. She had wanted only two things in her life—beauty and God's will. But the two always seemed to be in conflict. Her mother had been beautiful—so people said—but Kathryn had no memory of her. And the Lord certainly hadn't seen fit that Kathryn should inherit her beauty. Even on the empty platform Kathryn ducked her head at the thought of the square jaw she hated to see in the mirror.

Their home in Edgar, Nebraska, had had beauty— green prairie farms, trees along the Little Blue River, and only last summer she had achieved her greatest delight— three rose bushes bloomed in the yard of their white frame house. But God had seen fit to lead them here—surely the ugliest, driest spot in all His creation.

Why, Lord? she asked, looking at the endless brown dirt.

And God, as He unfailingly did, answered her through Scripture her papa had taught her: *Wait on the Lord: be of good courage, and He shall strengthen thine heart. Wait, I say, on the Lord.*

Kathryn felt a warmth and a relaxing inside, knowing that God had answered. And yet she was dismayed. She hated waiting. But it seemed she had little choice. "Where's Uncle Isaiah? I thought he and Aunt Thelma would be here to meet us."

Adam pushed his flat-brimmed, black hat back on his head and scratched his thin, pale brown hair—a feature his daughter had inherited. "Well, I thought so too. Something must've come up. It isn't like my little brother to be unreliable."

The August sun blazed. Kathryn wiped the perspiration off her forehead and frowned at the brown smudge it left on her glove. The dirt on the train had been bad

8

enough—her gray serge suit was covered with smuts that had blown in the open windows from the coal-fired boiler. But always she had held in her mind a comforting picture of the green cropland and tree-surrounded farmsteads she thought they were going to.

". . . water in Indian Creek much of the year, but when they get this proposed dam built the whole valley will spring up with farms. The soil's rich—just needs water." She had memorized Uncle Isaiah's letter to her papa. "This project will bring in hordes of surveyors and construction workers and homesteaders—a field white unto harvest for your preaching, Adam. You can help me on my farm at first, but you'll soon want to stake your own claim."

Isaiah had gone on about the farming opportunities, but the line that had moved Adam was "We've got no preachers here closer than Boise City, fifteen miles to the northeast."

Adam was a man of decision. His was a strength of spirit, not of body. The very next Sunday he had preached to his little congregation in Edgar on the text "How shall they believe unless they hear, and how shall they hear without a preacher?" and told them he and Kathryn would be leaving.

Kathryn thought about another text: "How beautiful upon the mountains are the feet of him that bringeth good tidings." Well, her papa might have beautiful feet, but the mountains here were far in the distance. They looked cool and blue both in front of and behind her, but they provided little relief from the dust and 106 degree heat here. Kathryn had always hated being closed in—claustrophobic, Dr. Johns had said she was—but this seemed like too much openness to cope with. Would Papa really *stay*? There wasn't a living soul here to preach to.

"Might as well sit a spell." Adam picked up the biggest of their cases and shoved it over against the shack. Then he sat on the bare plank bench, which was fortunately on the shady side of the building. "Isaiah didn't send no directions, or we could walk."

9

Kathryn looked at the dust-covered toes of the high-top shoes sticking out beneath her skirt and was thankful for her uncle's omission. She rummaged in her carpetbag and drew out a small, leather-bound book and pencil before she took her place on the bench.

Adam smiled at her. "Someday you'll be mighty glad you kept that journal, girl. When I see you writin' in it I often think how I wish my mama'd kept one when she and papa came over from Ireland after his textile mill burned."

Kathryn smiled and nodded but didn't really listen to the story she'd heard so many times before. Although she did wonder what her English grandmother, who had followed her Scots-Irish husband first to Ireland and then to Canada and on down to the Great Plains to homestead in a sod hut, would think of *this*. She had read Grandmother Eliza's letters. How barren she had found the plains—how she had thought them brown compared to the soft greenness of her own land. Whatever would Grandma have thought of this?

Her thoughts turned to her own mama. Kathryn hadn't minded leaving Nebraska too much, since Uncle Isaiah and Aunt Thelma were here in Idaho. Living with Aunt Thelma would be something like having the mother she'd never known. But she had hated leaving her mama's grave in the tree-lined cemetery by the river. There had been tiny wild daisies growing all over it last week when she went to say good-bye. Ella Smith Jayne had died when Kathryn was five days old, so all she knew of her mama was the sepia photograph taken on the day Ella married Adam Jayne in 1883—nineteen years ago. The photograph and her grave were all Kathryn had. Now she had only the photograph. Kathryn turned to write in her journal.

She had finished only five lines, however, when Adam stood up. "Ah, here he comes. I knew Isaiah wouldn't let us down."

Kathryn looked at the storm of dust approaching from the direction her papa was pointing. It seemed an enormous brown swirl for just a buckboard and team to be stirring up, but, as powdery as this ground was, she guessed that shouldn't surprise her. She stood, shook her skirt out, and adjusted her broad-brimmed straw hat, preparing to wave to her aunt and uncle.

In a few minutes, however, her smile faded to a confused frown. A large brown coach with a team of eight horses thundered across the desert toward them. The driver pulled the stagecoach to a halt, and a violent fit of sneezing overtook her before she could get her handkerchief out of her reticule. The cloud of gray-brown dust rolled over them and on across the sagebrush.

A wizened little miner with skin like a piece of dried leather got off the coach. "Missed the train, have we?" He swore profusely when Adam told him that, indeed, he had. "Well, throw my bundles down," he called to the driver. "It won't be the first night I've spent in the open—nor the last neither." He examined the schedule posted on the side of the building. "Mail train west tomorrer mornin'. Reckon that'll do me." He caught the bundles the driver tossed to him from the top of the stage.

Then Kathryn realized Adam was deep in discussion with the stagedriver's assistant.

"Coach goes within hollerin' distance of Isaiah Jayne's place. It's just a piece on up the road. Take you both and your luggage for thirty-five cents."

Adam nodded and hoisted up his trunk. Relieved to be doing something, Kathryn accepted the assistant's rawhide-gloved hand to help her inside the coach. She sank back against the leather seat with a sigh.

"And where are you going, pretty miss?" A laughing voice with a Scottish burr made Kathryn jump.

Coming into the shade of the coach from the glare of the desert sun, she hadn't seen the two men sitting across from her. But she was spared having to answer by her papa, who followed her in.

Adam, always hoping for an opportunity to share the gospel, was good at engaging strangers in conversation.

11

He soon learned that the man who had spoken to Kathryn was Merrick Allen, that he had boarded the stage that morning at Idaho City, a prosperous gold-mining town in the mountains twenty miles above Boise, and was going to Silver City, an equally booming gold and silver mining town in the Owyhee mountains some thirty miles to the west. It was Merrick's smooth appearance and well-cut clothes more than anything he said that led Adam to guess. "Gambling man, are you, Mr. Allen?"

Merrick threw back his head to laugh, knocking off his hat to reveal his thick black curls. Even in the dimness of the coach Kathryn could see how blue his piercing eyes were.

But then the coach wheels hit a rut in the sunken dirt road, and she had to clutch wildly to keep from being thrown off the narrow seat, so she missed most of his reply, except something about Lady Luck smiling on him more here than in San Francisco.

The small, red-bearded man beside him remained sullenly silent.

When the coach righted itself and settled into its more usual bounce and sway, Kathryn nudged her papa. Why didn't he say something about the evils of gambling? Mr. Allen looked far too fine a man to let go unwarned into eternal darkness. But then she looked out the side window where her father was gazing at a small brown shack with two unpainted wooden outbuildings and realized that the coach was slowing. Was this Uncle Isaiah's place?

They climbed down, and moments later the stage rolled on with a shout from the driver and a snapping of reins, coating them with yet another layer of dust.

Kathryn felt even more desolate than before. *This* was a farm? Something seemed to be growing in the cleared field behind the shed, a cow stamped in the corral, and a few chickens scratched around the door of the shack, so she supposed it *was* a farm. But it was too quiet.

"Is this Uncle Isaiah's, Papa? Where are they? Why isn't Aunt Thelma out here to meet us?"

12

She hadn't seen her aunt and uncle for two years, since they left Nebraska to move West. Working as a hired hand Isaiah couldn't save enough money to buy his own place, and he was determined to have his own farm—his own land. So they had packed everything they owned, which was little enough, and headed West where, even in the new-turned twentieth century, a man could still stake a claim on a quarter section of land. If he irrigated and farmed it, it'd be his free and clear in five years. Just a little over three more years to go.

Kathryn shook her head. She couldn't imagine what it must have been like—what it was going to *be* like—living here. In all this time Uncle Isaiah had managed to clear and plant only one small field. And those brown-tipped leaves—were they bean plants?—hardly looked alive now.

"Why is it so quiet?" Kathryn's voice was unnaturally loud, as if her insistence could call up an answer.

Adam shook his head and walked toward the house, not even bothering to carry his suitcase—the one with his Bible in it, which he had hardly let go of during the whole trip.

Kathryn followed with dragging feet. She didn't like it. Something wasn't right.

"Well, no sense in standing out here." The hinges creaked as Adam pushed open the unlocked door. "I'll start the stove, and we can make some coffee and biscuits while we're waitin'."

"Cook? In all this heat?" Kathryn was sure the temperature must have risen at least five degrees while they stood outside. But she didn't argue. She took off her hat and suit jacket, hung them on the iron bedpost, and tied on an apron she found hanging on a nail behind the door.

Adam picked up a couple of sticks of gray, gnarled wood that reminded Kathryn of the driftwood she had sometimes gathered from along the Little Blue River in Nebraska. "Seems they've found something useful to do with this sagebrush." But before he could get them in the stove

13

they heard a strange humming sound outside the cabin, and a dark cloud shadowed the small window beside the stove.

Kathryn took two steps toward the window to see what was happening, then jumped back as the entire cloud swarmed down the stovepipe and into the room. She stifled her desire to scream as she realized the danger of opening her mouth. The air was full of tiny flying balls of soot. She swatted wildly and backed toward the door, emitting strangled cries from her sealed lips.

Suddenly the door swung open, and Kathryn backed into the solid form of Uncle Isaiah. The cloud fell lifeless, covering table, chairs, bed, floor, and people.

"What is it?" Kathryn leaned heavily against Isaiah's strong arm supporting her around the waist.

"Flying ants. We get them almost daily during the hot season—about now—in the hottest part of the day."

The floor crunched when Kathryn took a step forward. "Are they dead?"

"Yup, coming down the stovepipe they get covered with soot. It kills 'em." Isaiah pulled a broom and dustpan from behind the stove. "That way we don't have to swat 'em dead, but it's a mixed blessing. Everything they touch gets covered with soot too."

No one said another word while Isaiah efficiently swept up three dustpanfuls and dumped them outside the door. The chickens fluttered over, cackling and scratching. Isaiah turned back to the room, and then Kathryn saw how haggard and stooped he looked—anyone would have thought him five years older than Adam rather than the five years younger he really was at thirty-five.

Especially when compared to the frailer Adam, Isaiah had always seemed to Kathryn to be the epitome of strength with well muscled, tanned arms and a long, firm jaw ending in a cleft, square chin. But now it was Adam whose energy seemed to be supporting the drooping Isaiah and Kathryn.

"Where's Aunt Thelma?" Kathryn asked in a small voice that revealed the cold foreboding she suddenly felt. Then she noticed the band of black fabric around Isaiah's arm.

Isaiah sank onto the saggy bed with a sigh. "Our little Josiah came two months early. She had an awful time. The doctor came out from Nampa, but he couldn't do anything."

Kathryn stifled a sob and moved to her uncle's side.

"I thought I'd have time to finish the burying and then meet your train—I didn't forget you—but in this heat you can't delay a burying."

"Don't you worry one bit about us, Isaiah." Adam put his hand on his brother's shoulder. "You weren't all alone, surely?"

Isaiah shook his head of thick brown hair, cut square above his collar, but before he could reply they heard the clop of horses' hooves and the creak of a buckboard.

A tall, thin man with a black moustache and a plump woman with blonde braids wound around her head came in laden with baskets of good-smelling food. They introduced themselves as Ned and Nelly Brewington, the Jaynes' nearest neighbors, homesteading on the next section. They had gone to the cemetery with Isaiah, they explained, but had stopped back by their place to pick up the children and the food.

"This here's Alvina—she's almost fifteen. She'll be company for you, Kathryn." A tall girl with brown braids smiled. "David here's eleven. Shake hands with the folks, Davey." David wiped his sweaty palm on his overalls before he obediently stuck out his hand. "And Lucy's eight." Lucy bobbed her blonde curls. It was easy to see she took after her mama.

"Best neighbors God ever made," Isaiah said. "Nelly kept me fed and Thelma comforted the whole time she was sick."

In a few minutes the table was covered with a clean cloth, Nelly having quietly discarded the soot-spotted one, and the cloth covered with a platter of fried chicken, a big bowl of applesauce, green beans, and potato salad. Kathryn and Adam were given the two chairs in the room, Isaiah and Ned sat on stools, and the Brewington children crowded onto the bed while Nelly served everyone.

"This is the best fried chicken I've ever eaten, Mrs. Brewington," Kathryn said after her first bite.

"Call me Nelly. Everyone does. But that's not chicken."

"Long-eared chicken, you mean!" Davey laughed.

"Jackrabbit," Alvina responded to Kathryn's confused look. "It's the only fresh meat we have in the summer—anything else spoils before we can get home with it from Nampa or Boise."

Shadows stretched long across the desert, and the blue mountains turned purple, before the Brewingtons climbed back into their buckboard and rattled off across open land.

"Aren't there roads?" Kathryn asked.

"There are, but it's a lot longer going around the sections," Isaiah replied.

When the company had gone the brothers spoke quietly about Thelma's death, Adam offering what comfort he could.

"I'd take it mighty kindly if you two'd go back to the cemetery with me tomorrow," Isaiah said. "Ned prayed and read the Twenty-third Psalm over her grave, but I'd feel better to have a real preacher."

Adam readily agreed. Then they turned to the still unpacked trunks and cases.

"I've just got one room back here." Isaiah pulled a woven blanket away from a doorway at the back of the cabin. "But I divided it so's you'd have some privacy."

The room was long and narrow. Isaiah had made it into two cubicles, each just big enough for a single bed and a trunk, by stretching lengths of unbleached muslin floor-to-ceiling down the middle and tacking them in place with strips of lath. "Sorry. I know it isn't what you're used to."

Kathryn was so exhausted after her days of travel and the strains of the past few hours that any bed looked palatial to her. "It's fine, Uncle Isaiah, really. But there's just one thing—I'm so terribly dirty. I know it's a lot to ask, but could I possibly have a bath? If you could just set the tub out, I'd be glad to heat the water myself."

Isaiah looked distressed. "I'm right sorry, Kathryn. But you see, we have to haul all our water in barrels from the Snake River—fifteen miles away, that is. We manage to keep the cattle alive and a small garden if we're lucky—but water for a bath is an unheard of luxury."

Kathryn settled for a small bowl of water and a sponge. The water was so dirty when she finished she couldn't imagine its doing any good to the vegetables Isaiah asked her to pour it over.

When she stepped out the door she looked about in disbelief. First she noticed the chill. The temperature must have dropped forty or fifty degrees since the sun went down. The next thing was the silence. It had been quiet in Nebraska, but there were always crickets, frogs, night birds—comforting, melodious sounds to fill the night and make the dark friendly. Here there was nothing. No tiny creature rustled in the brush. No sound carried from a near neighbor. It was as if she had stepped off the face of the earth into a great void. Dauber, Isaiah's horse, moved in the corral, and the noise startled her like thunder. She jumped back into the house and slammed the door.

"It's so quiet!" Her own voice sounded as if she had yelled.

"Yup. Took Thelma a long time to get used to that too. Said she missed crickets more than flowers."

"But why? You have those awful flying ants. Don't you have any other insects?"

"Not unless you count jackrabbits. And the ants only come in the heat of the day. Nope, it'd be a good fifteen mile trip in the buckboard to get close enough to water to hear a cricket or a frog this time of the year. Of course, in the spring when there's water in the creek we get a few. But it won't be quiet all night. Soon's the moon comes up you'll hear plenty from the coyotes."

It was a good thing he'd warned her. Kathryn was just drifting off to sleep when a blood-curdling howl brought her bolt upright. The shrieking yip-yip-yip seemed to come from right under her window. The cry was answered by another beast some distance away. Then another and another. How many were out there? It sounded like hundreds. Could the creatures get into her room?

Surely they would eat the animals in the corral before they'd break into a house to attack humans. It was hardly a comforting thought, but it gave Kathryn the courage to overcome her fear of being closed in enough to put her pillow over her head. She lay down again, but she didn't relax.

This was the most awful place in the world. What could God have been thinking of to make anything so ugly? She knew it was wicked to question God, and she knew the pillow over her head couldn't hide her thoughts from the Almighty. But she couldn't help it. Silently she screamed at Him: *Ugly, ugly, ugly!*

And then she had an even more wicked thought—it was horrible to be glad Aunt Thelma was dead—but now surely Papa wouldn't stay here. How could anybody live without water? Aunt Thelma was the lucky one—she had escaped. Kathryn shivered under her quilt at the thought—would she have to die to escape this place?

Another coyote howl tore through the dark, more piercing than ever. Maybe it would be worth dying to get out of here. Her pillow did little to muffle the sound. Would the shrieking and yowling keep up all night? Kathryn was just despairing of ever getting back to sleep when a deep, soothing voice came from the other side of the muslin wall. "Yea, though I walk through the valley of the shadow of death, I will fear no evil . . ."

Kathryn slept.

2

The first rays of sunrise peeping in her tiny, uncurtained window woke Kathryn. She slipped silently out of bed and put on her long black skirt and high-necked white blouse. She didn't have a black blouse, so this would have to do for mourning clothes. She tiptoed to the door. Uncle Isaiah must be awfully tired, because even the creaking hinges didn't disturb him.

Kathryn stood in open-mouthed amazement. How could a place change so in such a short time? From the intense heat and dust of afternoon barrenness the desert had last night turned into an icy black void filled with blood-curdling howls. This morning it was a place of peaceful, golden serenity. Even the sagebrush looked almost pretty with the morning sun gilding it, and the air that had first so stifled, then chilled her, was now cool and refreshing.

She walked a bit just for the pleasure of moving—certainly not for any variety in the scenery. Was this really the same world she had been willing to die to escape from last night?

The words of a favorite Bible verse came to her so vividly she flung out her arms and quoted it aloud. "Weeping may endure for the night, but joy cometh in the morning." She knew she had better fix this moment strong in her mind. She had the feeling there was going to be a lot of weeping in this rough land, many times when she would need to be reminded that joy would come in the morning. Because she also knew that, no matter what, once Adam Jayne was in the place he believed God wanted him, no hardship, death, or drought would move him.

The distant mountains—had Uncle Isaiah called those in front the Sawtooths?—were a rosy pink below a sky already intensely blue. Surely that was a sign of heat to come. She turned back to the kitchen. Best she get the coffee boiled and bacon fried while the air could still cool off the house.

Instinctively she picked up her skirts to keep them dry as she walked through the brush. Then she kicked a stone and raised a little cloud of dust, and she realized—there was no dew. At home in Nebraska her skirts would have been damp to her knees. Here all was as bone dry as it had been yesterday afternoon. And already the sun was heating the air.

"Help me remember the joy," she whispered as she strode toward the little brown shack that was now home.

After breakfast Isaiah hitched Dauber to the buckboard, and they set out on the three-mile ride to the cemetery. They rode for some time with only the clop and creak of horse and wagon to break the silence, following the tracks of the old stage road that had sunk a good two feet into the ground.

At last Kathryn spoke. "Good thing Dauber's a dappled gray. The dust doesn't show on her." She brushed at the folds of her black skirt but only succeeded in raising more dust.

The sound of her voice seemed to loosen Isaiah's tongue, however, and, probably to take his mind off his loss, he turned to Kathryn. "You wouldn't believe it, but twenty-five years ago when they were building the railroad a hundred people lived here. Before that the place was called Fifteen Mile Station—the first major stage stop out of Boise on the way to Silver City. People could get a good hot meal and relax a spell. Then when the railroad construction camp set up on the banks of Indian Creek they called it Kuna for an Indian word meaning 'the end.'"

"The end of the world?" Kathryn was ashamed of her words. She should be comforting Isaiah, not venting her frustration.

But Isaiah just gave a wry smile. "Lots of people have thought so. It's supposed to mean the end of the railroad line—which it was then. But Thelma claimed she believed another translation—some say the word means 'ugly.'"

Kathryn bit her lip.

Thelma's grave was recognizable only because the mound was higher than others, not because the dirt showed any signs of being freshly turned. Isaiah took off his hat, Kathryn folded her hands, Adam opened his Bible —although he knew the words by heart: "In my Father's house are many mansions. . . . I go to prepare a place for you . . . that where I am there ye may be also." He closed the Bible and prayed.

Kathryn still had her eyes closed when he startled her with a request. "Now, Kathryn, suppose you sing for us. Isaiah and I'll sort of follow along so you won't feel too lonesome."

Kathryn choked. Why hadn't he warned her? Of course she'd sung a lot in Edgar—for weddings and funerals and Christmas programs—but she'd always had her little pump organ to accompany her, and her heart hadn't been so heavy nor her throat so parched. She swallowed. The lump wouldn't go down, but she forced a few words out. "Amazing grace, how sweet the sound . . ." Her voice came out in a thin, cracking rasp, but Adam and Isaiah didn't seem to mind. They joined in and carried on to the end. "When we've been there ten thousand years, bright shining as the sun . . ."

Adam ended the service by having them say the Lord's Prayer together. But Kathryn couldn't leave just like that. She had loved Aunt Thelma and knew how much she had longed for the infant that lay buried with her. How different it would all be here if they could have been met by a smiling Thelma and a cooing baby Josiah. She wanted to give them something. Leave some offering. If only there were flowers in this God-forsaken place. She absolutely refused to place a sprig of sagebrush on Thelma's grave.

She walked some distance beyond the graveyard before she found it—a brown, dried weed that in the spring had been a tiny purple daisy. It was now baked to straw but retained a glint of yellow in its center. She broke off three stems—carefully so as not to shatter them—and carried them to the grave.

With a sense of completeness at having done the best she could, Kathryn looked around her. There must have been about twenty mounds, all with wooden markers bearing the date 1882. On closer look she saw that most were the graves of children. "What happened?" she asked.

"The construction camp I told you about," Isaiah answered. "They'd just completed the railroad when the entire community was wiped out in a diptheria epidemic."

"All?" The thought was so staggering that Kathryn's mind couldn't accept it. "You said a hundred people—they all died? A whole town just gone?"

"That's what they say around these parts. 'Course they haven't found a hundred graves. Some would have been lost, but probably when the women and children died those that were left just drifted on."

Thelma's rough-hewn cross and the tiny one beside it for Josiah blurred before Kathryn's eyes. She had been too young to know when her mother died. Neighbors and friends in Nebraska had died, and Papa had preached their services and prayed over their pine boxes as they were lowered into the ground. But never before had Kathryn thought of a whole village being alive and active one week and in the graveyard the next.

The impermanence of life struck her so hard she felt she must sit down. She looked around and saw a big rock. She sat. But that was all. She tried to pray, but words wouldn't come. She had always figured she had strength within her for anything—but she had never imagined a situation like this.

It hadn't been easy in Nebraska—taking care of Papa, going to school, raising chickens, keeping a garden, and helping with the church—but at first there had been Aunt Thelma to help and then neighbors and women from the church when she moved. Now there was no one. The joy Kathryn had glimpsed that morning was gone. She felt it would never return.

If only she could pray. But her mind was as silent and barren as the desert. Then the words came—not words for her to speak to God, but words from Him: "Lo, I am with you alway, even unto the end of the world." Well, Kuna was the end. All she could do was trust. Even if her heart didn't feel like it, she had to keep the truth in her head. She could trust Him.

"Be of good courage, and He shall strengthen your heart, all ye that hope in the Lord."

Kathryn blinked. Were Papa's words for Isaiah or for her?

Apparently for Isaiah, although the Lord had quickened them to her heart as well, for Isaiah stood shaking his head at the dilapidated old signboard that said "Kuna."

"Yup, like I said, it's the end. I reckon this is it for me." He turned away. "I just don't see how I can go on."

"No!" Kathryn jumped at the sound of her own voice, but the words of Scripture were still ringing in her mind. Uncle Isaiah needed to hear them too. "No, God promised to be with us, even in such an awful place as this. And you can't let Aunt Thelma down. She put up with living here for two years so you could have a place of your own.

"And what about us? We sold our place in Nebraska and came all the way out here because you said this was a

23

land of opportunity where Papa could farm and preach. Well, we're here—and you know Papa is a wonderful preacher and a terrible farmer, so you can't quit on us.

"Like Papa said—we have to have courage—courage to hope in the Lord."

She stopped suddenly and clapped a hand over her mouth. What had she said? What had she done? A woman, little more than a child, telling a grown man what to do. "I—I'm sorry—I don't know—I didn't mean—" She took a step backwards, then saw the twinkle in Adam's eye.

Papa agreed with her.

Isaiah just put his hat on his head and turned back toward the buckboard. "I'll think about it. Have to do the chores today anyhow. And tomorrow we have to haul water."

When they arrived back at the shack, Kathryn put on Thelma's apron and set to work. She had gotten herself into this; now she had to make good. What had come over her? If she'd taken Isaiah's side and begged Papa maybe they'd all be packing to head back to the prairie, now golden with ripe grain, rather than being stuck here with a patch of dried up lima beans.

When the flying ants descended on them that afternoon all she could do was repeat over and over again with as much spirit as she could muster, "Lo, I am with you alway. . . . Be of good courage. . . . I am with you."

3

If some at the Jayne place had lost their sense of direction, however, the area around them had not. That fall the whole desert hummed with activity all driving toward a single goal—water. The Reclamation Act of 1902, popularly called the Irrigation Law, required the federal government to begin large-scale irrigation projects in the arid Western states rather than leaving the job of securing water to state governments or to individuals. The prospect of ample water for this rich soil fired people's imagination. When water came they would be ready.

All across the desert, homestead shacks—tiny, one-room structures built of unpainted upright boards, the cracks sealed with battens—sprang up on every quarter section. Anytime she stepped out the door Kathryn could spot a cloud of dust rising in any direction she looked—a sign that another settler was clearing land to be ready when the miracle of water arrived in the wilderness.

And Kathryn, too, like the homesteaders around her, was fired with a new goal. At first she had been determined merely to survive. Then had come the drive to succeed. On the heels of that—because she felt the responsibility of her firm speech in the cemetery—she resolved to help Adam and Isaiah succeed too.

Adam and Isaiah now worked every day clearing more land of sagebrush. Isaiah harnessed a newly purchased iron disk to Dauber, and hour after hour men and horse strained at the stubborn plants, grubbing them out of the ground. Kathryn thought it was the hardest work she'd ever seen, but Isaiah was jubilant. His pioneering spirit had gradually returned, and now he talked endlessly about the fine wheat, corn, and alfalfa they would grow when the Irrigation Law was put into effect.

"This new disk is great. It's so much easier than last year, you can't imagine."

"What did you do then?" Kathryn asked.

"Same as most of the others—drug railroad ties over the land—back and forth, back and forth—until those ornery plants finally broke off."

"Isn't there an easier way?"

"Well, some burn the sage. But it's pretty much a last resort—lazy man's way that ends in no good. We need the sage. It's our only fuel all winter. I've been meaning to ask you, Kathryn—I know you have your hands full with cooking and taking care of the house, but if you have any spare time, do you suppose you could chop some of the grubbed bushes for firewood? It'll take a mighty heap of it to keep us through the winter."

And so, in addition to her other chores, Kathryn began spending an hour or two a day chopping sagebrush into two-foot lengths and storing it in the lean-to behind the house. The fact that the gnarly wood seemed to fight back with scratches and splinters did nothing to improve Kathryn's appreciation for the plant. When one of the scraggly branches dug deeper than usual and left a long red gash in her arm, she could hold in her exasperation no longer.

"Why an all-powerful God would create anything so *awful* is beyond me. It's enough to make me doubt my religion."

Isaiah laughed. "Better not let your pa hear you say that. He might not be as understanding as God probably is."

26

But Kathryn wasn't laughing. "The only good I can see in it is it helps me believe in original sin—if I'd ever doubted *that*."

"Well, maybe it does a little more than that. It feeds the jackrabbits, they feed us, and it even furnishes the fuel to cook them over. That's not too bad a deal."

"Yes. But God could have created something pretty that would have done the job just as well. I'll bet jackrabbits could eat roses."

Kathryn grabbed the broom and began swinging at the bits of sage that littered a trail from the door to the woodbox. Just burning it for cooking fuel made the house stink constantly with its acrid, oily smell. She couldn't imagine what winter would be like.

Time after time Isaiah urged Adam to go stake his own claim. "This'll be mighty valuable land one day. No sense in missing out just for the sake of a filing fee."

But Adam resisted. "The law says you have to irrigate the land. We've got all we can handle right here. What if we had to haul twice as much water from the river? That's all we'd get done."

Isaiah shrugged. "Shouldn't let that worry you. Plenty of folks in these parts just throw a bucket of water on their claim and say they've irrigated."

Adam shook his head. "Might be good enough for the government land office. It's not good enough for God. Besides, when I saw G P in the sky God was telling me, 'Go preach,' not, 'Go plow.'" And that was the end of it.

There were plenty of opportunities to plow—or at least disk—because Isaiah had one of the few iron disks in the area. He and Dauber were in great demand to hire out for custom work, grubbing sage for other homesteaders.

When the brothers saw that Dauber seemed to tire faster than they did and figured they could work twice as fast—or nearly so—with a team, Adam rode in to Nampa and bought a rangy-looking Appaloosa, an Indian horse bred to the desert terrain, to work alongside Dauber.

"I can well believe he was born here." Kathryn shook her head at his red and brown spots. "He's as ugly as sagebrush."

But Buckshot also proved to be as strong as the sagebrush, and the custom work flourished.

They harvested only a few pitiful handfuls of beans from the dry field. What hadn't parched, the rabbits had eaten, but Isaiah went right on and planted winter wheat.

"Is it really worth the bother?" Adam asked.

Isaiah shrugged. "Never can tell. If we have a good wet spring, it might produce all right."

And through it all Adam never forgot that, for him, G P meant "Go preach." Every new homestead shack that appeared received a visit. Everyone within traveling distance was given a warm invitation to come to the Jayne place for Sunday Bible reading. And everyone received the invitation gladly, then shook his head over all the work to be done. The Brewingtons were the only regular attenders, but no one could have brought a brighter spot to Kathryn's week than her visits with that exuberant family.

Nelly was her best friend, and Kathryn was sure that without her cheerful good sense and practical advice she would never have survived.

"Give them a good meal," was at least part of Nelly's answer to any concern Kathryn expressed about her father or uncle. Whenever Kathryn was tempted to complain— something she had vowed never to do—Nelly's stalwart example was before her, showing her how to trudge forward.

The second week in November brought a change to their lives. Rain! It had been so long since Kathryn had seen any that it took her a bit to figure out what was happening when she first heard peppering sounds on the tin roof. Then she realized and rushed out, leaving the door open and her head uncovered. She flung out her arms and whirled round and round, her face held up to the wonderful refreshing drops. In a few minutes, though, her feet slowed. The flourlike dirt was turning to paste, sticking in globs to her high-top shoes.

Adam and Isaiah came in from the field and helped her set out pans to catch the precious liquid.

"Oh, it's like back home when we had a rain barrel," Kathryn cried. "Maybe we'll get enough so I can wash my hair in it." The mineral-hard river water she had used the past months left her hair dry and brittle. She longed for the silky feeling of a rainwater wash.

But the dry air absorbed most of the moisture, and the soil remained powder dry two inches below the pasty surface. Kathryn captured enough to wash her face and to give her hair a final rinse, but that was all.

That night, however, snow came—just a light frosting on the ground but enough to give Kathryn her second revelation of beauty in a desert morning. She so hated the endless brown that to find the world around her suddenly transformed to glistening white with pink and purple mountains beyond was to be transported to a fairyland. By noon the dancing crystals melted to gray sogginess to match the gray sky, but the vision remained.

"There won't be much plowing for a while now." Isaiah poured himself a cup of coffee and sat down at the blue and white gingham-covered table.

"Good, then we can concentrate on the preaching." Adam followed him with a steaming mug.

"Might get more folks out to a Sunday service now, but there'll be fewer to invite."

"How come?"

"Not much to do in the winter. Folks'll move into Boise and look for work. Most with kids to put in school or family to live with have gone already."

"And just leave their places here unattended?" Kathryn had heard plenty of stories about claim jumpers taking over the sod huts of settlers on her native prairie a generation or two earlier.

29

Isaiah shook his head. "Not much to worry about now. 'Bout the worst that could happen would be a few jackrabbits burrowing down. But just wait, when water comes everybody'll want our land."

It was always the same—when the water comes. Kathryn wondered if they'd live that long.

But the Brewingtons, who against all odds had managed to keep a small patch of alfalfa alive and were slowly building up a few dairy cows—not that their three or four head could yet be called a herd—would stay for the winter, and Nelly would teach Alvina, David, and Lucy their lessons at home.

A new family responded to Adam's invitation. In early September the Sperlins had staked out their claim a few sections to the southwest. They pitched a tent and spent every daylight hour clearing land until freezing nights forced them to build a shack. Like many others they had been happy enough to receive Adam's invitation to Sunday service but hadn't acted on it.

The Sunday before Thanksgiving, however, Adam was just leading out in a booming version of "When the Roll Is Called Up Yonder" when the door creaked open, and suddenly the room was full. Adam had probably mentioned to Kathryn that the Sperlins had three sons, but she had had no idea . . .

At the end of the first verse Adam stopped to greet the newcomers. "Harold Sperlin, welcome to the house of the Lord. Well, really the house of Isaiah Jayne, but today it's the Lord's house. Introduce this fine family of yours."

The six-foot-three, broad-shouldered man pulled off his hat to reveal thick, sandy hair and beamed on his family. "This here's Willa. Believe it or not she mothered these three great hulks and manages to keep us all fed."

He pulled his wife to the fore as if taking her out of his pocket, and everyone laughed. Willa Sperlin was barely five feet tall and as lean as a jackrabbit, but her brown eyes danced and her brown hands were strong as she shook hands around the room.

"And these here are Jules, Myron, and Elmer. We got three mules back on the place—'cause my dad always preferred mules to horses—but I'm here to tell you these boys can outwork any six mules."

No one doubted his word. When the three Sperlin boys moved, the shack trembled.

Nelly made room for Willa beside her on the bed. Kathryn held her breath. If those boys tried to sit on Uncle Isaiah's bed. . . . But they wisely chose to lean against the wall, and the service continued with four bass voices sending the hymns rumbling across the desert.

After the service Nelly issued her invitation for the Jaynes and Sperlins to join them for Thanksgiving dinner, and the women clustered around the table planning their menu and deciding who would bring each dish.

Kathryn thought the six pies she had made and the huge basin of mashed yams and sweet potatoes topped with crispy golden marshmallows that Nelly had told her how to fix would surely last them till Christmas, knowing how much the other women were fixing as well.

When they arrived at the Brewingtons' just after noon on Thanksgiving Day she was sure she'd never seen so much food for thirteen people—as much as at a potluck dinner for the whole church of sixty people in Edgar. She was even more sure that her pies would be left over when she saw that Nelly and Willa had each made a cake as well.

Ned had set up a trestle table the length of the kitchen to hold all the food, and the diners would sit all over the house, on stools or floor as seemed convenient. At least there was almost ample room.

Being the closest homestead to Indian Creek the Brewington place had water more of the year than any other in the area, and therefore was more prosperous. They had been there since 1900 and had already built two additions onto their original shack.

After months of living with bare, rough-hewn wood, Kathryn thought the red building paper that lined Nelly's walls was the most elegant thing she'd seen since the flowered wallpaper of their home in Nebraska.

After Adam offered a Thanksgiving prayer and everyone began heaping his plate with turkey, dressing, corn, mashed potatoes, gravy, and all the rest, Kathryn saw how foolish she had been to think she'd have to worry about leftovers. Those Sperlin boys were on their thirds and showed no signs of slowing by the time she was halfway through her first helpings.

At times like this Kathryn was aware of her strange position of being a girl filling a woman's role. Her impulse was to sit with Nelly and Willa and talk about cooking and housekeeping—chores that occupied her from sunup to sundown. But really, she was far closer in age to the Brewington children.

When Alvina burst out in a merry laugh at something her brother said, Kathryn decided to join their group in the bedroom off the sitting-room. She would like to hear about Alvina's lessons. It seemed like heaven to be allowed to spend part of each day doing nothing but reading and writing.

Kathryn had graduated from the little school in Edgar two months before they moved, and there had been no question of her going on to a degree. Her papa had only finished the eighth grade. His remarkable knowledge of the Scriptures he had gained on his own, reading far into every night by the flickering flame of a coal oil lamp—and his knowledge of literature as well.

Kathryn had learned at least as much from Adam as from her schoolteachers, for evening readings in the Jayne home had included a wide range of the classics: Shakespeare, Dickens, Sir Walter Scott.

Although during these past months in the desert there had been no time for such luxuries, and Kathryn sorely missed them, Adam still read the Bible aloud every day, and she wrote faithfully in her journal. But that was all the time or energy she had for such things. Now to hear Alvina talk about *A Tale of Two Cities*, which she was reading, brought a stab that was unchristianly close to jealousy.

Then the Sperlin boys, their plates piled high with pie and cake, joined them. The two younger ones, Myron and Elmer, who were Alvina's age or a year or so older, sat on each side of her, leaving Kathryn to the complete attention of the older Jules. The maneuver was so dexterous it was impossible not to suspect connivance among the brothers, and yet it was equally impossible to think of the open-faced Sperlins as capable of plotting.

Still, Jules Sperlin seemed to be a man of surprising contrasts. In spite of his enormous size and booming singing voice, Kathryn was surprised how softly he spoke in the crowded room. And, in spite of the huge quantities of food he consumed, she was pleased to see how nice his manners were. Willa had done her work well.

Jules asked Kathryn about her move to the desert. When she recounted the death of Thelma and the baby his sympathy was so genuine she was amazed at the gentleness he revealed. And then she reversed the question.

"Well, things were getting a mite crowded in Iowa." He shook his sandy hair, and his blue eyes danced. "Not that some crowding by a good Iowa cornfield wouldn't seem pretty welcome out here. But Pa has three brothers, and after Grandpa died it wasn't practical to divide up the land four ways. Pa's the oldest, so he decided he should be the one to move on."

Kathryn frowned. "I don't understand. It seems like the oldest would have the most right to stay. Let the younger ones move."

Jules shrugged. "Legally probably. But Uncle Ben just had a new baby, and Uncle Joe's always been a mite sickly, and it'd like to kill Uncle Everet to leave the stock—so this seemed best."

"Such brotherly love, such kindness . . ." Kathryn couldn't finish, so she turned back to her plate.

When everyone had eaten considerably more than he was comfortable with, Ned Brewington brought out his harmonica, and they spent the next two hours in a hymn-sing that rocked the house.

"Oh, I can't think of a better way to work off a bit of worldly indulgence in gluttony than singin' praises to the Lord," Adam said at last. "Ned, how come you've been hiding your light under a bushel? You bring that sweet potato along with you every Sunday, and we'll have a lot better song service."

Kathryn agreed. It would be lovely to have accompaniment to keep their often off-tune singing on key.

The thought renewed a homesickness that ever lurked beneath the surface of her consciousness. If only they hadn't had to leave her little pump organ behind. Of course, there was no place to keep it here, and it was being well cared for by Marie Sykes, the neighbor in Edgar who had first taught her to play. But Kathryn desperately missed her organ and Marie. When water came in, this might become a good place to make a living, but she wondered if life would ever be worth living here among the sagebrush and jackrabbits with no time for books or music.

The others, however, were entering into enthusiastic plans. The hymns had been so successful that they would hold a carol-sing for Christmas. Adam would ride out to invite all the homesteaders within a ten-section radius. That might be a good first step to getting them to come to church—and if they didn't eat much, just refreshments, they wouldn't need so much space. Alvina suggested they might be able to use the Brewington barn if it wasn't too cold, and the plans progressed.

Kathryn was quiet. Why couldn't they live in a civilized place that had churches and schoolhouses for meetings? Yes, she had determined to survive, and she would. But achieving success seemed as likely as climbing to the moon. And they probably wouldn't have to grub sagebrush on the moon—it was supposed to be made of cheese, so you wouldn't even have to work for food.

Her fanciful, escapist thoughts were interrupted by Jules. "I was wonderin', Miss Kathryn. For this carol-sing— I mean—would you like it, if your pa'd permit—that is, could I call for you in my wagon?"

Kathryn blinked in surprise. "Oh. Well, yes, Papa would permit—" She was as flustered as he was. "Yes, I would like that, Jules." And suddenly the desert didn't seem quite so barren.

4

The coming of Christmas and the closing in of cold weather made that warm Thanksgiving day a memory Kathryn had to cling to desperately in the next weeks. The men were unable to work in the fields, and Isaiah spent most of his days sitting at the table or stretched out on his bed.

Adam said a few quiet words to help Kathryn understand that Isaiah was now doing the grieving he had for months held at bay with hard work. Kathryn had seen the half-finished carved wooden cradle in the lean-to, and the image of that and the bleak brown mound in the cemetery made her heart go out to the listless man. But having her grief-stricken uncle under foot all day did little to raise her spirits.

Also, keeping the cold out of the shack required almost constant stoking of the stove. Now she understood why Isaiah had said they would need so much sagebrush cut for the winter. Sage burned bright and hot, but it burned fast. Some days Kathryn thought all she got done was carry prickly sticks from the lean-to to the wood box to the stove.

But after a few days she realized one advantage—with such constant burning she no longer noticed the biting smell that had bothered her so last fall. It was odd that too much of a problem could be its own solution. She won-dered if a lesson could be there but didn't have time to think about it as she turned to stir the pot of beans on the stove.

When Adam came in for mid-day dinner he invited Kathryn to ride out with him that afternoon. "It's cold, but you can bundle up against it. Have you noticed how the cold doesn't seem to penetrate so much here? Might be ten degrees colder than it was in Nebraska, but with no wind and no moisture in the air, you hardly notice it."

Kathryn wouldn't say she "hardly noticed" the cold a short time later when she was sitting beside Adam on the buckboard seat, but it was good to be out of the house. And the chill air was invigorating. "Thought we'd drive over behind Kuna Butte and see if those new folks are still there. Invite them to the carol-sing if they are. Robinson the name is, if I remember rightly. Young couple. Hope they make it homesteading."

They rattled along for some time over the hard-frozen, trackless ground. Nothing was in view but the long, bare hump of ground that people called Kuna Butte. On the prairie, a hill rising three hundred feet from the level ground might have been referred to as a mountain, but here, with foothills of the Rockies behind them and snow-capped Owyhees before them, the hump was given no such dignity.

Kathryn occupied her mind with wondering what in the world they would do for Christmas. The distant moun-tains were rich in pine but were much too far to go for a Christmas tree. They had brought no decorations with them.

And then, what would she do for presents? Adam or Isaiah would soon be making their monthly trip to town for supplies. She usually just sent a grocery list with them, but maybe she could go along this time and do some shop-ping. She still had some of the egg money she had brought with her from Edgar, although Isaiah's chickens hadn't laid well enough since she'd been here to add much to it.

Maybe they could even go into Boise. How wonderful it would be to see a big city with streetcars going up and down a paved street. To have lunch at the Idan-Ha Hotel. She closed her eyes with a sigh.

Suddenly her thoughts were interrupted. Buckshot was the first to notice. He pricked his ears forward and began sniffing the air. At first Kathryn thought the trembling of the wagon was the horse's increased pace, then she realized the ground itself was rumbling. She gripped the side of the spring seat.

Did they have earthquakes in this country? Uncle Isaiah had referred to volcanic ash in the soil, but she had not thought there might be such a thing as *active* volcanoes.

Then she saw. Just as they drew level with the butte, a band of wild horses thundered toward them from the back side. It was a thrilling sight—perhaps fifteen horses led by a magnificent golden stallion, his pale mane and tail flowing across the landscape, followed closely by his black, gray, and brown band, all at full gallop, heads up and nostrils flaring in the winter air.

Buckshot reared and whinnied. Kathryn again clutched her seat, realizing the danger. But Adam had a firm hand and voice and soon steadied his horse, which at first gave every sign of wanting to plunge after the cayuse band. The Jaynes sat until the horses had thundered out of sight on toward Owyhee County.

"Oh, they're wonderful!" Kathryn cried. "Uncle Isaiah told me some of the paths to Indian Creek had been worn by wild horses, but I had no idea!" She felt a strange, compelling attraction, as if she wanted to run after them herself.

"The way they pound the earth, you'd think they'd break into the cave up there. It'd sure be a sorry thing if one fell through a tunnel."

"Cave?" Kathryn asked. She'd heard of no caves. "In the side of the butte, you mean?"

"No, haven't you heard folks talk about it? Just a deep hole flat in the ground. Don't suppose anyone's explored all the tunnels they say are down there. One fellow I called on showed me some mighty fine arrowheads he'd found in one of the chambers—obsidian and smoky topaz, he said —I wouldn't know."

Cave. Kathryn shuddered. She was so claustrophobic she didn't even want to think about caves—deep holes, dark tunnels getting smaller and smaller—closing in on her. She put her hands to her face, and her breath came in rapid, shallow gasps.

Adam picked up the reins and clucked the Appaloosa into motion.

Kathryn's fear vanished as quickly as it had come. The vision of the horses returned. For the first time since Thanksgiving she felt like singing. This was her third surprising glimpse of the possibility that life here could be worthwhile: her first golden morning in the desert, her first gentle snowfall, and now the breathtaking sight of these noble animals. Perhaps God did have His hand on this country and, if on it, then on them too. For the first time in many months the words returned to her *Be of good courage . . . I am with you.*

The last ten days before Christmas, Kathryn threw herself wholeheartedly into preparations. She did get her shopping trip in Boise, even if there was no time—or money—for a fancy lunch. At the general store on Main Street, as streetcars clacked along the rails outside, she bought sacks of raisins, dates, and mincemeat along with tiny packets of cloves, cinnamon, and ginger. The next day the homestead shack smelled deliciously of steamed pudding from Aunt Thelma's recipe and the gingerbread that had always been Kathryn's favorite holiday treat.

Kathryn had also spent a delightful time at the mercantile, selecting small packages that she carefully wrapped with brown paper and bits of colored string before hiding under her bed. She even found herself humming Christmas carols as she went about her chores. If only they had a tree all would be perfect. Well, as perfect as possible in this place.

The day before Christmas Eve Adam returned from what he called his "pastoral calls" but which were really just friendly visits to let his fellow homesteaders know he cared about them—and that God did, too, if they seemed inclined to listen.

"Kathryn, come see! I've got a surprise!" In his exuberance Adam shouted as if she were in a far field rather than in the next room of a tiny shack.

Because of the extra time she'd spent on baking lately Kathryn had let the cleaning slip. Dust continually sifted in the cracks between battens and boards. Now she had determined to have things spic and span for Christmas. Therefore she emerged from the back bedroom carrying a pile of cleaning rags, her face and the apron over her oldest dress streaked with dirt, her wispy hair escaping the tie that had earlier held it neatly at the nape of her neck.

But the sight that met her drove any concern for her appearance or that of the house from her mind. A huge piece of sagebrush filled the space between Isaiah's bed and the table. It reached almost to the ceiling, and crystals of melting snow twinkled like stars in the lantern light.

"I brought you a Christmas tree."

"Papa! It's wonderful!" She raced across the floor and flung herself into his arms. "I can't believe it. Where did you ever find one so tall?" Most sagebrush was knee- or waist-high to a man. She had seen some that would reach Adam's shoulder, but this was above his head.

"Sunny side of a draw, out south a piece." He motioned with his head.

And then she cried out in alarm as the tree began to topple. "Catch it!" She didn't want it falling on the table and breaking her crockery.

A tall figure stepped out from behind the tree, grinning broadly, and she realized Adam had more than one surprise for her.

"Er—hello. I'm sorry. I didn't see you there." She smoothed a few strands of hair behind her ears.

"Didn't mean to startle you, pretty miss. But my horse went lame halfway out of Silver City, and your papa's being a good Samaritan."

Kathryn struggled to remember. Where had she seen those laughing eyes and heard that softly burred, mocking voice before?

"I can see you don't remember me. But I never forget a face as pretty as yours." He pulled off his hat. "Merrick Allen. We met on the stage last summer. Can't say I blame you for forgetting, though."

"Mr. Allen was on his way to Boise for Christmas, but since his horse needs a few days to rest a pulled ligament I invited him to spend the holidays with us."

Kathryn gulped. It couldn't have been a worse time for entertaining a guest—even tonight's beans and cornbread were left over, since she'd been concentrating on other things.

But Adam seemed oblivious to her discomfort. "Why don't you air out Isaiah's bed while Mr. Allen and I take care of the horses? I expect Isaiah's out with the cow—I'll tell him he's bunking with me." Adam leaned the piece of sage against the wall, and the men went out leaving Kathryn still open-mouthed with surprise.

But there was no time to stand gaping. By the time the men returned from the corral she had Isaiah's sheets hanging on the clothesline by the lean-to, her face washed, her hair combed, and her apron changed. She was frying salt pork to add to the beans and melting some sugared honey for the cornbread when the men came in.

"Now that's a mighty friendly smell!" Merrick beamed at her. She resented the way his blue eyes danced when he grinned at her, and yet she realized it was just a natural part of the man.

After dinner Isaiah hammered pieces of wood to the sagebrush to make it stand up, while Kathryn popped corn for stringing and dug in her sewing basket for strips of bright cloth to hang on the tree. She had been saving scraps for a patchwork quilt, and Nelly had recently contributed several pieces of calico, so she soon had the tree blooming with bright bows.

The men were less successful with stringing popcorn. Beside the fact that they ate more than they strung, the fluffy white puffs kept breaking when they poked them with a needle.

Kathryn popped a fresh pan and sat down with them. "If my guess is correct, I'd say you're from Scotland, Mr. Allen," she said after everyone had worked quietly for a spell.

"Aye. Originally from a little town in the border country—Selkirk by name."

Kathryn wondered if it was only her imagination that the twinkle went out of his eyes.

"Been here long?" Adam asked.

"Five years."

"Your family must miss you." Now Kathryn was curious about the shuttered look on his normally open countenance.

"Doubt it." He shrugged.

After another long silence Adam asked, "Think you mentioned being in San Francisco?"

As if to make up for his earlier reticence, Merrick Allen launched into a lively tale of living by his wits in the city. "But it was getting too civilized for me. Now this right here, this is truly the last frontier. Like I told Bo when I left San Francisco, this is the last place a man can make his way on his own from nothing without being crowded by society."

Kathryn wasn't quite sure what he meant by everything he said, but one impression was clear to her: he was exactly like those wild horses she had seen that day out south of the butte. She could just see him, head up, black

42

hair tossing in the wind, racing where he pleased, obeying no rules but his own.

Everyone was in a holiday spirit by the time for the Christmas Eve carol-sing the next day. Kathryn put on her best dress of deep maroon taffeta with an ecru lace yolk and deep lace cuffs on the sleeves and spent extra time swirling her hair into a graceful up-sweep. It embarrassed her when Mr. Allen called her "pretty miss"—she longed so to be, and knew she wasn't—but she was determined to do her best, even if her unruly hair was sure to escape its pompadour before the party was over.

She hummed as she packed her gingerbread, steamed pudding, and popcorn balls into baskets while her father hitched the team to the buckboard. Isaiah even unearthed some bells to tie to the harness. Tiny, light snowflakes were falling and tickled their noses as they tucked quilts around themselves in the buckboard.

Isaiah had no more than picked up the reins and clucked to the team than they heard the *clip, clop, creak* of a horse and wagon behind them. Kathryn looked back. Her hand flew to her mouth. "Oh, no! I forgot. Jules! Whatever will he think?"

Apparently Jules didn't know what to think. He pulled his hat off, and his sandy hair was quickly frosted with white. "Er—good afternoon. Am I late?" He looked uneasily from Kathryn to the handsome stranger beside her. "Or did you change your mind, Miss Kathryn? I mean, if I'm intruding . . ."

"Not at all, Jules." Kathryn began unwinding the quilts wrapped around her. "I'm pleased to see you. It was just that in all the hurry of getting ready, I—uh—got confused." It was the best she could do. "Mr. Sperlin, meet Papa's guest, Mr. Allen."

The two men nodded at each other, but neither smiled much.

Then Merrick broke the tension. "Allow me." With one leap he sprang over the side of the buckboard and held up his arms. In a single smooth sweep he grasped Kathryn around the waist and set her on her feet by Jules's wagon. "Up you go then, pretty miss." He boosted her up to Jules's outstretched hand. "Oh, ye'll take the high road, and I'll take the low road, but I'll be at the carol-sing afore ye!" He tossed his head and laughed as the buckboard rattled off.

Just like a wild horse, Kathryn thought as the gentle Jules tucked a blanket around her. Had Merrick meant it when he called her "pretty miss"? Perhaps her gray eyes were attractive enough, in spite of her other deficiencies. It was a terrible stab to her hard-won courage to think he might be mocking her. She turned to Jules with a shaky smile.

The Brewingtons' house was packed. Every homesteader who had chosen to winter on the desert was there, delighted to share in the celebration and fellowship. Nelly and Willa passed around steaming mugs of hot spiced cider while the neighbors visited.

Kathryn soon found conversation with Jules a little heavy going, and she noticed that although Alvina was well occupied by Myron and Elmer, David and Lucy were growing restless.

"Let's take the children out to build a snowman," Kathryn said to Jules.

"Well, I don't know . . ." he began, but Kathryn was already pulling on her knitted tam and mittens.

"Yeah! A snow fight!" Davey Brewington issued a general invitation.

Kathryn was surprised to see Merrick pull on his jacket and join them. She was even more surprised when she tried to roll a snowball. "What's the matter with this snow? It won't stick!" She looked at the loose white mounds on her gray mittens.

Jules nodded. "I tried to warn you. Dry snow. Not enough water in it to make it stick."

Kathryn brushed off her hands in disgust. "What good is it then?"

Jules shrugged. "Well, it's pretty. Makes it look right Christmasy-like."

And Kathryn had to agree, although it was an awful disappointment. "At least it lies flat on the ground. In Nebraska there was always so much wind with the snow that the ground would be bare and the snow'd all pile up against the buildings."

Davey and Lucy, who were used to the powdery stuff, knew what to do with it. Shrieking, they chased each other around the house with handfuls, trying to wash each other's face.

"Might do for a game of Fox and Geese," Merrick suggested. No one had heard of such a thing, but they obediently followed him around, dragging their feet to trace a wide circle with intersecting lines like the spokes of a wheel. The fluffy dry snow didn't cooperate by staying in obedient mounds on each side of their pattern, but with enough tracing they finally had marked trails.

Alvina, Jules's brothers, and even quiet, pale Mrs. Robinson, whom Kathryn had met the day she saw the cayuse band, came out to join in the game.

Merrick was the fox first, and the geese scattered in every direction around the wheel. Shrieking and laughing, all escaped until at last he tagged Kathryn.

"Persistent, aren't you, Mr. Fox?" She gave him a saucy look, then yelled, "Run, geese, run," and the game was on again.

Finally, rosy-cheeked, noses stinging and running from the cold air, the geese all flocked back into the house for mugs of hot cocoa. The adults had already begun singing "O Come All Ye Faithful" to the merry accompaniment of Ned's harmonica.

Adam led them on through the entire repertoire of familiar carols, and it was long after, when everyone was sprawled languidly, voices tired of singing and stomachs full of Christmas treats, that Kathryn wandered to the back bedroom to get a fresh hanky out of her coat pocket. With her hand to the door she stopped.

It hadn't been her intention to eavesdrop, but the intense tone of the voices told her this was not a conversation to interrupt.

"No sir. I hear what you're saying. But I can't believe in a God who allows all the injustice I've seen in this world." In spite of the unaccustomed bitter note, she recognized Merrick Allen's voice. "I've talked to lots of preachers, and no one has ever been able to answer that."

Adam's reply was so gentle she could barely hear it through the narrowly opened door. "God's not unjust. Man is. God allowed us to choose, because He didn't want to be worshiped by a pack of puppets. And man chose to do wrong."

"Yeah. I've heard that before. But I say, if He's God, He could have stopped it. I just can't accept that He lets all the unfairness go on."

"Can't accept or won't accept?" Adam paused, then his tone changed. "Where do you get off, Merrick Allen, telling God what you will and won't accept about the Almighty's behavior? What gives you the right to make the rules for God?"

Merrick was quiet.

Kathryn smiled and breathed a prayer for her papa.

After a bit Adam continued. "Besides, you're asking the wrong person. If you're really looking for answers and not just shouting excuses, why not ask God?"

"What?" Merrick's voice held shock and amusement.

"Well, the Scripture says He stands at the door of every heart knocking, and for anyone who opens that door He will go in and sup with them. Have supper—and a nice visit. Now if I wanted to know why—say Ned out there—was doin' something I didn't think was right, I'd ask him round for coffee and gingerbread, and we'd sit a spell and talk it over. I sure wouldn't go to some third party and yell my head off about it."

Just then Alvina called Kathryn, so she missed the reply. But later that night her papa's words came back to her. Mr. Allen wasn't the only person she knew who inwardly screamed at God and challenged Him for doing things the way He did. Of course, she didn't refuse to believe in God just because she hated the desert, but she hadn't done a very open-hearted job of accepting His will.

She was just considering praying about it when a pack of coyotes, driven closer to settled areas by the snow, began howling. No, she could believe in a God who made sagebrush and coyotes, but she didn't have to like it.

5

The days of January and February blurred into one long sameness of gray cold, broken with occasional spells of piercing bright sunshine that somehow seemed to make the cold even sharper. Then came windy March, blowing even more dirt into the homestead shack. No matter that the strips of batten filling the cracks between the upright boards were designed to seal out dirt and weather.

"This just doesn't work! You'd think someone could figure out a better way to build a house than this." Kathryn hit at the gray dust on the floor rather than swept it.

Nelly, who had driven over with some exciting news that morning, patted her rounding abdomen and nodded her blonde braids sympathetically. "I know. I wish I had more of the building paper Ned lined my walls with. If Isaiah has a good crop this year maybe he can buy you some. But in the meantime we can do what I did before."

"What?"

"Use newspaper. I've been saving Ned's all winter—there's a whole stack of *Statesmen* in the buckboard. I could have brought them in, but they're pretty heavy, and Ned is always at me to be careful these days."

"Oh, yes! You must be! I'm so happy for you!" In spite of the restrained behavior she had been taught by the Nebraska church women, Kathryn flung her arms around her friend and kissed her before running out to haul in the heavy bundles of newspaper. "Isaiah has a hammer and some tacks in the lean-to."

She ran around the side of the house. The shed was much emptier now at the end of a winter of full-time sagebrush burning, in spite of almost daily chopping as well. Thelma's half-finished cradle now stood forlornly forsaken in the corner. It made Kathryn breathe a prayer for Nelly's safe delivery before she hurried back to her task.

"If I could talk Papa into keeping our papers I could do this all the time," Kathryn said from her perch on the stepladder. "But he always takes them to someone when he goes calling. Says it would be selfish not to share."

"Your papa is one of the kindest men God ever created. Don't you worry about papers. I'll keep saving ours for you. If we can put a fresh layer on every spring—and maybe in the fall, too—you'll be amazed how snug this place is in no time."

That night when the March wind howled around the shack, accompanying the howl of a lone coyote, Kathryn was sure that it was more than just her imagination that made her feel cozier than before. If she shut her eyes she could even pretend that the paper had yellow roses on it.

If I had some yellow paint, I could paint roses on it. And she didn't care if it was a silly idea. It made her smile.

Eventually March winds turned to April showers, and even Kathryn reveled in the intoxicating fresh scent of sagebrush after rain—a sagebrush now golden with a tiny yellow bloom. All across the desert it was almost possible to believe in the prophet's vision, for even though the desert didn't blossom as a rose, patches of soft green moss appeared under the sage bushes, and tiny purple, yellow, and white wildflowers sprang up everywhere. Kathryn began taking long, rambling walks across the desert, as she so often had across the fields of waving prairie grass back home.

"Papa, guess what I saw today!" She burst into the shack late one morning, in a rush to fix their mid-day meal so that the men could get back to the fields. "A whole nest of baby rabbits!" She didn't wait for him to answer. "They were the dearest things. I'd love to have one for a pet."

Isaiah exploded in a guffaw. "You can't make a pet of a jackrabbit! Might as well take in a pet coyote or rattle-snake."

She set a steaming bowl of succotash on the table beside the slices of fried ham and turned to take from the oven the sourdough biscuits she had set earlier. "But it would be nice to have a pet. Henny Penny and Chicken Little's chicks are precious."

She didn't say more, but she began thinking: a dog. A dog to go on walks with her and to sleep by her bed at night. If he didn't spring up and growl, she'd know the coyotes were howling from the butte and not really under her window as it always sounded.

But the hens never laid more eggs than the Jaynes needed themselves, so she had no hope of earning the price of a dog with egg money, which was the way Nelly and the other women earned money here, just as they had in Nebraska.

This place offered one commodity, however, that her former home hadn't—the ever-present sagebrush. If she could chop enough to get ahead on their needs, she could send a load to town with Papa or Isaiah when they went for supplies. She had heard they paid two dollars for a wagon-ful at the seed store. She wondered how long it would take her to chop that much.

Three days later she found a new opportunity. Isaiah had hauled a fresh supply of water in from Indian Creek, so Kathryn took on the enormous project of heating water in the copper washtub and scrubbing every piece of dirty laundry in the house on a washboard, wringing it out by hand, and hanging it up. She was almost finished when she heard a ruckus like none other she'd ever heard.

She rushed to the window, but as it hadn't rained for a few days, she could make out little through the swirls of dust. Horses stomped, men shouted in a strange language, and dogs barked, all above a wave of bleating and baaing.

When Kathryn stepped out the door it appeared that the whole desert was alive. Hundreds of sheep, their white woolly bodies rolling along like ocean waves, were passing within a few feet of where she stood.

"What's happening?" she shouted to one of the sheepmen riding near her, but he only waved and flashed a broad, white-toothed grin beneath his black mustache before calling something unintelligible to his dog.

Kathryn turned to see if she could spot Adam or Isaiah planting alfalfa in the field they had cleared last fall, but they were out of range. And then a familiar figure rode into view.

"Jules! I'm so glad to see you!" She ran to him as he dismounted from his tall roan horse. "What's going on here?"

He tipped the broad brim of his cowboy hat in greeting. "Basque sheepherders. They winter along the Snake between Boise and Twin Falls. Taking their flocks to summer pasture in the Owyhees. I've heard tell they come through every year. Got your chickens out of the way? They'll scatter to kingdom come."

With a cry of concern for her fuzzy yellow babies Kathryn flew to the far side of the house. Fortunately they had been pecking on the side away from the sheep, and the mother hens were doing their best, with admonishing clucks and flapping wings, to keep their broods in line.

Kathryn began scooping the soft, squirming balls into her apron, while Jules filled his hat. By the time they had all three dozen rounded up and shut in the lean-to with the hens Kathryn was laughing so hard she couldn't have caught another chick if its life had depended on her.

The sea of sheep was still undulating past, their constant baaing becoming almost a familiar background by now.

"Oh, no! I left the door open," Kathryn wailed as a fresh cloud of dust rolled right into the house. Then a worse thought struck her. "My laundry!" She ran to the other side of the shack, where Isaiah had strung clothesline between house and barn. The white sheets that had so glistened in the morning sun just half an hour earlier now hung limp and streaked with dust. But before she could bemoan the work all to be done again she had a still worse thought—the towels she had spread on sagebrush bushes.

There was no point in looking. She was too discouraged to bother protesting the unfairness—the stupidity—of this place. She set her jaw and turned to the house, slamming the door behind her. She'd heard such an action referred to as "wooden swearing," and she had to admit that the sharp bang did give satisfying expression to her anger.

A moment later there was a gentle knock on the door, so soft she didn't hear it at first. She responded to the third set of rappings, flinging the door wide in an equally angry reverse of her earlier slamming.

"Yes?" she growled.

"I—er—thought I might be able to help." Jules stood there, his arms piled high with the soiled laundry, looking as apologetic as if he had dirtied the sheets himself.

"Oh, come in." She knew she should be grateful—at least polite—but she couldn't muster such gentle emotions at the moment.

As easily as if it had been a pan of dishwater Jules carried the copper tub out and dumped the dirty water on a patch of Isaiah's winter wheat that had managed to survive. He refilled the tub from a partly empty barrel and set it on the stove to heat.

By the time the linens had been once again scrubbed on the washboard, rinsed, and wrung out by hand—an activity Kathryn had to admit Jules was particularly adept at with his enormous hands—the wave of sheep had passed by.

"Now, there may be compensations. Let's go look." Jules started toward the door.

"Compensations? What about hanging up these sheets?"

"When we get back. Come on."

With a sigh, Kathryn followed him. Around the far side of the barn he stopped and grinned. "Ah ha. Now that's what we were looking for." He pointed to four scrawny lambs standing on wobbly legs, bleating with wavery voices as their mothers' white tails disappeared beyond the sage bushes. "Herders call them bummers—lambs that can't keep up. Aren't worth their time, so they're left—to help make up for any damage in crossing your land, if you want to look at it that way."

A baby with a black nose and one black foot turned to Kathryn with a mournful baa. She knelt and gathered it into her arms. "Oh, you darling!" But her delight turned to dismay when it began sucking at her cheek. "What will I do? I don't know how to feed a lamb."

Jules chuckled and picked up the remaining three. "Got an old work glove?"

Kathryn found one of Isaiah's. Jules cut tiny holes in the end of the middle finger and thumb and filled the glove with milk.

"Can only feed two at a time, but this should work." He sat with two lambs on his lap. In no time they had sucked the glove dry.

Kathryn gave a cry of delight and poured more milk into the glove. "How did you know about all this?"

Jules shrugged. "Neighbors warned us about Basque coming through. Raised lambs in Iowa."

It took six glovefuls to quiet the lambs, and then the laundry was still to be hung out, but Kathryn's spirits were restored. "I'm going to name them Flopsy, Mopsy, Cottontail, and Peter—if that suits them—I mean . . ." She reddened. She didn't know a polite way to ask.

53

But it didn't bother Jules. "You got it just right. That'un—" he pointed to the one with the black nose "—that's Peter. The others are his sisters—or girl cousins, at least."

Kathryn laughed. "Just wait till Papa and Isaiah see this! They told me I couldn't keep pet rabbits."

"Oh, I plum forgot. Mentioning Adam and Isaiah puts me in mind of my errand. Tell them, meeting of the Boise-Payette Water District in Nampa next Thursday. Hope to have a good delegation from Kuna. If we can get that proposed New York Canal dug hereabouts this summer there'll be no limit to what we can do with this land."

Jules helped her shift the lambs to the corral before he left but advised her to keep them in by the stove at night.

She shook her head over the thought of what that would do to her attempts to keep her floor clean, but she was determined to make good in her new role of shepherdess.

By May the lambs were strong enough and the weather warm enough that they no longer had to be brought into the house. This gave respite to Kathryn's housewife chores but brought the added concern of protecting them against coyotes at night.

It was a help to have the lambs taking less time, however, for now that all danger of frost was past the garden must be planted quickly to get in as much growing as possible before the really dry season came. It seemed they had three seasons there: dry, dryer, driest. So now Kathryn worked long days planting rows of beans, carrots, cabbage, beets, carrots, and corn, then carrying water to it all by hand every day.

Midway through her second week of garden tending, Kathryn had a particularly long, hard day. She had begun by setting her bread to rise, then realized how low they were on fuel for the baking so spent an extra hour chopping sagebrush.

Then the lambs, who had graduated from their bottle-feeding, had to be put out to forage. Sheep were God's hardiest grazers. They could survive and even fatten on the sparse, tough weeds of the desert.

She watched the four curly white backs for a moment, listening to the soft tinkle of their bells. Yes, she could survive here, too. With God's help and sheer willpower she would survive. But she doubted that her soul could fatten. There was no time to dwell on it, however, for there was the mid-day meal to fix, the garden to water, the floors to scrub.

After supper when she went back to gather the sheep for the night, Peter, true to his name, had wandered off. She put Flopsy, Mopsy, and Cottontail in the barn, then had to walk nearly a quarter of a mile toward the butte before she even heard his bell. It was growing dark by the time she got back and barred the barn door.

"Oh, Papa, Isaiah! Thank you so much for doing the dishes!" Their thoughtfulness nearly made her cry. They had worked longer and harder than she all day, and still managed this kindness.

"Go to bed, daughter." Adam put his hand on her shoulder. "I had no idea what a hard life I was bringing you to."

"It's all right, Papa. We'll make it." She gave him a quick peck of a kiss, then stumbled off to her bed.

Many hours later a ruckus in the barnyard startled her awake. She had long ago learned to sleep through the coyote howls. But this was different. Closer. More urgent. Clucking. Cheeping. The beating of wings.

Suddenly she knew. The chickens. She had forgotten to put them in the shed. "Papa! Isaiah!" She grabbed her shawl. "The coyotes are in the chickens!"

Isaiah, in his long nightshirt, was the first out the door with his shotgun. Around the side of the shack two long-legged, sharp-eared critters made black silhouettes against the moonlit desert. Two rapid explosions of the shotgun tore the night. A coyote yelp rang above the noise of frightened farm animals. The dark forms disappeared.

"At least one of 'em won't steal any more chickens," Isaiah said.

Adam brought a lantern.

Kathryn started to sob at the sight of scattered chicken feathers, legs, heads, and wing parts, which was all that remained of her once downy brood. Then she set her jaw as she had learned to do months ago and began rounding up the survivors.

As if that hadn't been the final straw, the next morning Isaiah presented her with a long, stout stick that had a small fork on the end. "It's gettin' pretty hot most afternoons now. Time you started watching out for rattlers."

This wasn't exactly new information to Kathryn. She had heard plenty about rattlesnakes when they arrived last summer, but she hadn't ventured far enough from the house to have to go armed. By the time she started working farther afield chopping sage, the weather was cool enough that the major danger was past. But now it was coming on again, with new nests of snake eggs fresh-hatched.

An instant vision made Kathryn shrink: gray and black diamondback snakes coiled under every sage bush, rattling their tails ominously. Then she took a deep breath and held out her hand for the stick. "And what do I do with this?"

"Best thing to do is freeze stock-still and hope the snake will go away. If he don't, place to pin him is right behind the head. Don't get his tail—he'll coil around and strike you."

Kathryn nodded. She got the picture. "And this?" She pointed to the sharp little penknife tied to one end with a leather thong.

"If you ever have to know—a snakebite will just be two little puncture marks on the skin." Isaiah opened the knife and held it above his wrist to demonstrate. "You take this here knife and cut an X right through the center. Then suck and spit and suck and spit as hard as you can to get the venom out. You hear?"

Kathryn more shivered than nodded—but she heard. She wasn't sure she could ever do such a thing. But she heard. And she never again went beyond the barn without her snake stick.

At least there were two bright spots on the horizon that summer: the coming of water and the coming of Nelly's baby. Talk of water was on every tongue. Meetings of the irrigation district became more and more frequent as survey teams planned laterals that would reach many homesteads from the New York Canal, and D. R. Hubbard began selling subscriptions in his Idaho Lateral and Canal Company to build reservoirs in Ada County. Those homesteaders with land below Indian Creek dug channels to carry water to their fields. Even though the sandy soil caved in constantly, rabbit and gopher holes undermined the digging, and once completed only the merest trickle of water reached the fields, optimism still ran high.

And Nelly bloomed. Late July or early August the doctor in Nampa had said, and the more excited Alvina, David, and Lucy got about the arrival of their new little brother or sister, the quieter Ned got. But his grin just got broader and broader until it seemed it would split his face. His harmonica playing every Sunday morning got more and more joyful.

They made plans to build another room onto their house. Adam, Isaiah, the Sperlins, and Joe Robinson would all help as soon as the crops were in that fall. With everyone working, the project could be finished in a day.

And although the room-raising was still several months off, it, as well as the coming of the baby, was a favorite topic of conversation after Sunday services. Kathryn noticed that Manda Robinson never entered in, however. It just seemed that her dark eyes got bigger. In spite of the summer sun, her skin got whiter, and she got quieter.

Kathryn worried about how all this rejoicing over the coming of a baby would affect Isaiah. Just a year ago he and Thelma had been as happy as Ned and Nelly. He never said anything, and Kathryn avoided the topic when around him. But still she worried.

One day in mid-summer, Kathryn came back from the garden with a mess of leaf lettuce, thinking about how good it would taste for supper with hot bacon bits and vinegar poured over it. She heard the strangest noise coming from the hut. At first she thought someone had been hurt, then she smiled. What on earth could make Papa sing so off-key? He usually had a lovely voice. Suddenly she realized it was Isaiah. She had never heard Isaiah sing alone before.

Inside the shack an even more startling sight met her. Isaiah had hauled the half-finished cradle from the lean-to and was sitting in the middle of the floor, whittling the second rocker. He looked up at Kathryn in the doorway and grinned. "Ned mentioned as how they'd loaned Nelly's sister the crib the others used, and her little'un was still using it—so it seemed unneighborly to let this sit in the woodshed."

Isaiah's mourning was over.

Kathryn was learning to cling fiercely to the bright spots, so she held Isaiah's victory in her heart and made it her own victory too. She needed it as the summer wore on.

This one, everyone said, was hotter than ever before, and the flying ants came sooner. Indian Creek dried up. So did most of the crops that had been planted with such high hopes a few months earlier. At least Isaiah's winter wheat yielded a crop, so they were better off than most. The talk of irrigation now seemed forced, almost desperate. There was no action. No reclamation workers. No new laterals. But they had to believe it would come.

Now clothes hung out on the line at nine o'clock in the evening would be bone dry and stiff in fifteen minutes. Henny Penny and Chicken Little, who had survived the coyote raid, refused to lay in the heat, so they were without eggs, and the cow gave little milk. Such commodities couldn't be brought from town because they would spoil on the long wagon ride home. Kathryn was getting so hungry for fresh meat she was almost tempted to try imitating stories she had heard of Silver City miners eating rattlesnake.

Then Adam came in from one of his pastoral visits with two jackrabbits. Kathryn gave a cry of delight, thinking of the delicious stews the young Molly Cottontails, as they called the females, had made that spring. "Oh, Papa, I'll fry one and stew one with carrots and potatoes, and we'll have a feast!"

She grasped them by their long hind feet and almost skipped out to the chopping block. With one swift motion apiece she had their heads off, then took her butcher knife and slit the tough gray skin from neck to tail. Taking a firm grasp on each flap of skin she pulled—hard. The skin pulled away, and Kathryn stared in horror. She was too appalled to scream. Then, after a long, frozen moment she flung the rabbit from her and fled.

"Maggots!" she shrieked at Isaiah. "Maggots! Crawling all under the skin—white—squirmy! *Ooh!*" She put her hands over her eyes to blot out the sight.

Only when he put his arms around her did she realize the man by the door wasn't Uncle Isaiah. "Oh, Jules, it was awful. The rabbits—Papa just shot them, but it was like they'd been dead for days!"

He held her as a shudder shook her body. "I'm so sorry, Miss Kathryn. Ma knew you'd be short of meat, what with the coyotes gettin' your chicks last spring, so she sent me over with a pot of fricassee."

"Oh, Jules," was all Kathryn could say as she leaned against him.

Willa had sent an enormous pot. "This is far more than we can eat, Jules. You'll stay and help us, won't you?"

His ready acceptance told her he'd been hoping for just such an invitation. She boiled carrots and made a cabbage slaw from the few vegetables she had been able to rescue from the jackrabbits. Supper turned out to be the feast she had promised after all, especially since she had made a pie from the apples Isaiah brought from town last week. Kathryn served it all on her mother's best china, which she had brought in a special chest from Nebraska and had used only at Thanksgiving, Christmas, and Easter so far.

After supper she cringed for the safety of her dishes as Jules insisted on helping with the washing up, but, as before, she was amazed at the gentleness in his huge hands.

When they were through he asked, "Would you like to take a ride with me?"

"Ride?"

"In the wagon. I thought maybe along the creek or around the butte, whichever you'd like."

Kathryn suppressed a bitter retort. Why bother driving out? One could see a lifetime of sagebrush from the doorway. But Jules was so kind and obviously so pleased to offer her a treat. She couldn't disappoint him. "Let's go toward the creek. I haven't seen Nelly for almost two weeks. I'd like to see how she is."

The week before, Kathryn had gone with Isaiah to take the finished cradle to Nelly, and it seemed her time must be near. Kathryn couldn't imagine how uncomfortable it must be to be so enormous in such heat, but Nelly had just mopped her forehead and laughed.

"It'll all be worth it. Woman was meant to bring forth her babes in pain, but joy cometh in the morning."

Kathryn wondered how long it'd been since she had thought of that verse. She had once clung to it desperately as a beacon of promise, but lately it seemed she had given up waiting for joy. How did Nelly manage to radiate it?

So Kathryn and Jules stopped to visit the Brewingtons, and Kathryn promised to return early the next week. Nelly was sure the baby would come anytime now, and even with her energetic family she needed all the help she could get.

Afterward, with the long evening shadows bringing cooler temperature, they drove on toward Indian Creek. Although the creek bed had been dry for weeks, a few sumacs and greasewood bushes had roots deep enough to survive. To Kathryn's green-starved eyes it was like a park.

"Oh, this is nice." She sighed.

"I hoped you'd like it." Jules's gentle blue eyes sparkled at her. "Whoa, girl." He pulled on the reins, and the wagon creaked to a halt.

When his arm went along the back of the spring seat Kathryn knew she should move, but she was so tired.

"Miss Kathryn, I—uh, I—"

Oh, no! Don't let him propose! Now she did move, but there were only a few inches to the edge of the seat.

"I was wondering—I mean, I think most awful highly of you. Would it be all right if I came courting?" He stopped to clear his throat. "Just once in a while, that is. I wouldn't want to make a nuisance of myself."

"Oh, Jules." She knew she should say no, but she was so relieved that he hadn't asked a harder question that all she could do was nod weakly.

Jules's arm left the back of the seat and nestled around her shoulder. For one alarming moment she thought he might try to kiss her, but one tight squeeze was all he attempted.

"I think we should be getting back," she said weakly.

Fortunately, driving a wagon required two hands.

6

The following Tuesday Kathryn raced through her chores, put beans, cornbread, and cherry pie out for the men's dinner, and set out at a brisk trot astride Buckshot, her long skirt bunched under her. A whole day with her friend would be a rare treat.

"That you, Kathryn? Come in." Nelly's cheery voice greeted her knock. "I'm just too comfortable to get up." Nelly sat in the rocking chair, her sewing balanced on her knees beyond her protruding abdomen. "I thought maybe we could finish hemming these shirts today."

Kathryn took off her sunbonnet and sank into a cushioned chair. "What comfortable furniture you have." She picked up a tiny shirt and threaded a needle. "Where is everybody?"

"Ned's in the south field. Vina took Davey and Lucy to the dentist in Nampa."

"You let them go all that way alone?"

Nelly laughed comfortably. "Vina grew up in this country, and she's been driving the wagon since before she was ten. Ned said he'd take them next week, but I wanted that done before the baby comes, and I don't think it'll wait another week. I sure hope not. Oh, look at that!" Both women watched her abdomen jerk as the baby kicked.

"Oh, my. Looks like he's trying to get out now. Doesn't that hurt?"

"Well, in a way. But it's such a satisfying feeling too. This little human life just stretching away in there—I don't know, it's hard to explain. Someday you'll know, my dear. There's just nothing nicer." Nelly's conversation slowly faded into the faraway smile that had become characteristic of her these last months.

Kathryn thought how nice it would be to be so contented. She wondered if she would ever know.

Nelly was just telling Kathryn what to prepare for the mid-day meal when the first contraction made her cry out. "Oh, Kathryn, it's too early, but that felt like the real thing."

Kathryn wasn't sure whether she was more delighted or frightened. "What shall I do? Shall I get Ned? Is there time to ride for the doctor? Boil water, don't they say?" She started to reach for a kettle.

Nelly laughed. "No hurry. I'll have hours yet—if this really is it. Ned will be in for his dinner soon, then he can ride to Nampa for Dr. Marsh. Pity we didn't know to tell the children to bring him back with them."

"How can you be so calm?" Kathryn felt fit to be tied, while Nelly continued to rock comfortably.

"Oh, I'll be plenty excited when I'm sure it's really coming. But after all, this is my fourth—it's not exactly unknown territory for me."

So, in spite all her instincts to rush to the field for Ned or to the nearest neighbor for another woman to be with them, Kathryn took the cast iron skillet from its hook and began frying potatoes.

An hour later, in spite of the heat of the day, the potatoes were growing cold in their bacon fat, for Ned still had not come in. Nelly refused to admit to any worry but agreed it wasn't like Ned to be late for his meals. And she had another sharp contraction.

"No, I mustn't eat anything, in case the babe really is coming. But you go ahead and eat, Kathryn. If Ned isn't back when you're finished, maybe you should go look for him. Maybe he went to Sperlins to talk about that water meeting, but it isn't like him not to tell me."

Kathryn put a slice of ham on a piece of bread. "I'll just eat this on my way. You're sure you'll be all right alone?" She tied her sunbonnet under her chin.

Nelly assured her she was fine, and Kathryn flew out the door toward the field Ned had planned to weed that day. Even in her hurry she took time to check that her snake stick was still attached to Buckshot's saddle. Constantly digging her heels into the horse's sides to urge him to go faster, Kathryn followed along Indian Creek over a small rise that concealed the bean field from the house.

She soon saw Ned's big brown horse grazing at the far side of the alfalfa field beyond. "Thank goodness, he hasn't ridden off to a neighbor." But her relief turned to perplexity when she couldn't see Ned's tall form anywhere in either field. Even if he was sitting down for a break he should be visible.

"Ned! Ned!" There was no response to her shout.

She decided the best plan was to ride toward the horse, but she knew better than to ride across a field, tearing out plants and irrigation furrows, so it was several minutes before she reached the far side of the field. "Ned! Ned!" she tried again.

This time she thought she heard a reply. Did something come from the other side of that sagebrush bush? She turned Buckshot into the uncleared land—and saw a dark form lying in the gray dirt. "Ned!" She was beside him in an instant. "Ned! What is it?" She grabbed his hand. It was burning, but that shouldn't be unusual in this heat.

Ned muttered something. And then Kathryn saw. Two tiny puncture holes on his arm.

She looked around wildly. There was no help for miles. Yet there was. In the time it took her to draw a breath the words came to her, *Be of good courage. . . . I am with you always.*

64

"Oh, God! Help me!" She stumbled to her feet. Her fingers were clumsy with haste as she untied the snake stick from her saddle. Too late for the forked stick. The rattler would be far away by now. But thank God for the knife on the end.

Could she use it? Could she remember what Isaiah had told her? It had to be done right after the bite—Isaiah had emphasized that. How long had Ned been here? Was it already too late? There didn't seem to be much swelling —surely that was a good sign. She had to try. Ned's life was in her hands. She wanted to shut her eyes as she drew the knife blade between the two red dots. But she had to look. She had to get it right. Not too deep—just the capillaries, Isaiah had said—don't cut an artery. She drew the knife. Then again, at an angle to the first.

Now she was acting on pure instinct, no time for thought. Lips tight over the cut area. Suck. Mouthful of warm, sticky blood. Spit. Spit again—don't leave any venom in her own mouth. Again. Suck. Spit. Again. And again. Occasionally Ned moaned and shifted restlessly. Sweat poured down Kathryn's face. Her heart pounded. She felt dizzy. Isaiah hadn't told her how long to keep up the process. But she knew she couldn't go on much longer. If she passed out, there would be no help for Ned or for Nelly alone at the house. One more mouthful. Spit. Her head spun crazily. She had to quit.

What now? She knew it was important to keep snakebite victims still—something about keeping the heart beating slowly—venom spreading less rapidly—if only she'd paid more attention to Isaiah's lecture. But she really had no choice. Even if it would be safe to move Ned, she wasn't strong enough to lift him onto his horse. She would have to go for help.

This time she didn't worry about the bean crop as she galloped Buckshot across the field. It must have been a good twenty minutes' ride through crops and sagebrush, every pound of Buckshot's hoofs raising clouds of dust in her eyes and nose. Coughing, choking, sobbing, she at last arrived at the Sperlins, her sunbonnet flung back, hair whipped wild around her head, face streaked with dirt, tears, and blood.

"Jules! Myron! Help!" Fortunately they were working the field nearest the Brewingtons'. Young Elmer was the first to reach her, but all three boys were there by the time she had choked out her story.

Jules took charge. "Myron, your horse is fastest—you ride to Nampa for the doctor. Tell him snakebite and a baby so he'll know what to bring."

Myron was in the saddle by the time Jules had finished instructing Elmer to go get their ma and take her to Nelly. "And don't do no harebrained thing like blabbing to Nelly about Ned. Tell her he's delayed in the field. That's all. You hear?"

Elmer headed to the house at a run.

Jules considered for a moment. "It'll be quickest to take our wagon. You better wait here—your horse looks about foundered. I'll be back in a flash."

Suddenly, after all that frenzied activity, Kathryn was alone in an empty field. Papa had always told her waiting was what she was worst at. He was right. She put her elbows on the saddlehorn and dropped her head into her hands. Now she had time to worry. She knew she should pray, but at times of great stress she could never think of the words.

Then, slowly, as her heart stopped racing and her eyes closed, the words came to her that Papa had quoted on that first awful night here almost a year ago, *Though I walk through the valley of the shadow of death . . . thou art with me.* And then she could pray. *Yes, Lord, and be with Ned and Nelly.*

Then she was rattling back across the field in Jules's wagon, directing him to the place she had left Ned.

Ned was unconscious, but alive. The sun had shifted so that the sagebrush gave him some shade.

Jules looked at the brown splotches on the ground. "Land sakes! You did some job. Did you leave any blood in him?"

"I didn't know, so I just went on as long as I could. Will he live?"

Jules examined Ned's swollen wrist. "Looks like you got a good clean cut. No telling how long he'd been here, though. Sucking has to be almost immediate to do any good." He shook his head. "Still, we can hope it was a dry bite. Snakes don't always inject venom, you know."

Kathryn wanted desperately to cling to that hope, yet she had to be honest. "But would he go unconscious from a dry bite?"

Jules shrugged. "Shock can do 'bout anything, even to a strong man. Here. Help me hold this blanket tight. We'll roll him onto it—easiest way to get him on the wagon."

The next hours were a blur in Kathryn's mind except for details that remained with her forever: Jules's saying, "You go in and tell Nelly. Gentle as possible. No way we can keep it from her now—have to take him in." The cool splash of the washwater from the pan on the bench by the door, so she didn't have to go in to Nelly with Ned's blood streaked around her mouth. Sitting by Nelly's bed, waiting for a long, hard contraction to pass before she could tell her the fearful news.

Nelly's courage. Willa's calming presence as she bathed Nelly's forehead with vinegar water. The building tension of waiting and waiting, with Nelly's pains coming ever closer and closer.

Jules reviving Ned with spoonfuls of whiskey, kept in the cupboard for medicinal purposes, then pouring some over his wrist. "Pa says it prevents infection—don't know why, but we allus do it on cuts."

And at last the clatter of a buckboard, horses, and voices as the three young Brewingtons arrived with Myron and Dr. Marsh.

Soon after, Elmer, who had gone to the Jaynes' with the news, returned with Adam and Isaiah. Kathryn made coffee, then went with Alvina and David to do the evening chores when the Sperlin boys went home to do their own.

Kathryn thought they should offer to leave, and yet she couldn't. She had to see Nelly delivered and talk to the doctor about Ned. After nearly two hours more of waiting they heard a tiny wail from the bedroom. Kathryn, who was sitting by Ned saw the smile on her patient's face, but Adam restrained him from getting up too quickly.

"Just give 'em a minute. They ain't going anywhere."

In a few minutes Adam helped Ned to Nelly's bedside, and Dr. Marsh proudly presented the red-faced bundle. "Nelly tells me he's Ned, Jr."

Kathryn later was always so thankful the Brewington family had that time together, as she and Adam and the doctor left the room and the other children went in, because by the time she went back the next afternoon Ned was in a coma.

Nelly was sitting up in bed nursing Neddy, tears rolling down her cheeks. "Dr. Marsh said you and Jules did everything just right, bless you. But it was late. He's a strong man—maybe he can throw off the poison. Some do. All we can do is pray."

"We hoped it might be a dry bite. Or maybe the snake didn't have much venom." Kathryn wanted to say something hopeful.

Nelly shook her head. "Arm wouldn't have swollen if there wasn't poison. It must have been awful for you. I don't know how you did it."

Kathryn didn't answer but watched spellbound as Nelly pulled baby Ned's tiny mouth away from her nipple and turned him to the other side, tickling his cheek to make him open his mouth.

"Wake up, sleepyhead. You've got work to do here." He fluttered his eyelids and with a tiny gurgling sound began sucking.

It was all so wonderful. And so awful. Kathryn kissed her friend and went out to walk by the creek, staying carefully to the path and grasping her snakestick firmly. What if Ned died? How could God let anything so awful happen? Just when everything should be so perfect. Like Thelma and her baby.

Why do You do it, God? She thought again, as she had so often, of that overheard conversation Christmas Eve between her father and Merrick Allen. Merrick was right. The world *was* full of cruelties and injustices.

The thought came to her: *Why not just abandon God?—He's abandoned you.* And yet she knew she could do no such thing—for without God what would she have left but the cruelties and the injustices? Without God she would have to go through the valley of the shadow of death alone. But she didn't want to go through it at all. Even with God, she didn't want to go.

The next day, though, she sat by Nelly's bed and held her hand and walked through the valley with her.

Davey came for Adam just after breakfast that morning. By the time Isaiah arrived, after seeing to the stock, Ned was dead. Whether from snake venom or from infection was hard to say, but it didn't really matter. They had all done their best; it just wasn't enough. Nelly and baby Ned went in to say good-bye after Dr. Marsh left, and Adam and Isaiah went down to the cemetery to make preparations.

That afternoon Kathryn stayed with Nelly while the others went to the service. "It wasn't even a year ago you and Ned were helping Isaiah," Kathryn choked.

Nelly squeezed her hand. "And now my Ned's laying beside your Aunt Thelma. The desert's a cruel place. I thought we could beat it, but I don't know." Tears slipped from the corners of her eyes.

"What will you do now?"

"I don't know. I haven't thought. Ned loved it here. My sister's my only family, and she doesn't have any extra room. If Davey were older, we might hang on. I don't know."

Kathryn shook her head in amazement over Nelly's words. *Why in the world would anybody want to hang on here? All this country's good for is funerals.* "In the midst of life we are in the midst of death," Papa said. *What life?* she thought. It all seemed like death to her.

After the brief burial the Sperlins came bringing food just as the Brewingtons had done for the Jaynes less than a year ago.

"Would you like to take a ride, Miss Kathryn?"

Why did Jules always have to be so kind? And would he ever quit calling her "*Miss* Kathryn"?

She shook her head. But when they got home she wished she had accepted. The flying ants had returned.

7

Kathryn clamped her jaw and hung on, because that was all there was to do. Then one morning she woke up and discovered that she had survived not only one year, but two. Two whole years of living without water. Who would ever have thought it possible?

Nelly had hung on as well. Alvina was now almost eighteen and Davey thirteen, so they could do the work of adults. They no longer had the days of study Kathryn had once envied them, and now she was ashamed of that envy. She was glad they had had that happy time. For although she was nearing twenty and had for several years done the work of an adult in the house, she had been asked to take on very little field work as Alvina now did.

All the men in the area did what they could to help as well. The Sperlins, as always, were the soul of kindness far beyond the call of mere neighborliness, especially Myron, whose smiles at Alvina were sometimes returned. Isaiah, it seemed, spent almost as much time on the Brewington land as on his own.

As a matter of fact, Adam and Isaiah had cleared little new land the past year. Kathryn thought she had detected less enthusiasm for planting this past spring—more acknowledgement of the fact that crops couldn't be kept alive with water hauled from the Snake River and that all

71

their irrigation meetings had produced no actual surveying or digging.

The New York Canal Corporation, financed with Eastern money, went bankrupt, leaving a few miles of unconnected canal dug in the desert beyond Boise. There was only one bright hope in the struggle for water. Former Governor Frank Steunenberg, famous for being a strong leader, had accepted a position on the water council. With the political knowledge of an ex-governor who could call powerful friends all over the state and in Washington to their aid, surely something would be done this year. Steunenberg was their only hope.

Kathryn had taken on only one new project. Well, really two as it turned out. When butchering time came she couldn't bear to have Flopsy, Mopsy, Cottontail, and Peter slaughtered. They were pets. She couldn't let them become lambchops.

"We have Peter. Couldn't we breed them? Raise sheep? They grow better here than beans, anyway."

Isaiah had to agree she had a point, so he began calling her Bo-Peep and built larger pens for the expanding flock.

The next time he returned from town, strange squeals and grunts from three crates in the back of the wagon drowned out even the squeak of the iron wheel that needed greasing.

"Now don't you go making pets of these, young lady. I fancy my sausage. We'll raise these for food while you're coddling that rack of lamb."

"Oh, Isaiah, they're darling!" She couldn't decide whether to hug her uncle or the little pink piglets.

"No pets, I said." Isaiah sounded like he meant it.

"No, uncle. I really don't want to start a piggery, either. I know what I'll do. I'll name them Ham, Bacon, and Sausage—that way there'll be no doubt in anybody's mind about their future."

Early in 1905, when they had been there two years and five months, it seemed that the long-hoped-for miracle of water would at last become a reality. Governor Steunenberg apparently had captured the attention of someone in Washington, D.C., because the Corps of Irrigation and Drainage Engineers sent a survey crew to map out laterals, canals, and ditches. There was going to be a dam. There was going to be water.

Almost overnight the population of the area doubled with the establishment of a tent town for the crews. Kathryn felt she had some sense of what it must have been like in Silver City when gold was discovered. People. Excitement. Hope for the future. Except that water was much better than gold.

Adam saw something far more precious than gold or water—souls. Here indeed were fields white unto harvest, for the survey crews were tough men, used to living in isolated areas for long periods of time without the civilizing factors of families and churches. These were men who needed the gospel. He began immediately planning a great brush arbor meeting for Easter.

"But, Papa, that's two months away. Why wait so long?"

"Because I want it done right." He ticked off the reasons on his fingers. "We don't have a building or even a tent big enough, so we have to wait till the weather's good enough to have it outside. I want plenty of time to get to know these fellows—not just hand them a flyer and leave —that's not evangelism, and—" he paused for his announcement to take its full effect "—we need time for your organ to get here."

"Oh, Papa! That's wonderful!" Kathryn threw her arms around him. "I just hope I can still remember how to play. Which hymns shall we sing? 'Amazing Grace' for sure. How about 'Shall We Gather at the River'? We'll be by Indian Creek, won't we?"

"Whoa—" Adam held up a hand "—there'll be time enough to worry about all that. Better go slop your pigs now if Isaiah's going to get that sausage he's been dreaming of. But I do reckon a lot of folks who wouldn't walk across the street to hear a preacher would come out for some nice organ music."

At last the optimism of the area caught up with Kathryn. The coming of water was wonderful; the coming of her organ was—was—no word seemed to capture the deep joy she felt, so she lay down her pencil with a sigh. Besides, she didn't need to record this in her journal—she would never forget.

The fact that Kathryn had returned to writing in her journal was evidence enough of the change in her attitude. She hadn't touched it for months. There had been nothing to write. One day was the same as the next. But now, if joy wasn't exactly coming in the morning, it might arrive in about two weeks—as soon as Marie Sykes could get the organ crated and carted to the train station.

She must write to Marie for advice. Marie was a much better musician than she and could give her helpful advice even from a distance. Suddenly a wave of nostalgia washed over Kathryn. Not exactly homesickness, but a flood of bittersweet memories of her old home and gentler life, of Marie and the good times they'd shared at the organ. How she would love to see her beautiful friend again.

But she did have one dear friend close at hand. "I must tell Nelly," she cried.

Isaiah looked up from his newspaper. "I'll drive you over."

She started to protest that she could go by herself, but Isaiah was already buttoning his long, sheepskin-lined coat.

Two weeks to the day later Kathryn was gathering eggs in the new henhouse Isaiah had built for her after last spring's brood had thrived and outgrown the lean-to, when she heard Lucy calling.

"Kathryn! A man from the train asked me to tell you—there's something *huge* arrived for you at the station!"

From then on, every moment Kathryn wasn't absolutely required to be doing something else, she was sitting at the organ, her feet pumping an alternate heel-to-toe rhythm, her fingers getting reacquainted with the keys.

One thing she did take time for, however, was going with Adam to distribute flyers about their meeting to homesteads as far away as Meridian and Nampa. So it seemed perfectly natural for her to offer to accompany him one early March evening when he set out for the survey camp. She couldn't understand his reluctance.

"The thing is, I've made some right fine acquaintances among the surveyors," he explained. "Joe Robinson and Myron Sperlin and several other of the local men have hired on to work with them, so I've had a friendly introduction. But I'm not sure this is the best place to take my daughter. There's sure to be a fair amount of drinking and gambling going on—not the place for a lady."

Kathryn disagreed. "It's exactly the place for a lady. That's what's wrong with them. They need to see a lady to remind them how to be gentlemen." She sprang onto the buckboard beside him.

But when they got to the camp just beyond Ten Mile Station, where a major lateral was to be dug from the Ridenbaugh Canal, which had supplied irrigation water to Nampa for several years, she wondered if she had been overly optimistic. She could see the red glow of cigar tips and hear rough laughter as they approached the largest tent.

"You let me go in first and give them some warning. Then I reckon it'll be all right for you to come in and hand out the flyers. It's a sure thing they won't turn them down."

Standing just outside the doorway of the tent Kathryn heard the men greet her father and invite him to sit a spell. She smiled. Adam had often said men drank and gambled because they didn't have anything else to do. Their willingness to put their cards down to hear his news was evidence that his theory was right. She hoped they didn't keep her waiting long. With the coming of the evening dark, it was getting cold.

"Well, well, what have we here?" She felt a warm hand clasp her waist. "Who's the pretty miss?"

She jerked back, poised to slap her assailant, then gasped as the lantern light from the door fell across his face. "You! I didn't know you were a surveyor, Merrick Allen."

He jerked his hat off his head and held it over his heart as he bowed. "Forgive me. I wouldn't have taken such liberty if I'd realized—that is, we don't see many ladies—er, are you alone?"

Just then Adam stepped out of the tent. "Merrick! What a happy surprise. Come in, both of you. Get out of this chill."

In a few minutes Adam had introduced his daughter around, told the men that she would be providing special music at the meeting, and Kathryn had distributed her handbills. She assumed they could go then. But Adam and Merrick Allen were deep in conversation, so she sat quietly and listened. In the time since Merrick had been here three Christmases ago he had traveled the West from San Francisco to Santa Fe to Butte, Montana.

"And have you written that letter yet?" Adam asked.

Merrick looked embarrassed. "Time hasn't seemed right. But I haven't forgotten." Then he laughed. "Maybe now I'm here, you'll be my conscience."

Adam started to reply, but some men around the table began shuffling cards. "Hey, Allen! Come give us a chance to win back what we lost last night."

"Yeah, quit gabbin' with the parson. Let's have some action."

Merrick turned to the table, and Adam led Kathryn to the wagon. "Sorry about all that. Knew this wasn't any place to bring you."

76

She didn't reply. *What letter?* she wanted to ask. Why did she find it so hard to talk about Merrick Allen? Why should she find the memory of his flashing blue eyes and unruly black curls glistening in the lantern light so disturbing?

With only two weeks left till Easter, there was little time to worry about such inconsequential things. Adam and Isaiah and the Sperlins spent every spare minute building a platform and making benches from boards and sawed-off logs and arranged them in a sheltered spot by the creek. Only the most romantic imagination could style this an arbor—but it was the best they could do. There were a few sumacs, and the sage and greasewood bushes grew taller here than anywhere else along the creek.

When Nelly wasn't chasing toddling Neddy she helped Kathryn write out song sheets for those who wouldn't know the words.

"I hope our homesteaders will sing good and loud. I don't think those surveyors are going to know many hymns —if they come at all."

Nelly laughed. Life had been hard without Ned, but she had hung on and managed to keep her cheerful disposition—a continual inspiration to Kathryn. Now Nelly looked at her friend. "You sound nervous. I can't believe it. I thought you loved playing the organ."

"I do. And singing, too. When I'm all by myself, or just sort of lost in a crowd. Not up on a platform with everyone looking at me. What if people don't sing out—I'll be doing a solo. It's not so bad with you and the Sperlins and the Robinsons, folks I know. But these surveyors—I don't know . . ."

She laughed too. "I know it's probably wicked to wish they'd stay home and gamble—but I'd sure be less nervous. At least I don't have to worry about Merrick Allen. There's not much chance of his choosing church over a game." She turned her attention to copying.

"Surely they wouldn't gamble on the Lord's day." Nelly sounded shocked.

Kathryn shrugged. "Maybe not—just all night the Saturday before so they'll be too tired and hungover to worship God the next morning. That's more likely."

But Kathryn's doubts were no restraint to Adam. This was the real beginning of the work he had come for. His Sunday preaching in homestead shacks and his rounds of "pastoral calls" had all been laying the groundwork for starting a permanent church that one day would have its own building and minister to all the spiritual needs of the area. So every minute Isaiah could spare him from the fields, Adam worked on his sermon, and the week before the meeting he determined to make repeat calls on everyone in the area to be sure they hadn't forgotten.

In spite of Kathryn's pleas that he stay home when it started raining on Wednesday, he rode out every day to gather his congregation. "What better sign of the Lord's blessing could we have than rain in the desert?" he insisted when Kathryn shook her head at his sneezing.

"It'll be a fine thing if you come down with a sore throat and have to preach with a raspy voice," she warned.

But he had heard of a band of sheep herders living out toward Owyhee County, and he wanted to be sure they were invited.

"Papa, they probably only speak Basque." But Adam was determined. And when he returned late Friday night wet and chilled, her concern for him silenced any nagging she might have done as she heated water for a footbath and brewed a cup of strong tea with honey.

Saturday he was feverish and his throat so swollen he could barely talk above a whisper. Kathryn made a thick poultice of turpentine and grease to smear on his chest and neck and wrapped him in flannel, but by evening he was no better.

"How do we go about canceling the meeting?" she asked. "It seems a shame to let folks come all this way and then be disappointed. Of course, maybe it'll start raining again. That'd keep most of them at home." She looked skeptically at the new-blue sky.

"Cancel the meeting!" Adam croaked and struggled to sit up.

Isaiah pushed him back down on the bed. "You relax, big brother. We'll think of something." He signaled Kathryn to follow him out of the room.

"We'll not cancel the meeting," Adam rasped after them.

Kathryn began making kitchen noises, stoking the stove and banging pans to cover their conversation. "I'm worried what it'd do to him if we canceled. I'm afraid he'd fret himself right into pneumonia—if he doesn't have it already."

"So what can we do? I guess you can go ahead with the music all right."

Kathryn turned so sharply she dropped her wooden spoon. "What? The music—all by myself? I mean, I'll play the organ—I don't mind that, set way off to the side—but you don't expect me to announce the songs or anything?"

"Well, I was thinking—if Jules and I set the organ sort of sideways, so's your back wasn't really to the congregation, and you sang out real loud—"

"Isaiah—no!"

She thought of all those people. All those faces. All those eyes. All looking at her. And she'd have to look back. She put her hand to her throat, as the old choking feeling came back. She could feel the people closing in on her, could hear their voices, feel their breath. "I can't—" she started, then a racking cough from the next room made her stop. "I'll think about it. Maybe it'll rain."

Isaiah sat up much of the night reading Adam's sermon notes over and over. Kathryn, feeling the shack close in on her and, everytime Adam coughed, knowing what she must do, went out to the sheep pens. The night was crystal clear. She could hold out little hope for rain.

She could hold out less hope for joy coming in the morning. In the morning she would not be allowed to play her beloved organ in an obscure corner of the arbor, as she had envisioned, but she would have to take a position up front before all those people.

There was no hope for it, because although Isaiah would attack this challenge with the best will in the world, only a direct act of God could make that man sing on key. And she simply didn't have faith to pray for a miracle of that magnitude.

Flopsy, Mopsy, and Cottontail, each with a new lamb tottering beside her, came up and nuzzled Kathryn's hand. "The Lord is my shepherd," she said over and over. But even that didn't remove her terror.

When she went in after chores, she realized it was the time of day Adam usually read the Bible aloud. Tonight he was not able to, so she would read to him. Taking his well-worn Book she opened to Isaiah 41, where he had been reading. For a time she read placidly, happy that the words were soothing to him, until she came to verse 6: "Be of good courage." There was her special comfort again. She sat up and read with more emphasis. "Thou art my servant; I have chosen thee, and not cast thee away."

A weak smile played around Adam's lips as if he knew how the words were speaking to Kathryn.

"Fear not, for I am with thee; be not dismayed; for I am thy God; I will strengthen thee; yea I will help thee; yea, I will uphold thee with the right hand of my righteousness . . . For I the Lord thy God will hold thy right hand, saying unto thee, Fear not; I will help thee."

The next morning she needed that promise, for Adam was no better and it did not rain.

A full two hours before the meeting was to start Jules rode over to help Isaiah load the organ onto the wagon. Kathryn redid Adam's poultice and rewrapped the flannel, brewed him a big pot of tea, and kissed his hot forehead. When she had rearranged her hair for the fourth time and checked that all three hatpins were firmly in place, she could delay no longer. She pulled on her gloves, picked up her Bible and hymnal, and went out with her jaw set. That was one of the hardest parts—the knowledge that she couldn't get through the morning with her jaw set. She had to sing—loudly.

"You sure look pretty, Miss Kathryn." Jules handed her onto the spring seat beside Isaiah. She forced herself to smile at him as he crawled into the back to steady the organ on the drive over the rutted road.

She couldn't believe what she saw when they approached the arbor. People were already arriving. Those who came with children from a long distance had piled their wagons with baskets of food and blankets, set to make the day a full outing and picnic.

She cringed when she saw her organ placed in the center of the platform. The raised wooden floor hadn't looked particularly high when the men built it. Now it was absolutely lofty. She decided her best hope was to meet as many people as possible first. If she could see them as individuals—friends—they might not loom as such suffocating specters when she had to stand in front of them.

Nelly arrived with her family, Myron Sperlin driving her buckboard and Alvina sitting on the seat between her mother and their friend.

Kathryn turned to them. "Oh, Nelly, pray for us." She told Nelly what had happened.

"Oh—" Nelly gave her a quick hug "—you'll be just fine. Don't worry about a thing. How brave of Isaiah! He must be petrified. Where is he?"

Kathryn stared as her friend moved off through the rapidly growing crowd. She had turned to greet Manda Robinson when Jules came up.

"Isaiah says, can you play something while the people're coming in?"

"Yes!" What a good idea. This would give her a chance to adjust to the situation—with her eyes firmly on her music—and no singing. She picked up the skirt of her gray suit and hurried to the platform while Jules moved through the congregation handing out song sheets. Maybe she *could* do it after all.

She was just on the first step of the platform when a strange voice made her turn. Even in early spring they still had their suntans, and their snapping black eyes and flashing white smiles radiated joy. The sheep herders had come. Now she had to do her part.

No matter how off-key Isaiah sang, nothing could dampen Kathryn's enthusiasm for the first song. "Jesus keep me near the cross, there a precious fountain . . ." The words carried her through all four verses until she didn't even have to remind herself to sing loudly on the last chorus—"Till my raptured soul shall find rest beyond the river." She glanced over her shoulder toward the creek, running along happily in its spring freshness.

Then movement at the back of the arbor brought her attention to the congregation. She couldn't believe it. Part of her newfound comfort had been based on the fact that, although several from the survey camp had come, Merrick Allen had not. Now she watched his tousled head move through the congregation. He was taking his time, coming right down to sit in the front. He stuck his hat under the bench, folded his arms, and grinned at her.

Isaiah had to announce the next song twice to get her attention. "I Will Sing of My Redeemer." He looked at her. She realized that was the name of the song, not a statement of Isaiah's intentions.

This time, with Isaiah into the full spirit of the meeting, Kathryn found it nearly impossible to sing on key and find the right notes on the organ. No matter what Isaiah had said about following her, he was leading—leading them all far astray from the songwriter's intentions.

She pumped harder and pressed the keys with more determination. She began perspiring. It was a duel to see who could lead the voices, and Isaiah in innocent enthusiasm was winning. Kathryn would have given up and played to his leading if she'd had any idea where his erratic notion of melody would take him next.

Suddenly, on the second refrain, "Sing, oh, sing. . . of my Redeemer, with His blood . . . He purchased me . . ." A strong, clear tenor rang out from the front row, helping her fingers find the right keys. "On the cross . . . He sealed my pardon, paid the debt . . . and made me free."

She finished triumphantly. The rest of the service was given over mostly to singing, since Isaiah was understandably uncomfortable about reading Adam's sermon. It was a joy to Kathryn, who could now forget about the suffocating crowd and shut out Isaiah's cacophany in concentrating on the clear notes coming from just below the platform as surely as if an angel sang in her ear.

It was only on the last verse of the last song, "I Will Sing the Wondrous Story," that she dared look. She had known all along. Merrick Allen with his taunting smile was her angelic singer. When the service was over she was torn between rushing to him with her thanks and wishing he had kept his smirk at the poker table where he clearly belonged.

Then she repented of her wicked thought—she must be thankful for all the souls who had come to worship. And thankful for the help the Lord had sent her—no matter how strange His choice of messengers.

Those who remembered Merrick, including Nelly and the Sperlins, greeted him warmly, and Kathryn felt even worse for the meanness of her attitude. She was just gathering courage to add her own welcome when she heard Isaiah.

"Now why don't you just come along home with us? Adam's feeling mighty poorly, and you'd be good medicine for him."

"Oh, no." Kathryn hurried forward. "I hate to sound ungracious, Mr. Allen, but Papa needs to rest. Later, maybe—"

Again that mocking grin, as if he read everything in her mind. "I wouldn't want to put anyone out, pretty miss. Most specially not my friend Adam. You take him my greetings. Besides, Mrs. Brewington here has been so kind as to invite me home for Easter dinner. I can't tell you how long it's been since I've eaten scalloped potatoes, ma'am."

He offered his arm to Nelly, and Kathryn couldn't tell which was blacker—her feelings or Isaiah's looks.

But they had a whole congregation to greet. Everyone was so enthusiastic about the service, and appreciative of their efforts at substituting, that Kathryn and Isaiah had glowing reports to take home to Adam, who was improved enough to be able to sit up and eat his Easter dinner later.

It wasn't until Kathryn stepped outside to thank Jules for helping with hauling the organ and to send her greetings to Willa that she learned the truth. She really couldn't accuse the uncomplicated Jules of any desire to discredit Merrick Allen in her eyes—she was sure he simply found amusement in the story that had gone around from the survey crew after the meeting.

Merrick had been outspoken in his intention to avoid the service. "Haven't been preached to since I left Scotland. I didn't come seven thousand miles away from all that just to land back in more of it" were his reputed words. Then it seems he had a run of bad luck with the cards. An engineer with the crew had been in a sporting mood—offered him the chance to gain his losses back if he won—or go to the brush arbor meeting if he lost.

"He came to the service on a *bet*? She turned and stumbled blindly toward the house without waiting for Jules's reply. "On a *bet*!"

She slammed the door.

8

As summer came on, hot and dry as ever, anticipation of the water project mounted—and also anxiety. The engineers and surveyors extended their work to the southwest, leaving a trail of red-topped stakes in the ground and carrying with them an ever-growing stack of maps with little wavy lines marking the future placement of canals and ditches.

It became apparent that not all the land would be blessed with water. Some land was too high—the natural gravity flow of water from the canals would not reach it. Some land was too far out—the laterals would not extend so far. So tensions grew. To the normal stresses of drought and 100-degree-plus temperatures, jackrabbit plague, and flying ant invasion was added the stress of not knowing whose claim would suddenly become worthless. Who would have suffered all this hardship for nothing? Who would now have to start all over again on new land or seek employment in town?

The enthusiasm over the Easter arbor meeting led the recovered Adam to make such services a monthly event, held on Sunday evenings to avoid the heat of the day. Kathryn soon became so accustomed to playing her organ in front of the congregation that she now hardly gave it a thought, although she was ever grateful for Adam's strong, on-key voice to lead the singing. Especially since Merrick Allen never came back.

She told herself she was relieved. His presence made her so nervous she was far more likely to hit wrong notes, and with his perfect pitch that was an unthinkable embarrassment. But her relief turned to anxiety as stories of life in the camp began to reach her: hard-drinking late into the night, card games that more often than not ended in fistfights. Apparently the tensions of the entire area were working on the reclamation crews as well.

It was a gradual change but a significant one, when Kathryn realized she was concerned for Merrick Allen. Now when she thought of him while going about her chores, she prayed for his welfare rather than worrying about his effect on her.

Lord, keep him safe in all that. Show him what a wicked path he's chosen. Bring him to You. In her mind she would see him looking at her in his mocking way, and she was never sure whether she was embarrassed or pleased. She began looking forward to the next meeting, praying ever harder that Merrick would come and that he would find help.

There was no telling how much good her prayers did Merrick, but she soon found that they did wonders for her. Concern for another's welfare took her mind off her own hardships. Practically all her life she had cared for her father physically—seeing to his meals and laundry and cleaning house, but Adam had always been the spiritual shepherd, seeing to the emotional needs of all around him and especially to hers.

It was a shock to her to realize that someone so seemingly self-sufficient as Merrick Allen could have such needs. Now she wondered what his life was really like. How satisfying could the life of a gambler be, roving from one boom town to the next? What was he searching for? The money he won—apparently with considerable regularity—couldn't mean much. There was little to do with it out here except use it for the next night's stake.

And what about his family in Scotland? Didn't he miss them? He had never mentioned them. Did he have a girl-friend back home? A wife maybe? She paused long over that thought. What could have made him leave his home-land and come so far at such a young age? For all his so-phistication, she was certain he wasn't too many years older than she—perhaps twenty-five or thirty to her twenty.

What about that letter Adam had asked him to write? Was it home to Scotland or to another place he had lived? Was it to ask forgiveness? Right a wrong? Gain informa-tion? Grant permission? Ask a favor? Whatever it had been, Adam had asked about it as if it bore significance, no mat-ter how cavalierly Merrick responded. She determined to ask Papa about it—when the time was right.

Then Kathryn had another person to worry about. It was mid afternoon by the time she finished hanging out her laundry, scrubbing the floor with the wash water, and carrying it out to dump on her garden. She looked up and saw a thin trail of dust rising from the direction of Kuna Butte. She stood, shading her eyes with her hands, as the wagon rolled toward her.

Manda Robinson, looking more frail than ever, reined in her horse and clambered down from the seat.

"Manda, are you all right?" Kathryn ran forward to help her with the horse.

"Oh, Kathryn. I'm so upset. I had to talk to someone. I had hoped Adam—"

"I'm sorry. He and Isaiah went for water. I emptied the last barrel doing laundry today. Oh—" she turned with a start "—I forgot. Do you mind if we take these clothes in before we talk? They've been out for half an hour. They'll be stiffer than boards."

It took the women only a few minutes to fill their arms with the indeed bone-dry clothes and linen.

"Just dump them on the bed," Kathryn directed. "Isaiah bought some lemons last week. I've just enough left to make a pitcher of lemonade."

Manda sank into a chair while Kathryn squeezed lemons.

"Now," Kathryn said, "will I do to talk to since Papa isn't here?"

Manda's stifled sob came out like a hiccup. "I just heard. It's so awful I can't really take it in. A survey team's working on laying out a canal a mile or so west of us, so I drove over to watch—thought Joe might even be working with them. I see so little of him since he's been working with the crew—although goodness knows we need the income—but anyway, I got to talking to one of the men about when we could expect the canals to be dug. When there'd actually be water—that kind of thing . . ." Now she didn't even attempt to stifle her sobs.

Kathryn got a clean handkerchief and gave it to her friend.

Manda mopped her eyes. "He said—he said—it was unlikely we'd actually have water for three or four *years* yet—have to build a dam on the Boise River first. I don't know—he went into a lot of detail I didn't understand."

Kathryn nodded. It sounded just as bad to her. She'd like to break down with Manda, but she knew she had to be strong for her friend.

"Yes, I know—something about there not being enough water for the Nampa farms if they take it out of the Ridenbaugh Canal without having more stored higher up. I've heard talk, but it sounds awfully complicated." She took Amanda's hand. "Mandy, I know it's dreadful. We've held on so long with so little, and to have to wait so much longer—but it *will* come. Remember, last year we didn't even have any surveys. Now look—they're making progress. Things really are better. And Governor Steunenberg won't let them stop. He's wonderful on the water council."

Manda shook her head. "No, listen. You don't understand. You haven't heard the worst. At least we had hope before. But now . . ."

Kathryn waited through another spasm of crying with her arm around Amanda's shoulders.

"The man told me—our homestead's too high. We're above the water. When the whole system's running we might be able to *see* the water in the canal, but it won't flow to us."

Kathryn just shook her head. She couldn't imagine. The Robinsons had survived much worse conditions than her own. Uncle Isaiah had a two-room shack with barn, lean-to, garden, and a few animals all established when she and her father arrived. Joe and Manda weren't much older than she and had come to 160 acres of desolate sagebrush to put up a one-room hut and hang on for the coming of water. Now it was all for nothing. What could she say? Surely she should quote Scripture or pray or something to help Manda. But all she could think of was getting her a fresh handkerchief.

Then she thought of something else. "Manda, you only have that one man's say-so. Don't give up yet. Let's go to the survey camp and see what we can learn from the chief engineer. Maybe we can find Joe. He might be able to do something. He's worked with the crew for months— he has lots of friends there. Maybe they can do something —maybe change the plan. Why couldn't they just dig the canal on higher ground to the east of you? Did you ask that man?"

Mandy hiccupped. "No. I didn't think of such a thing. Do you think it's possible?"

Kathryn shrugged. "I don't know. But finding out is better than sitting here crying, and that's what I'm going to be doing in a minute if we don't do something. Besides—" she picked up her straw hat—it was cooler and more flattering than her sunbonnet "—if we're not here when the flying ants come, we won't have to clean them up."

The afternoon was wearing on. Adam and Isaiah would be back from their Snake River trek soon. Kathryn scribbled them a quick note, then added a postscript: "Here's dinner if I'm late."

She rummaged on the shelf and set a can of chili and a can of pineapple on the table beside the bread she had baked that morning. It didn't look like much. She added a packet of rice and a bottle of ketchup. "They'll survive."

Manda appeared to be too listless to do anything, so Kathryn drove the Robinson wagon. The underfed horse seemed to have as little energy as Amanda, and the trip was slow.

"Have you thought what you'll do if the worst happens and that man turns out to be right?" Kathryn asked.

Manda shook her head. "I don't know where we'll go. All I have is the aunt who raised me—I don't think she'll want me back. We could go to Joe's folks in North Dakota, but they couldn't afford to feed us. And now—now we're going to have three mouths to feed."

"Manda, that's wonderful!" Kathryn held the reins in one hand so that she could hug her friend. "Oh, I'm sure something will work out—God's in control. He'll have something for you."

Funny, she thought, when things seem to be the worst they can get, if you add one more reason for desperation, then faith will break through. "I guess sometimes we think we're at the end of our rope, but we aren't really. It's too bad that we have to be at the absolute bottom before we'll let God take over, but that seems to be the way." Her musings were really to herself. She didn't even know if Manda heard her. But at least she felt better.

Evening shadows were stretching out from the sage by the time they pulled into the camp. Most of the men were eating, filling tin plates from a big cookpot set over a campfire beside the cookwagon. The cook, wearing a dirty brown apron over his work clothes, was putting a tray of sourdough rolls on the table. A card game seemed to be in progress in the shade of a tent beyond the cooking area.

Kathryn imagined Merrick Allen was likely to be there, but she carefully did not look that direction. "Let's see if we can find Joe. Would he be eating with the men?"

Manda nodded. "He eats here. It's part of his pay." Her eyes were red-rimmed, and she looked as though a puff of wind would blow her over—if there were any wind on this breathless evening. But at least she wasn't sobbing as she held her head up and followed Kathryn.

They found Joe eating at the end of a long table and squeezed in on the bench beside him. He brought them plates of stew and rolls with tin cups of strong black coffee.

Kathryn was glad to see that the food seemed to buck up Amanda a little. But when they had cleaned up their plates they could no longer pretend this was a social call. Manda told her husband her devastating news.

It was clear this wasn't a complete surprise to him. "I've heard talk." He nodded. "I haven't really checked it out, though—been too busy working with our crew mapping the Mora Canal. Looks like the chief's about through eating. Come on. We'll ask him."

Kathryn was glad to see Joe Robinson put his arm around his wife's waist to support her. Kathryn followed at a discreet distance. This was a problem they would have to face together. There was little she could do for them now. She was standing in the doorway of the engineer's tent, wondering what she should do with herself, when angry voices around the side caught her attention.

As she stepped around the tent she saw that the attention of most of the camp had been captured. From every corner men came to see what was going on. Her eyes flicked over a red-bearded man sitting at a table. Hadn't she seen him before? Then her attention shifted to a gray-bearded surveyor with a purple nose and angry eyes, who

91

leaned across the table and pounded the cards scattered there.

"I've allus suspected it, Allen! Now I've got you red-handed!" He grabbed Merrick by the shirt collar and pulled him to his feet. "No one wins as much as you do without cheatin'. But this'll be the last hand you ever cheat on."

"Just a minute, Hank. You're wrong!" Merrick squared his shoulders. "Bo can tell you. He dealt."

Even from where she stood Kathryn could see that his eyes weren't mocking now. Their laughing blue had turned dark with indignation.

"Liar!" Hank's doubled fist slammed into Merrick's jaw, sending him reeling. "Leave MacLeod out of this—it's you and me!"

Merrick was back on balance in a flash, coming at Hank with fists ready.

The crowd closed around the fight, forcing Kathryn to move forward in order to see. She pressed a hand over her mouth, determined not to scream as she felt the tension rising in her throat.

The two men circled, punched, and blocked. The next connecting hit was Merrick's to the side of the man's eye, sending him sprawling. Hank rolled and sprang to his feet. A gun glinted in his hand.

Merrick, wiping the sweat from his eyes, didn't see it.

This time Kathryn screamed—just in time for Merrick to dodge the shot. He sprang forward, grabbing Hank's wrist.

They struggled, then fell, rolling in the dirt.

"Stop them!" Kathryn cried. "Why doesn't somebody do something?"

"It's their quarrel, lady," the man Merrick had called Bo muttered at her side.

Now the gun was out of sight as they rolled over it.

The shock from the explosion was so sharp that for a second Kathryn thought she'd been hit. The circle of observers drew back. Kathryn saw both men lying still.

"Oh, God, help," she sobbed.

Then Merrick rolled over and sat up, shaking his head. Kathryn would have run to him had not the circle closed in again around the wounded man.

"Somebody send for the doctor."

"Preacher, more like—look at all that blood."

Kathryn pulled at the shoulder of the man in front of her. "Is he dead?"

"Don't think so. Not yet. That Allen's a lucky son of a coyote—don't need no murder charges around here."

"Murder? It was an accident—you saw."

The man shrugged. "County sheriff don't take kindly to card fights."

Kathryn looked back to the circle. Hank hadn't moved. A dark stain was spreading over his left shoulder. All she could think of was how thankful she was it wasn't Merrick lying there. What if he'd died—right there? Gone into eternity without God. What if Hank did?

"Yes," she cried. "Somebody go get Papa—er, Parson Jayne."

No one moved. "Go!" she yelled to Joe Robinson, who just arrived. He went.

Now she looked back to the scene of the struggle and saw that Merrick had taken charge. "Get me a clean towel!" He was ripping Hank's shirt away from the wound. "And some whiskey!"

It was almost an hour later when Adam arrived. By then Merrick had staunched the flow of blood by putting pressure on the wound, removed the bullet with a buck knife cleaned in whiskey, and had the unconscious Hank carried to his bunk.

Merrick sat alone and limp in the dirt, leaning against a tentpole. Kathryn came to him and sat down without regard to her skirt. A lantern on a nearby pole chased a little of the darkness from where they sat.

"Papa's gone in to him. Will he live?"

Merrick raised his head slowly and looked up at her. "Maybe. Has a good chance if infection doesn't set in. Lost a lot of blood, though. If he lives the arm should be all right—the bullet just chipped the bone. Silly coot. Why'd he have to do that, I'd like to know."

Kathryn was quiet.

Suddenly Merrick turned to her with renewed energy. "Kathryn, I didn't do it, you know. I didn't cheat, and I didn't pull the trigger."

"It never entered my mind that you had."

When Adam came to them a short time later they were sitting silently, Kathryn's hand clasped in Merrick's.

"From what I could see it looks like you did a right fine job." Adam sat on the other side of Merrick. "How'd you know what to do?"

Merrick was quiet for a moment, as if deciding whether or not to answer. At last he sighed. "I thought of being a doctor. Once."

Kathryn was afraid Adam would let it go at that, but he pressed. "Must have done more than just think. You studied, too, didn't you?"

Merrick shrugged. "Read a lot. Worked with animals on the estate."

Kathryn longed for Adam to ask more, but the subject was closed.

After a while he went on in a different direction. "They'll get Dr. Marsh to have a look at him in the morning. I hope you won't feel you have to be moving on after this?"

Merrick shook his head. "Funny thing. I'd just been thinking of heading on to San Francisco with a friend, but I reckon this's the one thing that'll keep me here. Moving on would look like guilt. I can see that now. I don't think I could take it if it all happened again."

Adam got to his feet with such energy that the other two stood as well. He clasped Merrick's hand. "Good for you! That's just what I wanted to hear! And if it gets uncomfortable for you here, you know where I am." He paused for emphasis. "Any time."

"Thank you, Adam." Kathryn had never heard Merrick's voice so warm and genuine. "I do thank you—for everything."

"Even my prayers?"

"I just about think I do. Anyway, don't quit."

Fortunately Adam had driven the buckboard, because the Robinson wagon was nowhere in sight. Kathryn wondered what had come of her friends' inquiry, but it was far too late to ask anyone. She sat, nodding, on the seat beside Adam. At last she found the courage to broach the subject: "Papa, what did Mr. Allen mean about 'it all happening again'?"

Adam clucked to Buckshot in the cold, silent desert night. "Daughter, you know I can't talk about things told me in confidence."

Buckshot clomped on through the dark, the wagon swaying and creaking rhythmically. Kathryn's head dropped to Adam's shoulder, her eyes closed. Merrick's face was before her, his blue eyes twinkling, his dark curls falling over his forehead as always. But he looked different. Then she realized. His smile. It wasn't mocking her. How could she have failed to see the sweetness and beauty in his face before?

9

Sunday two weeks later was scheduled for a preaching meeting. Kathryn took extra care arranging her hair in a loose pompadour, with soft tendrils curling around her face, and pinning on her hat with the blue ribbons and lace that matched her blue dress. She wouldn't admit even to herself why she hummed softly all the way to Indian Creek, but when she took her seat at the organ, happily set to the side of the platform now, she did admit that Merrick's was at least one of the faces she sought.

She smiled at Nelly holding a wiggly Neddy and sitting beside Isaiah, as she so often did anymore. She nodded to Alvina and Myron, then hoped her smile at Jules didn't look as stiff as it felt. Manda and Joe Robinson were sitting far to the back, and Kathryn feared their long faces meant they had had no good news.

They were well into the second hymn before a small movement at the rear caught the corner of her eye. She looked up between verses and saw what she expected. That is, she expected to see Merrick, but she didn't expect him to look as subdued as even that quick glance had told her he was. Merrick Allen had come with none of the mocking bravado he had worn to the Easter service.

He left as quietly as he had come. Kathryn did not see him after the service, nor after the one that followed in two weeks.

By then the Robinsons were gone. Manda had driven over early that week to say good-bye. They had decided to move into Boise city, hoping Joe's small savings from the survey work would carry them over until he could find work in town.

Kathryn pressed two loaves of homemade bread and a jar of apple butter on her friend as a parting gift. There was little else she could do. "Try to send me word when the baby comes. If only we had mail service here!" She kissed Manda's thin cheek and waved her on her way.

The next Sunday there was better news. Adam ended the service, as was his habit, with an altar call, inviting any who so wished to come forward and pray. Kathryn prayed for Merrick, sitting on his usual back bench. But no one came. So Adam signaled Kathryn to stop playing.

"Well folks, I have something extra special to announce today. It seems that my little brother, Isaiah here, and pretty Nelly Brewington—" he pointed to where the couple sat smiling and blushing "—have decided to get married. They want to invite you all to their wedding, which will be right here after the service the first Sunday in October."

Kathryn greeted the announcement with the loudest anthem her little pump organ could sustain, and people didn't even wait for a closing prayer to rush to the couple to congratulate them. Kathryn looked at Myron and Alvina standing to one side, smiling, and wondered how long it would be before the daughter followed her mother's example.

The joyful news brought its own problems. Myron didn't seem to be the only one of the Sperlin boys who thought matrimony was a good idea. Jules, who had been undemanding in following up the permission Kathryn had granted him to come courting, suddenly increased his fervor until he became a regular presence around the Jayne place. As soon as his own chores were done he could always be found helping Kathryn feed chickens, fold sheep, or slop pigs.

He was ever polite and helpful, and even though Kathryn asked him simply to call her by her name rather than "Miss Kathryn," he often lapsed into the more formal form.

Kathryn found herself growing more and more edgy. She felt as she had in Nebraska, watching dark clouds gather on the horizon, feeling the sudden stillness in the air, and knowing that a storm was coming but not being sure when. It was obvious that Jules would soon propose. She just didn't know when. As a result she jumped every time he spoke to her.

The trouble, she mused one evening after he had gone, was with herself, not with Jules. He was so kind, so good, he would make a perfect husband. She did like him—a lot. Next to Nelly she considered him her best friend here. That was exactly the problem. She didn't want to marry him any more than she would think of marrying Nelly. And how in the world she could refuse his proposal, after accepting his courting all this time, without hurting his feelings and losing his friendship was beyond her.

"I can't leave Papa right now. With Isaiah getting married and moving to the Brewington place he'll need me more than ever," she rehearsed as she dug carrots from the garden. She knew the logical answer to that was that Adam now needed a son-in-law to help him with the Jayne place, and Jules would be happy to move in here and take over most of the work.

The more she thought about what a complete answer that was—a farm for Jules, more room for Elmer and Myron on the Sperlin place, and especially freeing Adam from the farming he disliked so that he could spend more time on the preaching and pastoring he loved—she almost

98

thought she could do it. She was quite sure she *should* do it, and that made her more edgy than ever.

But no worries of her own could dampen her excitement over Nelly's wedding. "Isaiah's going to ride into Nampa to get flowers for me to carry and to put on the table. I told him to try to get a bouquet to set on the organ too. Chrysanthemums should be in bloom now."

After Ned's death Kathryn thought she would never see her friend look so happy again.

"And come see." Nelly took her to the bedroom where she had almost finished sewing the ivory lace on her peach taffeta dress. She pointed to a soft green dress. "Alvina's going to wear this—to stand up with me."

They went on discussing the music Kathryn would play, although she had already begun practicing the traditional Mendelssohn and *Lohengrin*. Nelly's words presented an interesting question. Who would stand up with Isaiah? Adam, the logical choice, would be performing the ceremony. Joe Robinson was gone. At fifteen, David seemed a little young. That left one of the Sperlins or some other—no, it would probably be Myron Sperlin. That would make Alvina happy.

Then, as if she'd read Kathryn's mind, Nelly said, "And guess who's going to stand up with Isaiah—Merrick Allen."

Kathryn caught her breath. "Oh. I thought it would be Myron." Her voice was tight.

"No, Isaiah likes Myron fine, but he thinks Merrick Allen is something special."

In the coming days Kathryn scolded herself for letting Merrick's threatened presence at the wedding bother her. It was Nelly's wedding. Anything that made the bride and groom happy should be fine with her.

Autumn was the loveliest season in the desert, even nicer than spring, Kathryn thought, and Nelly and Isaiah's wedding day was one of the nicest. The sunshine was golden without burning, and the yellow bloom on the gray-green sage looked like the desert had been decorated for the marriage.

Adam kept the morning service short, preaching on the symbolism of the church as the bride of Christ and encouraging all there to be ready to attend the marriage supper of the Lamb.

"I know none of you would have wanted to miss this happy event today. Think how much worse it would be to miss that great marriage feast Christ is preparing for His beloved. We—each one of us—are His beloved. Would the bride miss the wedding today?" He looked at the glowing Nelly waiting at the back. "No less will you want to miss that great event. And all it takes to attend is having God's love in your heart, His robes of righteousness covering your sinfulness." He closed his Bible and stepped back, Kathryn's cue to begin "The Wedding March."

At a signal from Adam every head turned to watch Nelly and Isaiah walk down the aisle between the rough lumber benches. It was obvious they couldn't have been happier in the finest cathedral.

Kathryn smiled. She'd never seen her uncle look so handsome. Nelly's coronet of braids glowed golden above her peach gown. When they reached the platform, they paused to be joined by their attendants. Alvina, smiling as happily as her mother, took her place.

Kathryn concentrated very hard on the music for a full line, then forced herself to look. Fortunately she was at the end of the song, or she certainly would have hit a wrong note or—worse—missed her pumping and let the volume die. Merrick looked even more handsome than the groom. His gray suit, high stiff white collar, and black tie were breathtaking.

"Dearly beloved, we are gathered here in the sight of God and these witnesses . . ." Adam began.

After the ceremony, while the bride and groom greeted their friends, Kathryn served the cake she had helped Nelly bake.

"They're going into Boise City to stay at the Idan-Ha Hotel," Alvina whispered.

Kathryn had seen the six-story, French-chateau-style hotel on Main Street. Once she had even stepped into the lobby to admire the red plush Queen Anne furniture. She couldn't imagine what actually staying there would be like. She returned Vina's smile, then turned to serve a piece of cake to Willa Sperlin.

It was late afternoon when the bride and groom rode off in their buckboard to the accompaniment of friends' well-wishes.

Kathryn began cleaning up.

"Here, let me." Jules took the stack of dirty plates from her hands. "You sit and rest a spell. You must be tired."

She didn't even argue. She simply made her way to the edge of the arbor where several tall sage bushes offered some shade.

"Hello, pretty miss."

She started. She honestly hadn't seen Merrick there. She wondered if she would have gone that direction if she had.

Groping for something to say, she sat at the far end of the bench. "Are weddings in Scotland anything like this?"

"Not a lot different. They'd be in the kirk, of course— because it'd most likely be raining outside."

"Kirk?"

"The church. Ours was small, gray stone, with three bells in the tower." His voice was so soft she leaned toward him to hear better. "I think that's what I miss the most here—church bells. Miss them more than the green." He was quiet, then laughed. "Oh, sorry. You asked about weddings. Guess the biggest difference is that we'd have

101

the pipes—bagpipes. Can't get married or buried in Scotland without the sound of the pipes. 'Amazing Grace,' 'The Bluebells of Scotland'—nothing else like it."

"Mr. Allen, I think you're homesick."

He shrugged. "Not really. But something like a wedding—makes you remember."

She wanted him to go on, tell her more. "Where is your home?"

"Don't have one." He raised his eyebrows in his self-mocking way. "Oh, I know what you mean. Selkirk. Little village in the Borders. The Ettrick Water runs babbling through a draw in the hills. Good fishing." He held his hands more than a foot apart. "Trout and salmon that big. Hillsides all covered with fir trees. Dark, dark green, almost black. They raise sheep farther down, make lots of woolens—plaids and tweeds." He paused. "Sorry, didn't mean to bore you."

"No! I loved it. How I wish I could see it. Are there flowers? We had flowers in Nebraska. These chrysanthemums are the first I've seen for months." She felt she could talk to him like this forever. She felt so close to him.

They did talk more. He told her about his older, married sister and about his grandmother who was the family matriarch. But nothing he said gave her any clues as to why he had left.

"Miss Kathryn—" she jumped at the sound of Jules's voice "—your pa was feelin' awful tired, so Myron and I loaded the organ for him, and I told him to go on home, I'd bring you." He looked from Kathryn to Merrick and back again.

She suppressed her desire to sigh. "Thank you for helping Papa, Jules. You know, he never has fully recovered his strength from that fever he had last Easter. I beg him to take it easier, but he won't listen." She stood up and turned to Merrick, extending her hand. "And thank you for standing up with Isaiah today, Mr. Allen. I know he appreciated your support." They shook hands, and she walked off with Jules.

The wagon had rolled only a few hundred yards when Jules let the reins go slack and the horse slow to an ambling pace. "Miss—sorry, I mean Kathryn— I've been wanting to talk to you for a long time, but I wasn't sure what to say. Now I think I know, so I'd best go ahead."

She made a slight protesting sound, but he held up his hand. "No, don't say anything yet. I'd be powerful grateful if you'd just listen." He gave his head a little shake. "This isn't easy."

He concentrated on his driving for several moments. She sat with her hands folded in her lap, looking straight ahead. At last he took a great gulp of air and rushed ahead.

"Miss Kathryn, I love you. I have since the first time I saw you almost three years ago. And I can't think of anything more wonderful in the whole world than having you for my wife."

Again she made a sound, almost a groan deep in her throat.

"No," he said, "not yet. I'm not done. You see—" he turned to her, letting the horse find its own way "—you see, I know. I have for a long time, really, but I thought maybe I could win you. I wanted to try at least. But it was powerful clear today where your heart is."

She gasped, and he hurried on. "I just wanted to tell you how I feel. Just so's you'd know. I don't want to make you feel bad. And this way you won't have to worry about me asking you something you don't want to hear. Just so we can stay friends, that's all I ask."

Her eyes clouded, and her throat closed up so tight there was no possibility of answering him. She groped for his hand beside her and held it tightly in both of hers. She had never been so near to loving him.

10

Adam did take life somewhat easier that winter, much to his daughter's relief. There wasn't much work to do on the farm, and with many of the homesteaders moving into town for the winter there were few souls to shepherd. The surveyors finished their measuring and mapping, folded their tents and equipment, and seemingly melted away into the night, leaving the desert emptier than ever. In spite of the fact that they spent Christmas with Isaiah and Nelly, that was probably the most desolate holiday Kathryn had known. "Perhaps the New Year will be better," she wrote in her journal late the night of December 30, 1905.

The next day news swept across the desert of how much worse things had become. Former Governor Frank Steunenberg, on whom the area had pinned all its hopes for a speedy completion of the irrigation project, was dead.

Not just dead, but brutally murdered. Coming home late one night he had tripped the bomb that an assassin had attached to the white picket fence running around his quiet Caldwell home.

For days on end little else was talked of. New reports came flying: Governor Gooding had offered a state reward of $5,000 for the arrest of the murderer . . . other sources raised the total to $25,000 . . . a stranger registered at the Saratoga Hotel in Caldwell was suspected . . . the stranger,

Harry Orchard, was arrested . . . the Wobblies were behind it—the International Workers of the World had never forgiven Governor Steunenberg for using force in stopping union riots in the mines of northern Idaho . . . Harry Orchard confessed, naming big union bosses as his employers . . .

Then the rumors slowed, and routine returned to the cold, barren days in the desert.

Jules stayed true to his vow of friendship, and with Merrick gone with the survey camp Kathryn began to wonder if she had made a mistake in letting Jules decide the matter of their relationship for her.

The garden should have been planted by mid-May, but with nighttime temperatures still dipping well below freezing, there was nothing Kathryn could do but feed her sheep. They wouldn't even raise a pig this year—that had been Isaiah's pet project, and now he would raise all he wanted at what people persisted in calling the Brewington place.

Kathryn thought the title appropriate. No disrespect was meant to Isaiah, and it commemorated all the hard work Ned had put into building the homestead.

At last, the second week in June arrived, warm and sunny. Kathryn worked four days straight from sunup to sundown planting and watering her precious seeds, while Adam and Jules planted beans and sugar beets.

Now if it turned blazing hot in July, as it was wont to do, the tender sprouts would fry in the field, and that would be the end to farming for that year. At least they would have a few sheep to sell. Thank goodness for her tiny flock.

Kathryn couldn't imagine how others could hang on. Rumors persisted that reclamation workers would be back any day to dig the canals. But none materialized. Kathryn remembered the man who had told Manda it could be years yet—and that had been before they lost the powerful voice of Frank Steunenberg.

Kathryn mounded the last little hill of soil in the row she was planting, put in a spoonful of bone meal, dropped in her corn seed, and watered it. "One more row to go." She rubbed her aching back and looked to the end of the garden when a shadow fell across her path.

"Oh, Papa, you finished before I did. And I don't have your supper started yet."

"I'm not hungry," a soft Scots voice replied.

"Merrick!" She jumped to her feet, forgetting her aching tiredness.

"The bad penny returns."

"Merrick," was all she could think to say again.

He didn't seem to have much more in mind. He knelt down and helped her plant the final row of corn. And soon she thought of lots of questions: *Where have you been? What brought you back? How long will you be here?* But by then they were working so companionably she didn't want to disturb the silence, so they worked on to the end of the row.

By that time Adam had returned from the field, so she could let him ask the questions, and she simply listened while she prepared supper.

Merrick had gone to San Francisco with some of the surveyors seeking winter employment. While there he had met an old gambling buddy, A. J. Heston. "And Heston took me in as a partner in his construction company."

"What do you construct?"

"Dams, canals, ditches. Figured there's nothing more needed in this part of the country. Also figured it was about time I did something constructive—if you'll forgive the pun."

"Written that letter yet?" Adam asked around his coffee mug.

Merrick nodded.

"Mailed it?"

Merrick nodded.

"Got an answer?"

Merrick shook his head.

Almost overnight the months of waiting turned into hectic activity. Heston's company won a contract to construct a section in the vast network of canals, laterals, and ditches that would carry water across the desert from the Boise River to the Snake. The New York Canal, ending in the desert beyond Boise, had lain a vast, dry channel since Eastern funds to complete it had failed several years before. Now, with federal contracts going to a number of private firms, Diversion Dam would be built on the Boise River, filling the New York Canal which, when completed, would meet with Indian Creek just east of Kuna, fill the Mora Canal, and on and on across fifteen desert miles to Swan Falls on the Snake River. A jigsaw line of trenches across the desert carrying water as vital to its life as the system of veins and capillaries carrying blood to the body. And Merrick would be part of that project.

Now, with the renewed vigor that the challenge of preaching to construction workers brought, Adam returned to holding arbor meetings.

He thought to hold a special religious and patriotic service for the Fourth of July, and Kathryn, who had hardly touched her organ since Christmas, began practicing again. Hurricane lamps on shelves on each side of the music rack made the golden oak glow and shadows play across the organ's scrolled carving as her feet pumped and she set the range of eleven stops by ear.

It had been her mother's instrument, her wedding present from Adam. "Ordered it from Sears Roebuck for $79," she had heard her father say more than once. "Delivery anywhere in the U.S., and if you weren't pleased they'd pay return postage—but my Isabel was pleased."

Kathryn quit reminiscing and turned to practicing. The program would include all her favorite hymns, with

"America the Beautiful" and the national anthem as the centerpiece of the celebration. She considered including "Yankee Doodle," which sounded so good when she pulled the treble coupler all the way out, but decided that would be too irreverent for a preaching service. She did, however, include it in her practicing—just to warm up her fingers, she told herself.

She was never sure how much her increased practicing contributed to the mishap. As soon as she had the breakfast dishes washed one day she turned to her organ, which now sat against the wall where Isaiah's bed had been, making the tiny house seem almost roomy. She got as far as "O beautiful for spacious skies," when the pump pedal seemed to fall away under her foot, and with a gush of air the notes died.

It took all Kathryn's strength to push the organ out from the wall to open the panel in the back and find the cause. At first she thought mice must have been chewing the bellows. Then she realized this was the desert. Jackrabbits were their only vermin, and, nuisance though they were, she could hardly blame such damage on one of those long-eared gray creatures.

No, it was the perennial desert problem—dryness. The leather bellows had become so dry that with renewed use they had suddenly split at each fold.

Adam returned from the barn to find her sitting on the floor, her head in her hands. "It can't be repaired, Papa. It'll take a whole new bellows. What will we do about the service?"

Adam shook his head. "Maybe the Lord's trying to tell me something. Didn't seem like I was getting a very good response to my announcements, anyway. 'Spose we pray about it and see what happens."

Kathryn nodded. It didn't sound like much, but she couldn't think of anything else to suggest.

What did happen was beyond anything she could have imagined. The next day Merrick came to visit again.

She showed him the ruined bellows, thinking he might offer to get a new one for her at the Boise Music Company when he went into the city on construction business.

His proposal far outdid anything so modest. He didn't even ask—he insisted that she and Adam accompany him to Boise for the Fourth of July. By the time he had finished describing the parade, bands, theatrical entertainments, picnics, and shopping offered by the city of 17,000 people she was breathless.

She blushed and demurred, however, when he described the Natatorium, the elaborate wooden building at the end of Warm Springs Avenue that offered natural hot-water swimming. She did not have a bathing costume. The last time she had gone swimming she had been about ten years old. She smiled, remembering the hot summer's day and splashing in the Little Blue River with three other girls.

Adam, at first doubtful, showed increased interest in the excursion when Merrick reminded him that, if they went early, they might get seats in the courthouse for the trial of Big Bill Haywood for his alleged part in the assassination of Governor Steunenberg.

Adam nodded. "Been reading about that whenever I can get a *Statesman*. Sounds like that Clarence Darrow fellow's putting up a good show to get his client off."

Merrick agreed. "Not every day we get a fancy lawyer from the East in these parts. But the word is that the local prosecution's giving him a run for his money. My guess is we'll be hearing more from both James Hawley and William Borah."

So it was decided. The arbor meeting was postponed, Jules would take care of the animals, and on July 3 Kathryn got her long-cherished wish to spend a night in the Idan-Ha Hotel.

After breakfasting on scrambled eggs, muffins, and coffee at a small, round, linen-draped table in the hotel dining room, Kathryn straightened her hat, smoothed the skirt of her blue dress, and, wishing her outfit were as fashionable as those she saw around her, went out on Main Street to await the parade.

Boise's paved street had been cleared of traffic, leaving the two streetcar rails gleaming in silver solitude down the center. Ropes had been stretched over the street, and American flags fluttered in pairs every two hundred feet or so. Likewise, flags fluttered from poles atop the bunting-draped buildings. The highest, of course, was from the cone-shaped tower of the Idan-Ha.

The boom of a bass drum made Kathryn look to her left. Just in front of her the Columbia Band struck up a rousing version of "The Stars and Stripes Forever."

"I'm afraid that's better than 'Yankee Doodle' on the organ." She stretched up to speak right into Adam's ear so that he could hear her above the noise.

Next came Mayor John M. Haines, Grand Marshal of the parade, in a gleaming Ford "Black Beauty," its brass fittings sparkling in the sun.

Now it was Kathryn's turn to have someone speak into her ear as Merrick leaned down. "Did you know Boise has its own Ford assembly plant? Henry Ford's brother-in-law runs it out on the edge of town."

She stared open-mouthed at the amazing horseless carriage, wondering what it would be like to ride in one.

A contingent of Boise policemen marched by in blue uniforms with brass buttons and shiny badges, their bell-shaped hats and swinging nightsticks making them look like pictures Kathryn had seen of the Keystone Cops. Six white horses pulled the Liberty Car, filled with white-robed, flag-waving young women. Next came the Boise fire department with three horse-drawn wagons of the latest in fire-fighting equipment.

Later, bands, horses, and flag-waving children would blur in Kathryn's mind, but one group she never forgot: the half-block-long Chinese dragon that undulated down the street supported by members of Boise's Chinese community. The red, green, and gold cloth-and-paper dragon danced and skipped to the explosion of firecrackers under its pajama-clad legs. The fearsome fanged face suddenly rushed straight at Kathryn, making her step back to avoid its flowing beard. For an instant Merrick's arm steadied her. Then she was again firmly in balance, standing by her father.

Later she asked Merrick about the Chinese. "How did they get to Boise?"

"Came to work in the gold fields, then stayed to enter more stable businesses—laundries, restaurants, vegetable gardening."

Merrick led them just two blocks up Main Street to see Boise's colorful Chinatown. Kathryn loved the dragon-adorned, red-roofed buildings, but shuddered as Merrick told her of the vast system of tunnels the Chinese had dug under the streets to connect their various buildings.

"No, I would not like a tour, thank you." She would never voluntarily enter a place of close, dark underground channels.

At noon they picnicked in a cottonwood grove at Riverside Park, where they were serenaded again by the twenty-member Columbia Band. Merrick provided a hamper (Kathryn was never quite sure how) full of ham, cold chicken, potato salad, pickles, and those greatest of God's creations, fresh tomatoes and fresh peaches.

"Oh." Kathryn sighed, biting into her third tomato. "I've tried so hard to grow these, but they always blight in the heat."

At the end of the concert when the band, brandishing their instruments, got into waiting cars and drove off for a serenade of the city, Kathryn was amazed anew at how modern everything was in Boise,

She thought one day could hold no more excitement. But she was wrong. Merrick gathered up their picnic leftovers and suggested they go back to the hotel where Kathryn could have a rest before the theatrical that night.

"Theatrical?"

"A touring company from the East's been performing at the Columbia Theatre. I've heard tell they put on quite a show: Niagara Falls by moonlight with boiling mist; a working train engine with fourteen cars and a lighted caboose; and a horse race right on stage with real horses."

With all that to look forward to, Kathryn found resting difficult that afternoon, but she was glad for a time of quiet. She found that the excitement of the city and its crowds was tiring in quite a different way from the hard work of homestead life.

That night, after dinner at the hotel, an elegant affair served in five courses by white-jacketed waiters, Kathryn was enchanted with the Columbia Theatre. She had never seen anything like its black and white, zebra-striped stone arches and twin cone-topped towers. The play, whose numerous spectacular effects followed a plot line of the hero's falling into traps set by the villain and being rescued by the sobbing, golden-haired maiden, was punctuated with frequent explosions and billowing smoke. Kathryn felt the evening—the whole day—left nothing possible to be desired.

The next day Merrick was off about his business affairs before Kathryn and her father went down for breakfast. She and Adam ate quickly, then stepped onto the streetcar, as Merrick had directed the night before, to go to the Ada County Courthouse.

They were in luck. There were still a few high-backed wooden chairs empty in the back of the room.

At first Kathryn was fascinated by the scene before her. Dark-suited men sat at tables filling the front of the room. The panel of three judges sat to the right. The visitors' seats were packed with men and flower-hatted ladies who appeared to come from every walk of life.

The confessed assassin Harry Orchard sat in the witness stand, a stocky, dark-haired, mustachioed man. It seemed obvious to Kathryn, as to almost everybody, that Harry Orchard had not acted alone. The question at this trial was, since the motive for the assassination was trouble among the miners in northern Idaho, who had paid Harry Orchard? Who had masterminded the plot? Who was really responsible for the murder of Governor Steunenberg?

Three Colorado mining bosses had been extradited to Idaho, and suspicion fell most heavily on Big Bill Haywood, leader of the Western Federation of Miners. Harry Orchard was the star witness for William Borah's prosecution. The public had already been shocked by Orchard's blithe confession that he had committed more than twenty violent crimes against enemies of the miners' union. Now Borah was directing Orchard to testify that his salary for committing these atrocities came directly from the union payroll.

Then Clarence Darrow, Haywood's attorney from Chicago, cross-examined Orchard. Kathryn watched in amazement as the young, brown-haired attorney, forehead knit in a perpetual look of concern, elicited statement after statement from Orchard that cast doubt on his former certainties. Yes, someone had paid him. No, he never received a check signed by Haywood. No, Haywood never gave him any money in person. No, he had never dealt directly with Haywood. . . .

The crowded courtroom got hot and stuffy. Kathryn could no longer force herself to follow the intricacies of the trial. The fact was that a fine man had been brutally murdered. It was an act of unmitigated evil. Whether or not Haywood was responsible hardly seemed important to her, although she believed the guilty should be punished. The thoughts that filled her mind were of the evil in the world.

Just two days ago Adam had read aloud from Isaiah 6 the prophet's cry "Woe is me! . . . I am a man of unclean lips, and I dwell in the midst of a people of unclean lips." That was exactly how Kathryn felt. All around her was darkness and evil. Closing in. Oppressing her. She wanted to cry out, "Are none righteous, O Lord? Do none seek Thee?" The darkness came closer. She began breathing faster, her hands at her throat.

"Kathryn. Let's get some fresh air."

Adam's calm voice and steady hand led her from the room.

On the street, flags still flew from yesterday's celebrations. The sun was golden, the sky blue. Now she felt silly for her panic. Yet she knew that at least some of what she felt was true. Although one seldom experienced evil as a real presence, she did live in a world with much evil.

She sank against the leather seats of the hansom cab Adam hailed, closed her eyes, and prayed: *Dear God, You have made a beautiful world, but it has been so soiled by evil and the doers of evil. Help me to rely on Your strength and Your goodness. I have so little of my own. Help me find Your beauty when there is none around me.*

Then she looked around her. Adam had directed the cabbie to drive them up elegant Warm Springs Avenue, which was lined on both sides by fine mansions set in the midst of sculptured lawns and gardens bright with long-stemmed white daisies, delicate purple cosmos, and bright black-eyed Susans. In one yard a brilliant red climbing rose still bloomed in a shady spot.

"Thank you, Papa." She squeezed his hand on the seat beside her. "I needed to be reminded of the beauty in the world."

"I'm sorry you don't have more of it where we live, daughter."

Kathryn nodded. She was sorry too. But she said, "I know, Papa. But just knowing that it exists is a help. Remember when I was little and I was jealous of Betty Sue's porcelain doll? You told me to be glad she had it, that I could share in her joy and I could take heart from the fact that if someone had such a treasure it meant that it was possible I might have something like it—when the time was right."

"I'm not sure that's such a comforting analogy. You never got a porcelain doll."

"No, not a porcelain one. But don't you remember— my very next birthday I got that beautiful rag doll that I loved so dearly. I slept with her for years. The Lord knows you can't sleep with a porcelain doll. He gave me what I really wanted."

The cab stopped in front of the Boise Music Company just a block off Main Street, and Kathryn went in to buy her new bellows. She was a little worried since they didn't handle Sears & Roebuck organs. She didn't want to have to wait the weeks or even months it might take to mail-order the part.

But she was in luck. The bellows for their Esty organs were just the right size. And the man gave her a bottle of foul-smelling grease. "You treat your leather with this good —once a month at least—it'll keep it from drying out and cracking."

So her trip was successful in every way. As they rode homeward with the lowering sun, long shadows stretching behind them, Kathryn gave a contented sigh.

"Glad you came?" Merrick asked her.

"Oh, yes! It was all I could have dreamed of—no, it was far more than I could ever have dreamed of!" She sat silently for several moments, savoring her delight. She knew that the excitement of the parade, the fun of the pic- nic, the pleasure of the theatrical—much as she had en- joyed them—had not been the heart of the matter. She had found much of the beauty she always longed for in Boise with its elegant mansions and well-watered lawns. But the joy she took home with her from her trip was the knowl- edge that she was glad to go home.

Home to her brown, powder-dry desert with jackrab- bits and flying ants. Boise was filled with tree-lined streets of Queen Anne houses set in gardens radiant with flowers.

115

Home meant a two-room brown shack, the walls covered with newspapers. For the Lord knew that a rag doll was right for her.

She looked at Merrick beside her. She wondered how much of this joy was because Merrick was going home with them. As she thought of him she realized that the usual sparkle was gone from his eyes. "Merrick, didn't your business go well?"

"I'm not sure. Something worries me. Heston knows plenty about constructing canals. He'll drive that New York Canal across the desert in record time—probably way ahead of schedule. And he'll make a profit."

"So? Do you think he's dishonest?"

Merrick shook his head as if trying to shake off his frown. "Wouldn't have gone into business with him if I thought that. I spent all morning going over the books. There's not a flaw in them. I don't know what it is—like a weight here—" he put his hand on his chest "—that I don't understand."

Adam had been sitting quietly behind them in the bed of the wagon, going over his stack of mail that had been awaiting him at the Post Office. He handed Kathryn one from her friend Marie.

"Reckon she'll want to know how you're coming with your organ playing. You'll have a tale to write back to her." Then he pulled out another one. "Oh, Joe and Manda Robinson. Wondered if we'd ever hear of them again." He looked at the postmark. "Looks like they're in Nampa. It's to both of us. You read it first, daughter."

Kathryn was delighted to do so. As Adam had seen, they had moved to Nampa. Joe had a job working for a small mercantile store, and Manda was pregnant again. She hadn't written sooner, she said, because their first baby had been born sickly, and she didn't want to write bad news. But now little Joey was thriving, had more than made up for his slow start, and Manda was feeling much better with this child.

"I guess some people just aren't cut out to be home-steaders," Manda concluded. "I love living in this little town in my white house with lace curtains at the windows. Joe says he'll build me a picket fence next year. I want to plant a rambling rosebush on it. Do come see me when you're in Nampa for supplies."

"Oh, that's such good news! I'm so happy for her! I must write more letters. It's easy to forget how much pleasure a letter can give someone." Something about the silence on the seat beside her made Kathryn turn to look at Merrick. She couldn't tell whether the look in his eyes was anger or pain.

"What did I say wrong?"

"You didn't say anything wrong. I'm glad your letters brought you pleasure. *You've* never done anything to deserve aught but pleasure."

His strange tone puzzled her, but Adam seemed to understand. "Your answer came, did it?"

Kathryn interpreted the jerk of Merrick's head as a nod. "It's no good."

Adam shook his head. "I'm so sorry. I was sure that when you explained—"

Merrick's tone was now openly bitter. "They think it's an attempt to get their money—get back in father's will." He drove in silence for a long time, the wheels creaking, the horse clopping.

Kathryn longed to say something, but she knew so little of what he was talking about that she had no idea what to say.

At last he spoke again. "Funny. In the Bible the prodigal son is welcomed home with open arms."

Adam spoke from the back. "That's a picture of how Jesus welcomes us home, Merrick. No one ever needs to worry about the reception they'll receive from Him, no matter how far short of the mark we may fall as humans."

Merrick cocked an eyebrow. "If it's all true."

Adam answered very gently, "It's true."

117

11

They did reinstitute the brush arbor meetings that summer, but the heat was as hard on Adam's health as it was on the crops. Although Jules and Myron hauled all the water they could to the Jaynes', making almost daily trips to the Snake River in an attempt to supply both farms, all Kathryn could save were her animals and some of the most valuable garden vegetables. Carrots, potatoes, and beans they had to have. Beets, radishes, and even corn she relegated to the oblivion of luxuries.

Her holiday in Boise remained a bright spot in Kathryn's memory, even when she read in *The Statesman* of the acquittal of Big Bill Haywood—insufficient evidence to link the union boss to Harry Orchard, the jury said—although Kathryn had felt certain of his guilt. In spite of the prosecution's loss, *The Statesman* went on to report at length William Borah's powerful address to the jury and predicted a career of national scope for such an eloquent orator.

Kathryn turned back to her vegetables thinking of the perfect green rows in the Chinese vegetable gardens she had seen in Boise. She daydreamed of the luxury of having fresh vegetables from such gardens delivered at her kitchen door daily—a service the inhabitants of the Warm Springs mansions enjoyed.

More exciting to her than the thought of such service was the fact that she could contemplate it without any feeling of jealousy for those who enjoyed it. It simply encouraged her to thank the Lord for the carrots and potatoes she could save. She even asked Him to help those people enjoy their bounty. "And help them remember to tell You thank you, Lord," she added.

Adam's health was a far greater concern for Kathryn than her vegetable patch. He attempted to make his pastoral calls in the early morning or late evening, avoiding the heat of the day, but he often lay so still on his cot when he rested that it frightened her. More to relieve Adam's distress over the lack of spiritual guidance for his people than for any goal of her own, Kathryn came up with a plan.

"I've been thinking, Papa," she said one evening as they sat on a bench along the shady side of the shack, sipping lemonade. "I've done pretty well shepherding Flopsy, Mopsy, Cottontail, and Peter. Maybe I could help out some with your flock."

Adam smiled weakly. "Bless you, girl. But it wouldn't be proper for a girl to preach."

"Oh!" The idea so frightened Kathryn that she jumped and almost spilled her lemonade. "No, no, Papa. Whether it's proper or not, I couldn't do that. But I *could* teach Sunday school. What I was thinking of was starting a class for children and inviting their mamas to stay when they bring them. It'd be like teaching two classes in one that way."

She took a deep breath and rushed on with the rest of her audacious plan. "Also, I could keep playing the organ. And if the menfolk drive their families in for class and want to stay for a hymn sing, well, we might be able to find someone to help lead the singing." When she saw that her idea was well-received she added, "Mr. Allen has a fine voice."

"That he does indeed. I've noticed many times. But I don't think it'd be pleasin' to the Lord to have an unbeliever in the pulpit."

119

Kathryn sank back against the side of the shack. She knew Papa was right.

"But I suppose there wouldn't be any harm in his sitting in the congregation and singing out real loud."

Kathryn smiled at Adam's suggestion.

Nelly, Alvina, and Lucy were the first she invited to the new class, and they were the most enthusiastic recipients of the idea. Kathryn decided that in order to save Adam the work of transporting her organ for the services, they should simply hold the classes at their place. Then on those Sundays he felt strong enough to preach he could do so. On his poorly days he would be able to hear the singing from his bed.

Nelly offered to help Kathryn spread the word of the enterprise. She would go to homesteads to the northeast toward Nampa, as Isaiah was working that side of their section. Kathryn visited to the southeast, stopping to see Willa Sperlin first. Willa then went on with her to introduce her to the family that had taken over an abandoned homestead on the next section. Hazel Young promised that she and her ten-year-old daughter, Lila, and six-year-old Benjamin would attend.

The first Sunday school was to be the second Sunday in August. Kathryn practiced the organ until she was afraid the bellows would break again. With both feet pumping rhythmically she went over and over "Jesus Loves Me," "Tell Me the Story of Jesus," "Jewels," and all the other songs she thought appropriate for this new venture. And she worked on her lesson. She could think of no more appropriate topic for a new Sunday school than the story of Jesus welcoming the children.

She lay awake late Saturday night worrying. Would anyone come? Would so many come they wouldn't have enough room? Would the men stay for the hymn sing? Would Papa be strong enough to preach? Adam had been preparing a sermon with even more diligence than she had prepared her lesson, and she did not want him to be disappointed.

The next day the answers to all her questions were "Yes!" Everyone they had invited came—so many that, although there was enough room for the ten women and children who came to Sunday school to sit inside for the lesson, when time came for the hymn sing the men waiting outside, gossiping by their wagons, were required to drag logs from the lean-to to sit on in the space around the door. Some, wearing their everyday clothes, simply sat down in the dirt. Others remained on their wagon seats—a more comfortable solution, but one that added the sound of wagon creaks to Kathryn's playing.

And yes, Adam was strong enough to preach. At the end of the service he announced an exciting prospect he had been thinking on for sometime. "It'll be many months yet afore we have water in Indian Creek—clear next spring it'll be. But I want you all to start now praying and planning with me because when the water flows clean and precious, I want to hold a baptismal service. As far as anyone knows, this'll be the first baptismal service in these parts, and I can't think of anyplace we could more nearly recreate that great service in the Holy Land desert when John baptized our Lord."

It seemed that having the innovation of Kathryn's Sunday school and Adam's baptism service to look forward to brought new enthusiasm for spiritual things to the desert. It even held through the dreary, gray cold of winter when they could hold no community hymn sings because there was no building large enough and it was too cold outside. There could be no singing when your breath froze on your lips.

But Kathryn's Sunday school continued, with most of her students except Benji Young listening attentively to her stories. Benji, alas, for all the appealing sparkle in his eyes, was wiggly and headstrong, ignoring his sister's best attempts to keep him in line.

Merrick came as often as he was in the area with his construction crew. There were so many projects going, both direct government jobs and those contracted out to Heston & Allen and other companies, that one could be working anywhere from the mountains above Boise clear across the desert to the Snake River. The times he came were always special ones for Kathryn. And always he teased to be allowed to join her class.

"No. It wouldn't be proper. Women aren't to teach men," she insisted over and over again. "Saint Paul said—"

Merrick would laugh. "So why do they do it all the rest of the time, I'd like to know."

And although he would sit around the corner or in the next room with Adam, his back squarely to her class, it always seemed to Kathryn that Merrick was listening. She prayed that she might say something that would help him.

Unlike the previous year, the spring of 1907 came in warm and gentle, whispering promises of good days ahead for the desert. It was a time when one felt God's goodness and could see His hand in the ever-growing irrigation network around them. At such a time people wanted to praise God, so Adam, feeling stronger than he had in months, reinstituted the arbor meetings a month before Easter.

"That's a good way to build enthusiasm for our baptismal service," he said. "People who hear the Word of God preached on the banks of the creek will feel it a natural thing to undertake the symbolic identification with Christ in that same water."

As Merrick's crew was now constructing the part of the New York Canal that connected with the Mora, he was camped within a few miles of them and able to attend services regularly. Although he had made no indication of believing what he heard, he brought several of his fellow workers with him each time. And he sang as clearly as the most demanding choirmaster could have asked.

Adam had put a great deal of work into his Palm Sunday service, building up to the great Easter service, so it was a particularly sharp blow when he woke Saturday morning with a burning forehead and hands, parched throat, and aching back. Kathryn spent the day nursing him, bathing his forehead and chest in vinegar water, spooning small quantities of Dr. Marsh's elixer on his tongue, and encouraging him to drink from the fresh barrel of water Jules had brought from the Young's.

That new source of water had brought to the desert added excitement and faith for the future. The Youngs, like another family to the east of them, had dug a well. People laughed. But at four hundred feet they hit water. Dr. Marsh recommended it for the invalid since the water in Indian Creek had to settle several hours before it was clear enough to drink, whereas water from the well pumped up clear and pure every time.

But with the best nursing Kathryn could provide, and the special prayer offered by Isaiah, who drove over to see his brother, Kathryn had to admit that her father was even more feverish that evening.

"Papa, we'll have a great hymn sing, don't you worry. And we'll all pray that you'll be well for the baptism service on Easter Sunday. I know that will be pleasing to God. He'll help us."

Adam didn't argue. But Kathryn worried about her brave words, especially in the wee hours of the morning when a coyote howl wakened her and she found Adam sitting up in bed, awake but with glazed eyes. He appeared to be preaching, but the words made no sense to her.

She gave him another teaspoon of the elixir, bathed him all over in cool water, and took her place in a chair beside him to keep vigil the rest of the night.

When Merrick arrived next morning to drive her to the service, the dark circles under her red eyes told the story more clearly than her disheveled hair and the Saturday work dress she still wore.

"You're not going?"

She put her finger to her lips and led him outside. "I don't know what to do. I can't leave Papa. He's sleeping now, but he was dreadfully ill in the night. But all those people—how can I disappoint them?"

Merrick grinned. "Have you asked the Lord what He wants you to do?"

She looked at him sharply, but he wasn't mocking. She shook her head.

"Your papa would say it's a poor second to be asking me—or any person—when you can go straight to God. But let me make a suggestion. How about I stay here with him, and you go to the meeting?"

"Oh, thank you."

He shrugged. "Makes sense, since I am capable of spooning water into a sick man's mouth, but not of playing the organ."

"Oh, the organ." How would they get it there without Papa and Merrick?

Again Merrick had the solution. "While you get ready I'll ride over and fetch Jules and one of those mammoth brothers of his. Don't suppose it would be much trouble to them to just carry it there without the aid of a wagon."

As far as Kathryn ever knew, the Palm Sunday hymn sing, with Isaiah leading the congregation in prayer and making the announcement about the baptismal service the following Sunday, went just fine.

But if she had been required to recount who was there, what songs they sang, or how many, she would have been unable to do so. Isaiah announced each song, and her fingers found the notes. Her mind, however, was in the little brown shack three miles back across the desert. *Dear God, be with them. Let them both live. Let Adam live physically. Let Merrick live spiritually.* Then she started.

Dimly she realized that Isaiah had announced the next hymn—for the second time.

The notes of the last song had barely died away before Kathryn was on her feet. Indeed, the notes should have been sustained several beats longer, but her feet simply would pump no more.

"Jules, I must get home to Papa. Can you bring the organ later? I'll ride Davey's horse—he said I could."

She didn't wait for Jules's answer, but the comforting warmth of the hand he laid briefly on her shoulder stayed with her throughout her dusty gallop.

She had been so urgent about getting home that her impulse was to burst in the door crying, "I'm home. Are you all right?" But she knew that was no way to approach an invalid who might be just dropping off to much-needed sleep. So she tethered the horse and walked in quietly.

As soon as she was inside the door she heard voices. Did they have another visitor? Surely that calm, steady timbre could not be from the fever-racked Adam. And yet, a moment of listening told her it was. Even if she hadn't known the voice, she would have recognized the logic.

"If you can't accept the evil in the world, how can you accept the good?"

If Merrick made a reply, she didn't hear it.

Adam went on, his voice seemingly stronger with each new argument. "You say you can't serve a God that allows evil in the world. How can you serve a devil that allows love, truth, and beauty in the world?"

This time she heard Merrick's reply. "Serve the devil? What do you mean, man? I don't serve the devil."

Adam's voice was so calm, so reasoned. "Well, it has to be one way or the other. The Scripture says, 'Choose ye this day whom ye will serve.' Don't let that choice be made by default."

"The trouble with my family. The trouble with Heston. I didn't choose any of that."

125

"Course not. None of us choose our troubles. Scripture says it rains on the just and the unjust. All kinds of things happen to all kinds of people in this world. Thing is, when you get in trouble, who're you gonna ask to help you get out of it? Who're you going to listen to? When things go right, who're you gonna thank? When you're alone and want to talk to someone, which power are you going to inquire of?"

Silence.

"A man cannot serve two masters, Merrick. And there are two masters in this world—well, one true Master and one who would be if he could. Choose which one, Merrick."

In her mind's eye Kathryn could see him shake his head, his black curls bouncing. "No. No need to choose. I never meant to turn my back on Him. I thought He'd turned His back on me. But you've helped me see it all so clearly now."

Kathryn heard Adam's hand clap Merrick on the shoulder. "That's just what I thought all along. Now what you need to do, lad, is get alone with Him and talk it all over. He knows everything you've said and thought, but He'd sure like to hear about it direct from you. And you need to hear what He wants to say to you."

When she heard footsteps, Kathryn backed quietly out the door. She didn't want to interrupt.

Later that week when Merrick returned to see how Adam was and to tell them he would be among those to be baptized Sunday, he sought her out for a quiet talk.

"I'm so glad you got it straight with the Lord—so glad!" she said.

"'Got it straight' is just the right way to say it. You see, I realize now I never really did quit believing. I just had a lot of stuff tangled up in my head—confusing God with my earthly father, I guess. My father was unjust, so I labeled God unjust—I don't know. It'll take me awhile to sort it all out, but it sure feels good to quit rebelling. Sort of like growing up, so now I can be serious. Do something important."

Here, four years later, was finally her opportunity to talk to him as she had wanted to ever since the first day she saw him on that hot, dusty stagecoach. "What about your gambling?"

"Haven't done a whole lot of it since Hank was shot—sort of lost my appetite, you might say. Thing is, I just have a sense of the game—it's like I can see in my head where the cards are."

She wrinkled her forehead in thought. "Strange. That sounds God-given, but it sure is a funny talent for God to give. Maybe He wants you to use it in other ways."

Merrick cocked an eyebrow at her. "Maybe. But I haven't seen anything else yet. You know what they say —'Lucky at cards, unlucky at—'" He grinned. "Unless, of course, you consider this construction company venture a gamble. There are days I'd think it all to the good if somebody shot Heston."

Kathryn forced a calm tone to hide her shock at such a statement. "Why? What's he doing wrong?"

Merrick frowned. "Dunno. It's hard to put your finger on. Oh, easy enough to say he's a stubborn—er—that he's very hard to deal with. And that he has a terrible temper when anyone disagrees with him. But he *does* know a lot about digging canals."

"Is he cheating you?"

"Don't think so. I check the books pretty carefully."

Kathryn knew what she would do. She would pray about it. That sounded too preachy to say to Merrick, so instead she went to another topic that had long troubled her. She might never find Merrick in so open a mood again. "Merrick, what about your family?"

She saw the tightness in his face and thought he wasn't going to answer her. She was trying to find a graceful way to cover her blunder when at last he spoke.

"Guess this is one gamble I'm going to have to take—only I can't see where the cards are." He paused again. "It's a fair question, Kathryn, seeing how much I impose on your hospitality, but I've dreaded having to tell you. From the day I saw you—don't suppose you remember that scorching August afternoon—well, I expect you remember the afternoon—but it's a lot to ask to hope that you'd remember me in the middle of everything else."

"Of course I remember!" Kathryn wanted to fling her arms around him, but as years of lectures from older women had taught her, she suppressed her natural vitality. She was so happy—to think that he remembered those few minutes she had carried in her heart for so long. She remembered that he had called her "pretty miss."

"Thank you for remembering." He said it so quietly, it made Kathryn catch her breath. "Well, ever since then I've dreaded having your beautiful gray eyes look at me accusingly like my mother's did. She had gray eyes too."

Shyness made Kathryn close her eyes. But when she opened them he was still looking at her, smiling.

"Well, enough of this. If I'm going to tell you I'd best get on with it. It's just that I'm asking so much of you—asking you to trust me where my own family wouldn't."

Sensing how much he needed some sign from her, Kathryn broke through her own reticence and slipped her hand inside his on the bench.

"I shot my brother. My twin brother."

She didn't gasp. She just squeezed his hand tighter.

After another long silence she asked, "How did it happen?"

She saw the first hint of relaxation in his face. "Bless you. You said *how*, not *why*." Then he turned away. "Trouble is, I don't know. I don't see how it could have happened, but it did. We were hunting. He was in front of me. The grouse were off to our left. It doesn't seem my shot could have been that far off, but—" Now his words came fast, she had to lean forward not to miss any. "It was a beautiful autumn day. The firs on the hillsides a dark, dark green, the laurels and ash in the draw by the Ettrick Water all red and gold. We walked all the way up to Broadmeadows, and the grass was golden. Raynor shot a fine partridge. He was so proud—clamped it to his belt—went striding on ahead of me. Then we flushed a whole covey of grouse—" He put his free hand over his eyes as though to blot out the memory.

"Maybe it wasn't your shot that did it. Have you ever thought of that? Was anyone else hunting in that area?"

"Ever *thought* of it? For weeks I thought of nothing else. Argued with everybody that would listen to me. At last they quit listening. The more I protested, the worse it made it. You see, my family didn't even really believe it was an accident."

"What? That's a horrible thing to say! How could they possible accuse you of—"

"Murder? Ugly word, isn't it? Oh, they didn't make any accusations. Not out loud. Too much stain on the family name. But I know they were all relieved when I removed my uncomfortable presence. Relieved and smug. All except my grandmother—I think she at least wanted to believe me. I realized later that running away just confirmed their suspicions."

"But why would they think you'd do such a thing?"

"Jacob and Esau. I was the younger twin. With Raynor gone, I'd inherit."

"Oh, Merrick. I'm so sorry." She couldn't think of anything else to say.

"Does that mean you believe me?"

Now she gripped his hand with both of hers. "Of course I believe you. If you shot him at all it was an accident, and I'm not even sure you did that." She thought for several seconds, her square jaw clamped firm. "You're sure you didn't see anyone else? Were there places someone else could hide? Who knew where you were going that day? Who else would benefit from Raynor's death? Did any birds fall when you shot?"

"Whoa!" He laughed breathlessly. "Just a minute, Sherlock Holmes. I didn't see anyone. The draw was full of rocks, crevices, and trees, but I don't believe anyone was hiding there. Everyone at Woodburn knew the general direction we went. When I saw Raynor fall I didn't think to look for birds. Now that you mention it, Clarence did drag in a grouse later, but by then who knows where he got it?"

"Clarence?"

"My dog. Beautiful spaniel—white and liver with long, silky ears and eyes that melt right into your heart. But didn't I skip one of your questions?"

"Who else benefits?"

He considered for a moment. "Rowena, I guess. My sister. Well, not her directly. Women can't inherit. But her son, Robert Bruce—Robbie we call him. The estate will go to him. Hadn't thought about it before, but that's the way it works."

"I don't suppose Rowena or Robbie—"

Merrick laughed at that. "Hardly. She was in her child-bed at the time. Robbie must have been a full three hours old when it happened." Suddenly he turned sharply on the bench to face her full-on. "But that's not important. The important thing is, you believe me, don't you? You really do."

"Well, of course. How could you be so silly as to think I wouldn't?"

"No one has before."

"That's not true. You told Papa, didn't you? He believed you."

"Well, yes. But priests and parsons and the like have to—it's part of their job."

She shook her head. "They have to listen, they have to try to help, they don't have to believe. It's quite a different matter." After a moment she said, "Twins. I didn't realize you were a twin."

130

"That's another thing that made it so hard. We were really close, like twins are supposed to be—understood things between us that regular siblings wouldn't. That made it harder to take that they would suspect me, and harder to accept his death. I still miss him."

They sat silently in the spring sunshine until Adam, who seemed to have made a remarkable recovery from his recent bout of fever, joined them. He talked with excitement about his plans, relating everything to an analogy of the River Jordan.

Kathryn laughed. "Papa, next you'll be dressing in animal skins and eating locusts and honey—if we had any locusts around here."

Adam grinned. "No, my dear, I don't see myself as any kind of John the Baptist. But just think—seven people have asked for baptism—seven new souls for the Kingdom. If I accomplished nothing else in my life it would all be worthwhile."

That night, chores at last finished, Kathryn sat long by the lantern in her tiny, muslin-partitioned room, her journal open on her knees. She would like to have recorded all Merrick had said to her, and yet the words chased around and around in her head with such speed she couldn't catch any to write them down. In spite of her concern for Merrick's problems, she was overwhelmed with joy that he at last had shared them with her. She was simply invaded with a sense of delicious happiness, of rightness, of assurance that, as God had promised, He was with her.

She could even believe that Kuna wasn't the end of the world. Joy had come before morning. And she couldn't wait for sunrise.

12

Easter morning came with a glorious sunrise that had Kathryn singing, "Up from the grave He arose, with a mighty triumph o'er His foes . . ." as she went about feeding the lambs and chickens and milking Buttercup.

Later, it appeared that none in the whole wide expanse from Nampa to Owyhee County had refused the invitation to an Easter morning arbor service, in spite of the cold wind that cut through the gold of the morning.

Kathryn, worried about the cough that had been troubling Adam since his last illness, insisted that he wear a wrapping of flannel over his chest. But he firmly refused her coal oil and turpentine poultice on the grounds that it smelled so bad it would keep the congregation away.

"Just don't get any wetter than you have to, Papa. It's not as warm as it looks out there, and you've only been out of bed for a week. I don't suppose you could baptize people from Jules's boat?"

"Don't worry, daughter. I won't go in above my waist, and I've already packed dry trousers and my thickest wool socks to put on as soon as I get out."

After the morning preaching service, the three men and four women who were to be baptized, including Merrick, Lila Young, and Davey Brewington, prepared. The men removed coats, vests, hats, and ties, and rolled up their sleeves, while the women, who already wore light skirts and shirtwaists, simply lay their wide straw hats on the church benches and took off their leather shoes and belts.

Then Adam led his congregation of more than twenty-five souls to the creek singing, "Shall we gather at the river? The beautiful, the beautiful, river . . ."

Jules and Myron were first to step down the sloping, sagebrush-covered bank into a small rowboat waiting there. Myron, standing in the front, poled the boat a little ways out into the creek and held it there against the current. Jules sat in the back, ready to extend his arm to help any who might lose their footing in the flowing creek. Kathryn was glad he was there, thinking that if she were to walk out into that cold, running water, she would be glad for the assurance of Jules's strong hand just an arm's length away.

Merrick was the first to stride into the water. Kathryn smiled at his determined look. It was as if she could hear Peter saying, "Not my feet only, Lord, but my head and my hands also." There was nothing halfway about Merrick.

"Merrick Clarence Allen, I baptize you in the name of the Father, and of the Son, and of the Holy Ghost." Adam placed a clean white handkerchief over Merrick's face and lay him over backwards, supporting him in the water until the flood closed completely over his face, symbolizing his identification with Christ in His death. Then, symbolic of his resurrection to new life, Adam lifted him up, dripping and smiling.

On the creekbank Kathryn led in singing, "The cleansing stream, I see, I see! I plunge and, oh, it cleanseth me!" Merrick stood beside her, shivering inside a blanket in time to sing the final chorus, "Oh! praise the Lord, it cleanseth me! It cleanseth me, yes, cleanseth me!"

The service continued, down to the youngest one to be baptized, little Lila Young. They sang, "Lord, wash me and I shall be whiter than snow," as Lila stepped into the water in her white dress.

". . . In the name of the Father, and the Son, and the Holy Ghost . . ."

No one was ever quite sure what happened. Apparently Lila didn't realize she should keep her feet on the creekbed when she went over backwards, and certainly Adam wasn't prepared to take her full weight, even small as she was. But suddenly Lila, uttering a small cry, disappeared beneath the surface of the water.

Adam staggered backward before losing his balance with a wild flailing of his long arms. Lila bobbed up, sputtering. Adam lunged forward to help her, only to slip on the rocky creek bed and receive another thorough dunking.

It was all over in a minute. Many standing farther up the bank didn't even see it happen. Jules was over the side of the boat before there was any danger of drowning, lifting them both up in one motion.

But Kathryn was terrified for her father's health. She had no dry flannel strips to rewrap his chest. He borrowed a dry shirt, but it was lightweight—little protection against the bitter wind.

It seemed that she was right to worry, for from that day Adam's cough became increasingly heavier and heavier. Kathryn lay long at night, listening to him on the other side of the curtain, wishing the only sound she had to disturb her was the howl of coyotes on Kuna Butte. That would seem positively comforting compared to the racking cough deep in Adam's chest. Dr. Marsh's remedies availed little, and throughout the summer and early fall Adam grew weaker and weaker.

On a bitter, gray day in early November Adam's cough silenced. It was many minutes before Kathryn, in the next room, realized how quiet it was. She felt the fear at the top of her head, then draining downward. "Papa!" She rushed into his room. She sat a long time, holding his hand while the warmth faded from it.

Hours later she heard Jules outside. Dear, faithful Jules, who had come as always to help with the chores. Never had she been more thankful for him. Now at least the animals wouldn't suffer. She waited until he had tended to them before she went out to him in the darkness.

"Kathryn! I didn't think you were here. There was no light in the house."

"I know, Jules, I—" She choked and couldn't go on.

He folded her in his arms, and she sank limply against him, "Papa, Papa," she sobbed over and over again.

Jules carried her into the house, lit a lamp, and made tea and toast for her before he went in to Adam.

"You laid him out real nice," he said when he came back a while later, his own eyes red-rimmed. "There's no real hurry about the service. It's cold enough, we can wait two or three days if you want. Shall I take you home to Ma? You can't stay here tonight."

She thought of dear little Willa fluttering around her and shook her head. "I never realized—it was just so natural—but Papa and I have never been apart. Not one night in twenty-three years. I'll stay here."

Jules started to protest but stopped when he looked at her firmly set jaw. "Well, you can't stay alone, and it wouldn't be proper for me to stay. I'll ride over and fetch Nelly."

Kathryn didn't protest, but she hardly noticed when he was gone.

She hardly noticed anything the next two days. She ate when Nelly put food in front of her. She lay down and closed her eyes when Nelly put her in bed. She nodded when neighbors came to call and told her how sorry they were. But the rest of the time she sat by Adam's still form.

Isaiah, who had prayed over Thelma and their baby, and then over Ned Brewington, now presided at the burial of his brother. Kathryn didn't even notice that he was off-key when the little group, shivering in the frosty air, sang "Abide with Me." But she did notice when a rich Scots tenor rang out on the last verse, "In life, in death, O Lord, abide with me."

"Kathryn, I'm so sorry. I've been in Boise. I didn't know until I got back about an hour ago. Been fighting with that partner of mine again—had my head full of business troubles. I'm so sorry. I don't know what to say."

"Glad you're back, Merrick." Jules clapped him on the shoulder. "I've done what I could, but I know she'd rather have you." Jules turned away.

Merrick drove her home, the wagon creaking over the frozen ground. How many times had she made this trip from the cemetery? she wondered. How many more times would she make it? How long would it be before more of her family and friends were under the soil by Indian Creek than above it?

She looked back at the creek. "He was so excited about the baptism being like the River Jordan. Now he's crossed the Jordan." Somehow the thought was comforting to her. The first comfort she had found.

Alvina was at the shack before them. She had the stove well-stoked with bright-burning sagebrush, nourishing beans and cornbread ready to eat.

"Mama sent an apple pie, and the coffee'll be ready in a minute." She set three plates on the table. "Mama said I was to tell you I'll stay as long as you want me. Clear till you sell the place or—" she glanced at Merrick, blushed, and floundered for something else to say "—or until you make other arrangements . . ."

"What?" Kathryn shook her head sharply. It was like waking from a long sleep. "Sell? Arrangements? I don't know. I hadn't thought—" Suddenly she realized she had her whole life all to herself. Always she had taken care of Papa. Always his life had given structure to her life. Now she had to build an entirely new structure of her own. She had to make her own decisions. What would she do? Where would she go?

"Mama said you could come live with us. We're your nearest kin."

"Only kin." And she loved them. But she didn't want to live with them. Suddenly the whole world was a possibility—a frightening prospect. She could sell the homestead and move back to Nebraska. Back to gentle green prairies where flowers bloomed and she and Marie could play the organ together. Or she could move into Boise. She didn't have any idea what she could do there—perhaps get a job cooking in one of those elegant mansions where fresh vegetables were delivered to the door and hot water ran from taps.

"Thank you, Vina. I—I don't know. Please stay tonight. I need to think."

She did think. It seemed the only sound for miles around was the soft swish of Vina's skirt as she prepared the food and Merrick's gentle sipping of coffee as they gave her the gift of silence. Kathryn thought of the beauty of the desert at sunrise. She could still remember her amazement the first time she saw it so—fresh and golden. She thought of its serenity under a dusting of snow. Of the sense of newness when the sage bloomed yellow and sunny. Of the fun she'd had with friends.

But it was really the hard times that had bound her most strongly to this place. Not just the major distresses like funerals, illness, violence, but more. It was the daily struggles, the shortage of water, the long hours of work, the scratching and stinking of the sage. All that added up to each night's bringing a sense of accomplishment simply because she had survived.

That was it—the goal she had set her first night there and striven for ever since—she *had* survived, when many dear ones around her hadn't.

But that wasn't all; she had wanted also to *succeed*. She hadn't done that yet; she was still struggling. If she

137

gave up now and moved to a gentler place, she would never reach the goal she had worked toward for so long. Often that had been all she had—her goal and her determination to reach it. Often when she prayed she had felt the goal God-given, and He had never failed to fulfill His promise for joy in the morning—no matter how long and dark the night. Leaving now would be turning her back on all the good things God had done for her. For the first time in many days, she smiled.

Later, when Alvina had gone out to scatter the supper scraps to the chickens, Merrick took Kathryn's hand. "Kathryn, I'd like to make a suggestion for your future. You can't imagine how terribly I'd like to—but the time isn't right. Not for either of us. I guess all I can say for now is that I hope you won't move too far away." Suddenly his grip on her hand tightened. "It's not fair of me to ask, but please don't go."

All she could do was repeat what she had said to Vina. "I don't know. I need time to think."

It was Vina who started the idea forming in her mind. "Why don't you play the organ, Kathryn? Wouldn't it make you feel better?"

"I don't know what to play." Kathryn recalled the terrible listlessness that had overtaken Isaiah when he was mourning Thelma. Now she knew just how he had felt.

"How about some Christmas carols—it's only a couple of weeks till Christmas. Remember what fun we had that very first Christmas you were here? You didn't have your organ then, and Pa played his harmonica."

Kathryn smiled. "Yes. And Merrick and Papa brought me a piece of sagebrush to use for a Christmas tree, and I decorated it with sewing scraps." Suddenly warm memories flooded her mind. She hadn't lost Adam. All the times they had had were still with her. She went to the organ and played "O Come, All Ye Faithful."

Then her memory went further back. Back to Nebraska, back to being ten years old and having Marie, just five years older, guide her untrained fingers over the keys. Dear Marie, how she missed her sweet smile and sunshine-blonde hair. How much she wished she were here right now.

Then the thought came to her, *Why not?* Marie, for all her beauty and sweetness, was still unmarried in a household with five younger brothers and sisters. Surely she would welcome a change. And women homesteaders weren't unknown. Especially with Jules to help with the heavy work—although now she would insist on paying him instead of just accepting all his work as friendship.

She and Marie could run the farm if water came next summer as promised. If not, it wouldn't matter. It seemed unlikely that anyone would be able to hold on much longer without water.

That night she wrote to Marie.

13

"Marie! I'd forgotten how beautiful you are!"

Kathryn rushed to her friend, who had just stepped off the train. "Poor Marie, you look as horrified as I felt the first time I saw this place." She hugged Marie tightly. "That's why I wanted to be so sure we were here to meet you. I've made them all wait for hours."

A sweep of her arm indicated the welcoming group by the little brown hut. "There was no one to meet us when Papa and I came. You can imagine—oh, but I've got so much to tell you."

Jules stepped forward to pick up Marie's trunk, and Kathryn introduced him, then Isaiah and Nelly, Alvina, David, Lucy. "And this is little Ned." She ruffled his soft brown curls. "Oh, and Myron, Jules's brother," she added as Myron scooped up Marie's carpetbag and rush basket.

Marie looked overwhelmed, her delicate skin paler than ever.

"Don't worry none, miss. You'll get us all straight soon enough. There aren't that many folks out here on the desert for it to be much of a problem." Jules tipped his hat and offered Marie his arm to help her into the buckboard.

Kathryn sprang onto the seat beside her friend and talked almost nonstop until they got to the homestead. She had had no idea how desperate she had been for some

140

link with her old life. It was so good just to talk to someone who had seen a flower and a green tree recently. It was now July, and Indian Creek had for many weeks been nothing but a dry bed surrounded by brown weeds.

She heard Marie gasp when they stopped at the shack, and she grasped her friend's hand. "Marie, I'm sorry. I tried to prepare you, but you sort of get used to it—I'd forgotten how awful it looks because in my mind I see the people who have been here and remember the things we've done. Oh, Marie. Give it a chance. Don't go back yet."

"Back? My dear Kathryn, you haven't given me a chance to get a word in edgewise for the past three miles. I have no intention of going back. Even if I didn't know that my little sisters who now occupy my room would absolutely refuse to give it back. No—" she shook her head "—you didn't really prepare me—but I'm not sure anything could have."

Jules helped them off the wagon, then turned to pull the barrel of water off the back.

"We got a whole barrel just for household use to celebrate your coming," Kathryn whispered to Marie. "I remember how desperate I was for a bath when we got here. That was before the Youngs came and put in their well. It's lovely to be able to get some of our water from them." Kathryn led the way into the house, everyone following her.

Nelly and Alvina went straight to setting out lunch, while Lucy and Kathryn helped Marie unpack.

"Do you suppose I could have a glass of that water to drink?" Marie asked.

Lucy skipped off and returned in a minute with a tin cup still dripping cool, crystal droplets. "Mm, that looks so good." Marie took it in both hands and closed her eyes to savor the drink. "Oh!" She gasped and pushed the cup from her. "What is that?" She shuddered. "It tastes like—like—sheep dip!"

Jules rescued the cup from her limp hand. "Well, now, I expect that's pert near what it is all right. The Youngs are sheep people. That's why they put in the well—for the sheep. They use the ground next to it for dipping pens, so I guess a lot of sulfur does get into the water." He grinned at Marie's horrified expression. "Don't worry. Sulfur's healthful, and the water's wet. Pretty soon you won't notice it at all. But tomorrow I can go down to the Snake and get some good clean river water for you."

"Snake?" Marie inquired weakly.

Davey was the one to explain that Idaho's main river was so named by the Indians because it curves like a snake.

Nelly's coffee was strong enough to cover the taste of sulfur in the water, and a good nourishing meal of ham, potatoes, milk gravy, canned tomatoes, and peas, with canned peaches for dessert, seemed to restore Marie somewhat.

But suddenly Kathryn was worried. From the moment months ago when she thought of inviting Marie to live with her, and her enthusiastic reply had come so quickly, Kathryn had never doubted the rightness of her course. Now she doubted.

She remembered Manda Robinson's words *Some people aren't meant to be pioneers.* For a long time Kathryn had doubted that *she* was. Now Kathryn realized that the fact she had decided this was the right life for her didn't mean it was right for Marie. What would her refined friend think of rattlesnakes, jackrabbits, flying ants? What would she think of sagebrush?

"Time to get back to our chores, but first I have something to tell you all."

Kathryn blinked at the sound of Myron's voice. Nearing his twenty-fifth birthday, Myron was the biggest and the quietest of the Sperlin brothers. He never initiated a conversation and seldom responded to one. Kathryn had often wondered if he would ever have the courage to speak for

142

Alvina as he so obviously desired to do. Now—she put her dishtowel down and turned in his direction—was that what he had to announce? Were he and Alvina engaged?

"Well, I don't have to tell you folks there's a whole lot of things we don't have out here in the desert."

"Yeah, like water," David quipped.

"But we're working on it—next year . . ." Isaiah began, then turned back to Myron.

Myron cleared his throat. "Yeah, water, but I was thinking of something else—mail service. So I've drawn up this here petition. I figure if everyone this side of Owyhee County between Nampa and Meridian signs this and we send it into the the postal department in Washington, D.C., they'll see there's enough good citizens out here to send us a mail pouch of our own."

Alvina clapped her hands and beamed with pride. "Oh, Myron, what a wonderful idea! Just think of getting our letters straightaway instead of having to wait until someone goes to town for them!"

Myron looked justifiably proud of himself as the paper went around the room, collecting signatures. "Yup, and I figured I'd just toss my hat in the ring to see about getting appointed postmaster."

Everyone congratulated him and offered support. All but Alvina—she seemed too choked to speak.

In the coming days and weeks Kathryn helped Marie through her first experiences with howling coyotes, flying ants, and invading jackrabbits. And no matter how exhausting the days, it all somehow seemed worth it when they could sit down in the evening and take turns playing the organ.

Sometimes Jules would stay for a while after he finished helping with evening chores—as he had never once failed to do since Adam's death. Jules had staunchly refused to accept any payment for his services, but when Kathryn asked him to take small amounts of money or freshly prepared food to Willa he never refused, so all seemed satisfied with the arrangement.

Marie gradually took over more and more of the household chores, leaving Kathryn more time to work with her growing flock of chickens and band of sheep. Kathryn had no idea what she would do about crops when the coming of water made real farming possible—struggling with the garden seemed enough for her—but she loved the animals. When they had enough water to support a herd, perhaps she would consider taking on dairy cows.

One morning in mid-September she watched a wagon approach from the west, thinking it might be carrying early visitors. When the wagon drew close enough for its occupants to wave at her, Kathryn realized they were all children—five children from two homestead families driving to the new tent school Mr. Hubbard had provided for Kuna. In all, fourteen students came under the tutelage of Mr. Gaylord Green in Kuna's first school that fall. Kuna was becoming a real town.

With the promise of water closer to fulfillment every day, rumors flew: A blacksmith shop to open soon, a mercantile—then what? Lumber yard? Millinery? Bakery? Kathryn knew what she would most want, but it seemed too wild a dream to speak out loud: an ice house. Then, just when life seemed to have settled down to autumn mellowness, Merrick came back.

Kathryn was in the garden digging potatoes to store in the lean-to for the coming winter when the sound of a buckboard made her look up. At first she saw only Isaiah and went to meet him, then realized someone was beside him.

"Merrick!" Kathryn had spent most of her life struggling to suppress her natural vitality under society's injunctions for proper behavior for a young lady. But out here on the desert there was less worry about such things, and more and more of the real person under the shy exterior had bubbled to the surface lately. Now she could almost have flung her arms around his neck as she would have liked to welcome any old friend. Almost, but not quite. She settled for greeting him with a wide smile as he sprang down from the wagon.

"Merrick, I haven't seen you since—since . . ." It was still too painful to say "since Papa died."

But he understood. He took her hand. "I know. I've been tied up with water squabbles for months—even Nampa farmers who're getting water aren't satisfied—specially those at the lower end of the canal—wet farmers and dry farmers squabbling with each other—seems like every Water Users' meeting ends on a sour note." He paused to wipe the sweat from his forehead. "Sorry. I didn't mean to start in on that before I'd even said hello. How are you? I'm so glad you decided to stay."

"I'm fine. I have a friend living with me. She's a wonderful help. Come meet her."

At that moment the sound of an organ melody greeted them. "Aye, and musical, is she?" Merrick put on the thick Scots accent he often did when he was in particularly good humor. "And knows she's greeting a Scotsman true." Marie was playing "Annie Laurie."

Merrick stepped into the house, put his hat over his heart, and extended his other arm like a stage tenor, "But for bonnie Annie Laurie, I'd lay me doon and dee."

Marie whirled around on the organ bench, her blue eyes sparkling with delight, her blonde curls bouncing.

Merrick stepped forward, took the hand still resting on the keyboard, and bowed over it. "Aye, and what bonnie lassie is this?"

Fortunately Isaiah was there to make the introductions, for Kathryn could not have. "Pretty miss" had always been his special name for her. When he said it she felt pretty—could almost believe that her nose wasn't too flat, her jaw not too square, and her fine hair not too limp. When Merrick called her pretty she could forget that she had always wanted to be golden-curled like Marie—and

145

play the organ as well. A beautiful girl making beautiful music had always been part of the vision of beauty she sought. But Marie was the one that fulfilled it—for Merrick.

"Nelly says I'm to bring you all back to supper." Isaiah filled the awkward silence.

Around Nelly's boisterous supper table it was easy to remain silent, and no one noticed that Kathryn didn't eat anything. She didn't dare try. She knew the food would choke her.

Even Kathryn had to smile later that evening, however, when Myron burst in waving a piece of paper. "We've got it! Mail will come to Kuna! And I'm to be the first postmaster!"

"Oh, Myron! Does that mean we can get married now?" Everyone gasped and laughed at Alvina's straightforwardness. She hadn't been raised with the ladylike restrictions Kathryn had.

The quiet Myron didn't mind at all. He pulled her to her feet and stood with his arm around her waist. For a moment Kathryn even thought he was going to kiss her in front of everyone. But he just grinned more broadly still and said, "It sure does! This is a paying job—I get to keep a percentage of every bit of postage I sell."

Everyone fell to discussing the couple's plans, which included getting married next spring and building a one-room shack of their own on Sperlin property. Then Myron turned to Merrick. "I guess you've already heard the big topic of conversation in Boise?"

"I was just about to tell these folks when you burst in." Merrick grinned. "Go ahead, this is your night for news."

Myron held up his hand to silence the chorus of "What?" "Tell us!" "What happened?"

"Well, it seems Mrs. Steunenberg has been visiting Harry Orchard real regular in the state pen—"

Here he was interrupted with another chorus: "Mrs. Steunenberg?" "Visiting her husband's assassin?" "That was three years ago—she's still going there?"

146

Myron nodded. "She is. Regular, like I said. Other members of the family, too. Just like the Scripture says to do—and guess what—Orchard's become a born again Christian."

Talk of the hardened murderer becoming a Christian brought back to Kathryn's mind something that had been bothering her. There had been no religious services in Kuna since Adam's death.

"I've been thinking," she began tentatively, "now that they've got the school started with that nice big tent set up—I've been wondering if we could get a Sunday school started again—something really regular now. If they'd let us use the tent on Sundays we wouldn't have to stop for bad weather or worry about not being able to accommodate everyone in a house."

Isaiah slapped his thigh. "That's a right good idea! We need a real organization—a church board with everything set up proper so we can hire a regular preacher just like your Papa always wanted."

Two weeks later a dozen people met in the school tent in response to Isaiah's invitation. In spite of the broad spectrum of denominations represented, there was little objection to calling their church Methodist-Episcopal and agreeing to offer an invitation to the District Superintendent from Boise to hold the first preaching services in the tent. And they heartily accepted the services of Miss Kathryn Jayne to teach children's Sunday school.

Kathryn was glad to have a new occupation to take her mind off her worries as she watched the friendship between Marie and Merrick grow. Inviting Marie to live with her had seemed so *right*. Marie herself was such a godsend, and Kathryn so enjoyed her companionship in every way, except . . . Could Marie's presence mean the end of all her dreams—dreams of someday . . . Ever since she had met him, Merrick had been such a light in her life that the thought of life without him made the world seem unbearably dark.

14

February 22, 1909, was the day the whole valley had awaited for years. Kathryn felt she had been waiting her whole life for water to come to the desert, although it had actually been just over six years. She and Marie were up long before dawn that morning, milking Buttercup, feeding the chickens, and seeing to the other absolutely essential chores. Then they retired to their separate sides of the muslin partition to don their very finest clothes.

Kathryn shook her head over the blue dress and hat that had seen her through every special occasion since coming to Kuna. It had been made from the very latest New York pattern card, of the finest French taffeta and lace, and fit her perfectly almost seven years ago. Now she knew it was sadly out of fashion, and it felt uncomfortably tight in places where she had filled out since then, although her waist was as slim as ever. At least she would be covered by her cape most of the day, and she did like her cloak of dark blue wool with red piping—even if it was as old as the rest of her clothes.

Kathryn burrowed deeper into her cape, however, when Marie stepped out of her room in a long, wine-colored coat that nipped in at the waist and had a little white fur collar to match the hat topping her blonde curls. No matter how cowed Kathryn might feel by her friend's breath-taking beauty, though, she couldn't be mean about it. "Oh, Marie, you're beautiful! I love your coat!"

"Oh, I forgot—" Marie whirled back into her room and appeared a moment later with the large white muff that completed her outfit. "Thank you. I saved and saved for this—it's a whole year of what I could save from my piano teaching. My cousin in Philadelphia had her dress-maker do it for me."

The sound of Jules's wagon arriving spared Kathryn from having to answer, but the way Jules's eyes lit up at the sight of Marie gave her little comfort when she contemplated Merrick's reaction. Merrick, so stylish himself and with such an eye for women, who was so well acquainted with the latest fashions in Boise and San Francisco . . . Kathryn was silent most of the way to Kuna.

When they arrived at the little station, the excitement in the air wiped away Kathryn's worries about her personal shabbiness. "Where did all these people come from? There must be close to a hundred. I had no idea there were so many people in the whole desert!"

Jules laughed. "Nobody's going to miss this—the greatest day ever to come to this area."

It was Marie who pointed out that people hadn't come in just to catch the train—they lived here. "Oh, my, I can't believe how things have changed! This place was desolate when I came here eight months ago—now just look."

They all looked across the tracks to the Kuna townsite, and Kathryn blinked. She saw in her mind the single shack with the hanging signboard that constituted all of Kuna that scorching August day she arrived here. It *was* becoming a town.

The blacksmith shop was already operating, the general store looked almost ready to open, and another building was well framed. Had it really been that long since she'd left the homestead? No, she came within sight of this every Sunday on her way to the tent Sunday school, and, in truth, had seen the buildings. The fact was, she had been so focusing on her own troubles, still recovering from Adam's death, struggling to keep the homestead running, and, most of all, worrying about Merrick's attraction to Marie, that she had looked beyond herself very little.

Today would be different. Today marked the beginning of a whole new era for the area and all its residents. With her head high, Kathryn accepted Jules's hand and stepped aboard the special train that had been chartered to take residents of the Kuna region to the opening of Diversion Dam.

Kathryn waved to Isaiah and Nelly sitting just ahead of them and smiled when she noticed how close Alvina and Myron were sitting. She wondered if they were holding hands under the cover of Vina's full skirt. The wedding this summer would be a happy event.

No one on the excursion train minded that the route was a long one. Going by train meant traveling almost twice the distance one would in a wagon. The main line ran between Kuna and Nampa, then a recently laid spur took the train twenty miles east to Boise and continued five miles beyond to where the Boise River emerged from its rocky gorge in the foothills. It was comfortable and festive to go by train, though, and neighbors who had not seen each other since the last Water Users' meeting talked in glowing terms about the future of this land under irrigation. The two-hour trip seemed to fly. Soon frozen, brown foothills rose outside the windows of the carriage, and the train came to a halt.

"Oh, my!" Kathryn, standing in the open train doorway, caught her breath and stepped backwards. A brass band blared, the bright winter sun glinted off the bare hills, flags fluttered from poles, and those already arrived cheered as the new arrivals stepped off the train. Overcome with it all, Kathryn hesitated. Then a strong hand took hers and almost lifted her to the platform.

"Merrick!" She gasped. She had known he would be there, of course, but had expected him to be with the governor and other dignitaries since he was one of the major contractors.

She had no time to ask him what he was doing there, as he then turned to help Marie down the step. Jules followed, and the four of them were swept ahead by the crowd. The brass band led out, playing a Sousa march, followed by the governor and his constituents, then by all those who had come to watch the ceremonies.

The entire project, which included the building of a concrete dam, power plant, canal, and reservoir embankments, had taken three years. Now jubilant holidayers paraded out on the crest of the embankment and looked down at the great lake of beautiful water that would be sent down the system of canals and laterals to irrigate the valley's thirsty crops and cattle. A spontaneous cheer broke from the crowd.

The band arrived at the far side and became silent. Governor Frank Gooding greeted his happy constituents then, and the softened vowels of his English voice rang to the most distant listeners. "We are blessed to live in a state with unlimited opportunities and possibilities."

Here he was interrupted by a cheer, and Kathryn, having long abandoned her earlier unhappy thoughts, cheered as loudly as anyone.

"We have looked to our vast undeveloped areas, knowing that if only water could be brought, the land would spring up with thriving towns, schools, churches, all the amenities of civilization. Now, with water flowing to the thirsty land from the abundance of our snow-capped mountains . . ." From the bare, frozen ground he stood on, Governor Gooding pointed to the majestic peaks of the Sawtooths rising blue and white behind him, and again the crowd cheered.

"There has never been any doubt but that we have more than ample water flowing from our mountains to irrigate this entire desert. The problem has always been that

151

the flow occurs mostly when least important—in the spring of the year." Murmurs of agreement met his words. "But now, by the efforts of you all, and especially these men who stand here with me—the engineers, the builders—we have harnessed this great resource, and the prophecy shall be fulfilled—the desert shall truly blossom as the rose."

The crowd cheered, the governor waved, the band played. When it was quiet enough for a possibility of her being heard, Kathryn turned to Merrick, who was standing behind her—with Marie beside him, she noted. "Why aren't you up there with the governor? You were one of the contractors."

Merrick bent to speak so that she could hear him better. "Heston can handle all the glory for our company. He thrives on the hoopla."

There was too much confusion to discuss it further there, but Kathryn could tell by his voice that the rift between partners had not healed.

After a number of lengthy speeches by other officials, and applause for all the builders, at which Heston took repeated beaming bows, the crowd sang "America the Beautiful" and returned to the train.

Kathryn, Marie, and Merrick did not go back with the others to Kuna. The faithful Jules went on, promising to see to Kathryn's stock, and the three disembarked at Nampa to attend the gala dinner at the Dewey Palace Hotel that evening.

Although she had seen it many times, Kathryn had never actually been inside the elegant, Southern-style hotel built by the flamboyant promoter and mining speculator Colonel William Dewey. As they walked the two blocks from Nampa's ornate Victorian train depot, she couldn't take her eyes off the stately, four-story, red brick building with its gleaming copper-covered tower domes.

With one lady on each arm, Merrick led them up the stairs flanked by high white columns, and they strolled down the wide veranda that ran the length of the building.

"This is such a magnificent building." Kathryn looked around her. "I wonder why it's in Nampa? Wouldn't Boise be a more likely place for a grand hotel?"

Merrick laughed. "There's plenty of stories told about Colonel Dewey. If half of 'em are true, I'd believe anything. But apparently Dewey shook hands with a group of Boise businessmen on a deal by which they would build a railroad line to Dewey's mines in Owyhee County and in return he would build a big hotel in Boise. The Boise men reneged. The story is that Dewey said, 'I'll never do a thing for Boise as long as I live. I don't care if grass grows in the streets of Boise.' Apparently he came straight to Nampa and built his hotel."

"Well," Marie said, "it's simply wonderful. And I'm so looking forward to the banquet tonight. Thank you so much for inviting us, Merrick."

Kathryn had to admit that Marie didn't actually simper at Merrick. There was nothing she said that Kathryn couldn't have said herself. But she had the most terribly unchristian urge to step on the lace train of Marie's dress that dragged ever so gracefully over the boards of the veranda.

As the dining room on the main floor couldn't accommodate all the celebrants, the second floor assembly room, which was most often used as a ballroom, was set for the banquet. White linen-draped tables glowed beneath red glass lamps reflecting the warm colors of the red flocked wallpaper and velvet drapes. As they took their seats near the front of the room, Kathryn couldn't help noticing that Heston had managed a seat at the head table, only three down from the governor, next to an official from the Bureau of Reclamation.

In spite of the sumptuous menu, which included turkey, goose, chicken, guinea hen, consommé, nuts, and raisins, Marie seemed to be the only one of their party to appreciate it fully. Kathryn did her best to refuse to give way to her feelings of jealousy; she knew they were unworthy, and they accomplished nothing but to make her miserable. Yet they would not go away, even though Merrick paid at least as much attention to her as he did to Marie. Kathryn dipped her fingertips in the lemon-scented water of her fingerbowl and forced a smile.

Merrick seemed to pay most of his attention to his partner, Heston, who was drinking freely of champagne and talking loudly enough for his voice to reach their table.

"There'll be trouble yet," Merrick growled when one of Heston's overblown statements intruded on a quiet moment in their own conversation. "I try to tell him that promising people more than you can deliver is a disastrous way to do business, but he won't listen. Says I'm a tight-fisted, dour Scot and my understated way won't do here in the West."

Kathryn gasped. *"You* dour?" She had always thought of him as the most charming and adventurous person she had ever met—and so far from being understated that she often drew back from his flowery compliments. Although she had to admit to herself that her reticence was more from her own sense of not deserving his compliments than from his expansiveness. She noted that Marie never pulled back from a gentleman's compliment.

The next morning Kathryn had more immediate concerns to cope with. They had caught the final train back to Kuna last night, and it had been well past midnight when Merrick helped the ladies down from his buckboard and went back to Isaiah's. Kathryn awoke with a headache, in no mood to feed chickens and milk a cow, much less move a flock of dim-witted sheep to an ungrazed field, but it had to be done.

It was while she was carrying a pail of water to Buckshot that she realized how unprepared she was to teach Sunday school that day. She had looked at her lesson on Cain and Abel earlier in the week but had done little since then. Now there was barely time to change to her Sunday clothes and hitch the horse to the wagon. She would ask Marie to drive so that she could review on the way, she decided.

Marie took the reins willingly, but Kathryn's last minute review did little to bolster her confidence when she found the tent full of ten squirmy youngsters. Normally she would have been thrilled to find her usual flock of six students so expanded, but today the added numbers only increased her discomfort and added to their high spirits.

Many of them, including Lucy and Davey Brewington and Lila and Benjamin Young, had attended the great event with their parents yesterday, and they were bursting to share it all in great detail with those who hadn't been so privileged.

When she walked into the tent, a few minutes late—having failed in her usual practice of arriving before her pupils to greet each one and set the proper tone for the class—Benji Young was alternately drumming on the seats with a stick and tooting an imaginary horn to demonstrate the band, while the others marched around the inside of the tent as if it were the crest of the dam. All were followed by Jip, Benji's black and white sheepdog.

Kathryn got the dog outside, but repeated attempts to call the students to attention failed until she thought of a useful way to channel their enthusiasm. It was probably just as well she didn't have much of a story prepared—she'd never get them to listen. Instead she took a different tack. "All right, since you're so interested in construction, we'll think about buildings in the Bible."

She almost had to yell to be heard above the hubbub, but that got their attention. Longing for her organ, which they no longer transported for every service, she led them acapella in singing "Joshua Fought the Battle of Jericho," which their march around the tent had suggested to her. She feared for the walls of the tent when they came to "the walls came tumbling down," but the tent stood.

Then she got them to listen to a brief cautionary tale based on Jesus' parable about the importance of building wisely, linking it to the solid foundations required for building Diversion Dam. She thought some of them even got the application of building their lives on a foundation of faith in Jesus Christ. But when they began to wiggle ominously, she was unsure what to do with the rest of the time, so she asked if there were any questions.

Ten-year-old Benjamin Young raised his hand.

"Yes, Benji?"

"Are there stories of hunters in the Bible?"

Wondering what could have inspired such a question, she said, "Yes, there was a very famous hunter named Nimrod, but I'm afraid I don't know very much about him. Shall I try to learn more and bring you a lesson about him?"

Several boys' heads nodded, but Benji's response was more alarming. He pulled a pistol from inside his jacket and brandished it. "See what I got for my birthday? Now I can be a famous hunter like that Ninny guy."

Lila sprang at her brother. "Ben! Does Mama know you brought that to church? I bet she'll be mad. That's just for hunting jackrabbits."

Kathryn steadied herself by gripping the edge of the teacher's desk. "May I see it, Benjamin?" She held out a shaking hand and waited. She realized that with Ben's particular blend of mischievousness and stubbornness she could have a serious problem if he chose to disobey her. Fortunately, he chose to obey.

She looked at the small, engraved gun, then put it out of sight. She struggled with whether she should tie the appearance of a gun in Sunday school to the story of Cain and Abel she had planned to teach, or attempt to go on with the Scripture memory program she had started. She decided on the memory verses and had pulled her supply of prize pins from her pocket when the sound of wagons and adult voices outside told her that the Sunday school hour was up. *Thank you, Lord,* she breathed and sat down. Maybe next week she could hope to award more prizes as she had been doing regularly since Christmas—except for today.

As the congregation came in for church, Kathryn noted that the mood of the adults was as euphoric as that of their children had been. The Young family sat in front of her, and she returned Benji's gun to his father as unobtrusively as possible.

Then Bill turned around, as the service hadn't started yet, and began talking to Harold Sperlin. "Yes sir. This here valley's gonna be the Garden of Eden. Just you wait! That Mr. Heston promised me all the water I could possibly use—even have extra, he said. Do you know in the cities people bathe every week? Daily, Heston said, but I don't believe that. Just give me enough to water my sheep and to grow a good crop of alfalfa, I said."

"That's right," Mr. Sperlin agreed. "My user's permit cost me a pretty penny, but I figure it's worth its weight in gold—more."

Elmer, sitting next to his dad, joined in. "Yep, I heard that Mr. Heston say our land will be worth hundreds of dollars an acre in a year or two."

The talk went on until the preacher took his place at the front, but Kathryn couldn't help remembering Merrick's words "There'll be trouble yet."

15

Kathryn held the printed circular and read: "A Little Talk About Kuna, Idaho . . . This is a personal invitation to you to have a part in the building of a city. . . . On March 4, 1909, two hundred lots will be sold in the townsite of Kuna which stands on a beautiful plateau midway between the Owyhee and the Sawtooth mountains. Kuna has water now ready for irrigation of 35,000 acres of land."

She looked up at Isaiah, who had shown the brochure to her as soon as Nelly had greeted her visitor with a cup of tea. "I'm not sure I understand what's happening."

Isaiah explained. "This Mr. Hubbard who wrote that —you've heard his name—he was one of the contractors building canals and reservoirs—he filed on the Kuna Townsite property about six years ago. Now that we have water we're ready to be a real city, so he's selling the lots to people who want to build businesses here."

Alvina came in. "Just think, we'll have things like a milliners and a bakery—what luxury!"

"Lumber yard's what I want," Isaiah said. "I could do most of my carpentry in the time it takes me to drive into Nampa to buy wood and nails."

Kathryn was still scanning the flyer. "This man is a real visionary, isn't he? He says we'll soon be a town of four or five thousand people—that's hard to imagine. And electricity—ten to fifteen thousand horsepower. He says that's more than is available to all the towns in Boise Valley combined. I don't know, Nelly. Do you think we'll ever have electric lights?"

Nelly shook her head. "Hard to imagine—like you said, he's a visionary."

Vina sprang to answer a knock at the door, and Myron came in.

He, too was holding one of the circulars. "Have you seen this?" He looked at the paper Kathryn held up. "Oh, I see you have. What do you think? Sounds great, huh?"

Isaiah nodded. "Good opportunities for somebody. Can't say I'm interested in opening a business—all I ever wanted was my own land—but I hope the sale's a big success."

"Well, I'd like to do something besides farming, I can tell you!" Everyone except Vina was surprised by Myron's vehemence. Apparently she was well aware of his feelings.

"What would you like to do, Myron?" Kathryn asked. "I thought maybe being postmaster . . ."

Myron's enthusiasm deflated. "Well, I have to hope I can find something more lucrative than that if Vina and I are going to get married this summer."

"What's the matter?" Nelly asked. "I thought you were doing a fine job. Everyone is glad to be able to get their mail here."

Myron nodded. "Yep. But folks in these parts don't seem to be much on writing letters. If proceeds keep on at the same rate, I figure I'll make just over three dollars this year."

Vina's eyes filled with tears. "Oh, Myron—I thought —I mean, that was our nest egg."

He took her hand and squeezed it in both of his. "No, no, wait. That's what I came to tell you—I've arranged to buy one of the lots! I'm going to open a livery stable. Pa says he can let me have three of his horses cheap to start with, and I've talked to Mr. Carlson at the blacksmith shop

—if I can get the lot next to his it'll be real convenient for shoeing horses, and we can sort of work together."

"But Myron—" Vina, who was reading the flyer in his hand, interrupted him "—how can you possibly? This says the lots cost $100—$25 down and $5 per month. I guess that's pretty cheap—it says here lots in Nampa and Boise are $10,000—but if you only get three dollars from the post office . . ." She ended on a strangled sound.

Myron let go of her hand and put his arm around her shoulder. "I said not to worry. I've just come from talking to Mr. Heston—now there's a real fine man. Course he believes in this area after all he did getting our canals built and all."

Kathryn bit her lip. She had her own opinion of Mr. A. J. Heston.

"Anyway," Myron continued, "he's going to loan me the money."

The family exploded in lively rejoicing, especially Vina. She threw both arms around Myron's neck and squealed in a high pitch that must have hurt his ears, but he didn't seem to mind.

Only Kathryn held back. She couldn't have said why. Merrick said he didn't think Heston actually cheated his partners or investors, and the construction did get done. Of course he talked big, but so did lots of promoters. She smiled. The extravagant Colonel Dewey had probably possessed many similar qualities, and he had accomplished great things. Why couldn't she trust Heston?

Hubbard had spent every moment since the opening of the dam distributing his brochures and speaking to Boise Valley business groups so that when the special train arrived in Kuna from Boise on March 4 it was filled to capacity with prospective buyers. Except for the absence of the governor and the brass band, the day held all the excitement of the dam opening. A group of boys setting off firecrackers up the street made up for the lack of a bass drum.

160

Many people, like Kathryn and Marie, who had no intention of bidding on property had packed picnic baskets and come to see the doings. The Sperlins, their wagon loaded with three enormous hampers, tied up near Isaiah and Nelly, and the Youngs joined them on the other side.

Kathryn didn't really understand the process by which a potential buyer was to place a bid on a selected piece of property before the auction, but she knew Myron was nervous that no one raise his bid. He led them down the dusty main street to view the sagebrush-covered lot he had selected.

Kathryn smiled but was unable to think of anything admiring to say. To her it looked exactly like all the rest of the sagebrush-covered property for miles around.

But to Alvina this one lot could have been growing willows and roses. "Oh, Myron, it's wonderful! Oh, I do hope your bid stands. I prayed and prayed."

For Kathryn the day took on a new sheen when Merrick joined them.

"You thinking of buying a lot, Mr. Allen?" Bill Young asked.

"No, no. If I bought anything it'd be a farm—the more I see of business the less I want to do with it."

"Heston?" Kathryn asked quietly at his elbow.

He gave her a curt nod and muttered something Kathryn couldn't hear. Kathryn hoped Heston & Allen could end their partnership now that the irrigation was in. She knew it had been an unpleasant relationship for Merrick.

Bill Young took up the conversation. "Well, farming isn't a bed of roses either, I can tell you that."

"But it'll get better now that you have water, won't it?" Marie asked.

Bill growled. "Or worse. That partner of yours made a lot of fancy promises, Mr. Allen—about how much water we'd have—so I expanded my flock, took on at least a hundred head more than my well can support. So far I've had to spend three days a week hauling water from the river.

The pitiful trickle that reaches my place wouldn't keep ten sheep alive—when I get it."

"But there's plenty of water in the canal, and Indian Creek's full," Kathryn said.

"Canal's fine," Bill replied. "It's the system Heston engineered to carry water from the canal to my place. Those ditches collapse quicker'n we can dig them out. Ones that don't cave in on their own, the jackrabbits burrow under."

"Yeah, and he promised!" For the first time they all noticed Benji standing behind his dad. He held out blistered hands. "You should see Ma and Lila's hands—we dig out ditches all day and then don't get no water. I'd like to tell that Mr. Heston so."

"Now Benji, don't you go taking too much on yourself. This is man's business."

"Well, at least we can shoot the jackrabbits."

Everyone smiled at the youngster's assumption of a grown-up stance. Bill ruffled his son's hair and started to say something else, but Merrick cut in.

"Sorry to interrupt, Bill—but I just spotted a fellow over there I haven't seen since I was in San Francisco. If you'll excuse me . . ." He tipped his hat to the ladies and walked away.

Kathryn tried to see the man Merrick meant. In the crowd it was impossible to identify anyone, but she thought she glimpsed a red beard before a broad back blocked her view. She tried to shake off the heaviness she felt in her chest. There was no reason an old friend should spell trouble for Merrick, and, disappointing as the Youngs's water problems were, no one blamed Merrick for his partner's boasting. Why then did she have this sense of dread?

Now everyone's attention turned to the platform, where the auction was in progress. Alvina bounced up and down, trying to see over the heads of the crowd. Myron was down front with the other bidders, but she couldn't make out what was happening.

"Oh, it'll be so wonderful," Vina chattered to Kathryn or anyone who would listen to her. "Did you know Isaiah said he'd loan us the money for lumber to build the livery barn? And Jules and Elmer will help build it—just think, we could be in business in a few weeks! Oh, everything's so perfect!" Popping firecrackers accented her clapping.

It was several hours later, after the by-standers had considerably lightened their picnic hampers and many of those less closely involved had gone home to afternoon chores, that Hubbard's big gavel banged down on the po- dium. "The sale is closed! We're a success! Kuna is on the map!"

Everyone cheered, the men threw their hats in the air, and women waved hankies. Vina spotted Myron coming toward them and ran to meet him. But the couple returned with stooped shoulders and angry, confused looks on their faces.

"I don't understand," Vina said over and over.

Myron shook his head. "I don't understand either."

"You mean you didn't get the property?" Isaiah asked.

"But you had your bid in first, and Heston promised the loan," Vina argued.

Just then Merrick rejoined them. "What is it?"

"Heston," Myron answered between clenched teeth. "Oh, we got the property all right, but not for my livery barn. Seems the rules of the auction were that a person could only buy one lot. Heston bought one in his name for the warehouse he wants to build—and financed one in my name for his bank."

Amid the cries of outrage and questions that fol- lowed, Myron tried to give answers, but it took some time for a clear picture to emerge. Heston had agreed to loan Myron the down payment to buy a prime corner lot on Main Street. The purchase would be in Myron's name, but since Heston was financing it, he intended to dictate how the property would be used.

"So what it comes to is that you have to pay five dollars a month for Mr. Heston to build a bank, and there's no place for our livery stable."

Merrick's face darkened, and his fists clenched. "I told that shyster he'd go too far one day. Going through life taking advantage of people is not the right way to live. He wouldn't listen to me before, but now I'll make him listen." Merrick strode off.

"Hope he gives it to him good," Bill Young said. "That Heston deserves to get his."

"Wish I had my rabbit gun, Dad," Benji said. "I'd loan it to Mr. Merrick."

"Benjamin! You stay out of this, son. You hear me? Let men handle it."

But the angry voices that reached them from the side of the crowd where Merrick confronted Heston didn't sound as if it was being handled any too well.

"It was an honest deal. Is it my fault your greenhorn friend doesn't understand business?"

"He understands. I understand. I don't want anything more to do with our partnership, Heston. Forget the last payment you owe me. I wouldn't take your tainted money. I don't want my name linked to yours. But hear you me—if you try any more shenanigans I'll hire the best lawyer in Boise, and we'll get you."

Heston gave a scornful laugh. "Just you try it."

"Why don't you go back to San Francisco and leave these innocent people alone?"

Merrick ducked just in time to save himself a black eye. Heston's swing only knocked off Merrick's hat. But his return blow bloodied Heston's nose. A shout went up from the crowd at the sight of blood. Jules stepped between them just in time to block Heston's fist with his shoulder, and then Merrick's San Francisco friend pulled Heston away.

Bill Young slapped Merrick on the back. "Wish I could have given him just one good one. Benji told me he ran over and showed Heston his blisters while we were eating. Seems Heston laughed at him and called him a sissy."

Then Marie took over, wiping the dust off Merrick's face with her lace handkerchief.

A discouraged group returned home over the desert, the long shadows of evening stretching behind them. Kathryn was happy to let Merrick drive them home, even if Marie did sit closer to him on the spring seat than she did. Back at the homestead she was glad to have chickens to feed and Buttercup to milk. Routine chores were the best cure she knew for taking her mind off worries, and the animals always soothed her. She rested her head against Buttercup's soft, warm side as she rhythmically squeezed the milk into the tin bucket between her knees. She wanted to pray, but, as so often, words wouldn't come, so she just took comfort in the warmth and quiet of one of God's simple creatures.

"I got the sheep in." Kathryn jumped at hearing another voice.

"Oh, Jules. Thank you. If the chickens are in the coop I'll just give Buckshot a pail of water, and we can go in. I'm sure Marie's made coffee."

"I watered Buckshot. Let's go in."

Kathryn was so tired she could have sunk against Jules's arm, but she resisted doing so, as she didn't want to bolster his hopes unfairly. In all this time her feelings hadn't changed, and she knew they wouldn't. No matter what Marie and Merrick did.

But twenty-four hours later when Marie, Merrick, Jules, and Kathryn sat over another pot of coffee, her resolution was put to the test.

Merrick had come by to tell them he was returning to San Francisco. Kathryn forced a smile and carefully kept her hand steady while she set down her mug of coffee. "And what will you do there?"

"Bo MacLeod—you probably saw me with him yesterday—sorry I didn't introduce you, but I didn't realize then . . ." He took a long sip of coffee to cover what seemed to be uncharacteristic nervousness on his part.

Kathryn felt he was looking straight at her, and a lump came into her throat when he said, "Please believe me, I didn't plan for things to turn out this way—I—well, anyway, McLeod's actually a sort of distant cousin. He emigrated about the same time I did. Now he's in with the railroad, and he's offered me a job. It seems like the best thing to do—no matter what I really want."

Kathryn knew there was one consideration higher than anything Merrick wanted or anything she wanted. "Merrick, have you prayed about this? Are you sure it's right?"

He grinned and ran his fingers through his unruly locks. "That's what Isaiah asked me—almost the same words exactly. Like I told him—I sure have prayed." He grinned again, the brightest he'd been all evening. "Once you start talking to God the way your papa taught me, it's hard to imagine living any other way. But—" now the grin faded "—best I can say is it's necessary, so I hope it's right. After all, I figure God's in San Francisco too."

They sat in silence for a moment, then Merrick slapped the table and turned to Marie. "That's enough of these long faces—this isn't a funeral. Play us something on the organ."

Kathryn felt a small stab that he had asked Marie rather than herself, although she would quickly acknowledge that Marie was the better musician. Kathryn refilled their coffee mugs, and after a moment of pumping to get air into the bellows, Marie filled the tiny house with the lilting strains of "Jesu, Joy of Man's Desiring." Even the lantern flames seemed to glow and ebb in time to the rise and fall of the music.

Kathryn closed her eyes and felt herself relax to the beautiful melody. As her shoulders eased she realized how tense she had been. The peace in the room lasted perhaps three minutes.

A heavy banging at the door jarred the whole shack.

"Open up in the name of the law. We know you're in there."

Kathryn gasped and started to her feet.

Jules put his hand on her shoulder and pushed her gently back down. He strode to the door as the banging continued. Jules opened the door, and it seemed that the black of the night entered with the Ada County sheriff and his three deputies, all with drawn guns.

"Merrick Allen?"

Merrick stood. "That's me."

"You're under arrest for the murder of A. J. Heston. Hold out your hands."

16

The room spun around her, but Kathryn neither screamed nor fainted as a deputy frisked Merrick for weapons, which he wasn't carrying, and the sheriff snapped handcuffs on him.

At the door Merrick looked back. For one brief instant their eyes held. Then he was gone, swallowed up in the blackness with the sound of the slammed door echoing through the room.

Marie was the first to speak. "But I don't understand. Did he say Heston is dead? Why did they take Merrick? I can't believe that really happened—it must be a mistake— or a joke." Suddenly she flew to the door and flung it open. "Merrick! Merrick!" Her only answer was the howl of a coyote on Kuna Butte.

Jules went to the door, put his arm around her shaking shoulders, and led her gently back to a chair. "If you women'll be all right here alone for a spell I'll ride after them and see what I can learn. Guess we were all too stunned to ask any questions."

Marie was now shaking violently, little dry sobbing sounds rasping in her throat.

Kathryn got a blanket and wrapped her in it. "Yes, go see what you can learn, but first—let's pray for Merrick. I know he couldn't have killed anyone, but he must be in terrible trouble." She bowed her head and began praying even before the others responded. She was never sure what she said. This was one of those times when she had to rely on the scriptural promise that the Holy Spirit would make intercession with groanings that could not be spoken, because her own mind and heart were racing too fast to form coherent words.

Then Jules prayed—a simple prayer, strong for its unaffected faith. "Lord, help our brother. Help him look to You in his trouble. Let truth and justice win out. And help us hold steady in You. Thank You, Lord. Amen."

Marie's whispers were unintelligible, but when the brief prayer time was over, she was calm.

Jules picked up his hat but had not left the room before Isaiah came in. Kathryn ran to her uncle's comforting arms. "What happened? Do you know anything? They took Merrick away."

"I was hoping to get here first to warn you. I was at the townsite helping Timpson stock his mercantile for opening when they found the body. Carlson had closed up his blacksmith shop, then went back when Bill Young discovered his horse had a loose shoe. There was Heston layin' with his head in a pool of blood. At first they thought it was all an accident—that he'd slipped and fallen on the anvil, but then they found the bullet that grazed his skull."

"He was shot? Did you hear the gun?"

"But why Merrick? Lots of people hated Heston."

"When did it happen?"

"Where was everybody? Sounds like there were lots of folks in town."

"Was Merrick even there? Did you see him?"

They overwhelmed Isaiah with questions. He held up his hand and shook his head. "Whoa. Hold on a minute. I don't really know all that, but I'll tell you what I do know. They found the body early afternoon. Carlson had closed up to go home to eat, but he hadn't been in the shop for an hour or two before that."

169

"So anyone could have gone in. Why accuse Merrick? Was he the only one around?"

Isaiah took a deep breath before answering. "Everyone was there, finishing up business from yesterday's sale. Hubbard had a full house at his tent—successful bidders paying their money, unsuccessful ones hanging around complaining and hoping someone would default. Whole place was like a carnival—kids running all over setting off fireworks, dogs yappin'—"

"Did Myron make any trouble?" Jules asked. "I'm a mite worried about my little brother."

Isaiah shrugged. "Not what you'd call trouble. He was there all right, muttering about Heston's dirty tricks. Then he went to give Bill Young a hand. Bill and Benji'd come in looking for help—his feeder ditch collapsed last night, and it was more than his family could dig out by themselves."

Kathryn shook her head, recalling the blisters on Benji's hands. "That family's had more than their share of trouble. It's not fair, after they shared water from their well with everyone."

"But I still don't see why they suspected Merrick." Marie got them back on the main track.

"Seems he was the last one anybody saw with Heston. They were arguing outside Hubbard's office. Someone said they saw them walk off in the direction of the blacksmith . . ." Isaiah paused.

"But that's silly. Merrick didn't even carry a gun. He threatened to sue Heston, not kill him." Nothing made any sense to Kathryn. "Did they even question Merrick?"

"By the time someone fetched the sheriff from Boise, Merrick wasn't around. That MacLeod fellow said he and Merrick spent most of the afternoon talking business, but that doesn't change the fact that several people saw him and Heston walk off together."

Questions and answers continued to swirl around her, but Kathryn could take in no more. She could see nothing but Merrick's eyes as he went out the door. *The last thing he did was look at me.* His eyes—always so speaking, so full of humor and intelligence, so lively—had pled with her to believe him and to help him.

And something more. He was asking her for something she couldn't quite read—was it forgiveness? She couldn't believe there was anything to forgive, but if there was, he had it. For now, all she could do was pray for him, over and over. All she could say was, "Please, God, please. Be with him. Help him. Please, God, please. Please, God, I love him so much."

Then the answer came: *Yes. And I love him even more.*

"Oh!" No one really noticed Kathryn jerk up from her slumped position, but for her it was as if all the lanterns in the room had flared up. There was hope. God was in control. He had not abandoned Merrick, and He had not abandoned them. They could work in His guidance.

"Jules!" She grabbed his arm. "The sheriff is so stuck on his theory that all he'll look for is evidence against Merrick. Will you see what you can do? Talk to people, look for clues? I don't know—surely there's something we can do."

Jules placed his big hand over hers on his arm. "Don't you worry, Miss Kathryn. I'll do everything I can for you." He hadn't called her "Miss Kathryn" for years. "I'll start first thing in the morning. Soon as it's light, I'll see what I can find."

Kathryn started to thank him, then stopped. "No. Come for me. I want to help, too."

Jules looked skeptical, but he agreed.

The next morning Kathryn completed her chores by lanternlight, and by sunrise she and Jules were riding into Kuna.

They didn't have to wait long for Vic Carlson to come to open the blacksmith shop. The bald, stocky blacksmith frowned at them. "Thought I'd get here before the curiosity-seekers. Lost two days of work already—what with the sale Tuesday and all the excitement yesterday. I've got three wheel rims to make today."

171

He pulled a key out of his pocket and unlocked the black iron padlock on his door. "I hear tell they arrested that Allen feller last night. Too bad, nice feller. Figure he did us all a favor—nobody'll miss that Heston."

Carlson set about blowing up the embers of yesterday's fire with his bellows and placing more chunks of coal on it. "Body was right over there." He pointed. "Sorry about the blood on the anvil, Miss Jayne. Haven't had no time to clean up yet."

The blood on the anvil was oddly smeared, as if someone had put a hand on it. Kathryn remembered the sheriff examining Merrick's hands before he snapped on the handcuffs.

The hardpacked dirt floor also bore dark stains, which would be stamped out after a day's work.

Kathryn looked back at the open door through which the morning sun was streaming. Heston and someone had walked in there less than twenty-four hours ago, and only one of them walked out. She searched the floor carefully between the door and the anvil. If only the hard floor bore footprints. Of course, the sheriff and his men would have found any evidence there was to find. Still . . .

Carlson, at his workbench, was talking—more to himself than to them. "Fool kids—look at the mess somebody made playing with my rivets. Mixed up all the sizes. I don't know what it is about a blacksmith shop that attracts kids like a candy store. Somebody's gonna get hurt in here one day, and then their folks'll blame me."

Jules thanked Carlson for his time and, taking Kathryn firmly by the arm, ushered her out into the sunshine. "Kathryn, you look stunned. I'm most awful sorry I took you in there—I didn't think about there being all that blood."

"Oh, no, no." She staved off the suggestion that a little dried blood would bother her. "I'm thinking, that's all. Something Carlson said about kids. The town was crawling with them yesterday. Maybe one of them saw something. You know how kids are—get into places no one else

172

does and see things no one else pays attention to . . ." Her voice trailed off.

Jules nodded. "We could talk to a few of the young'uns. Seems worth a try. It's something the sheriff's not likely to do."

Not having any better ideas, they turned their horses toward the Brewington place. Less than halfway there they met Davey Brewington riding down the road with a young black and white sheepdog following at his horse's heels.

"Isn't that Jip?" Kathryn recognized Benji Young's two-year-old dog.

"Yup. He showed up at our place this morning, whining and scratching. Isaiah said I should take him back to Youngs' since he seems lost. Benji said he had him trained, but a sheepdog that can't find his own way home ain't much good if you ask me."

"Look," Jules said. "we'll be riding over toward Youngs' next. We'll take Jip for you. But first, were you in town yesterday?"

Davey had disgust written all over his face. "No! Got stuck with mucking out the pigsty—took all day. And I'd promised Benji we'd go target shooting. When you see Ben, tell him I'm sorry. Ma said maybe Saturday."

Kathryn and Jules turned east to take Jip home. At the corner nearest the Young place they met Bill.

"Howdy, folks." He patted Jip absently. "You got Benji? I was just going to fetch him from Davey Brewington's when I get this ditch set."

"What?" Kathryn went cold. "But we just saw Davey. He was bringing Jip home because Benji didn't go to his place after all."

Bill set his shovel in the ground with a forceful shove of his foot. "Fool kid! What's he got up to now? I don't want his ma to hear about this. She'll go crazy with worry." He thought a moment. "I suppose he might have gone home with the Sullivan kids when it didn't work out with Davey. I'll go saddle up and ride over there."

By then Jip had begun an insistent yapping and was even nipping at the heels of Jules's horse.

"Is Jip trying to tell us something?" Kathryn asked. "Bill, you go ahead and check with Sullivans. We'll see where Jip wants to go." She turned her horse without waiting for the men to assent.

Kathryn and Jules rode for almost an hour, Jip trotting ahead of them, until they were nearly at Kuna Butte.

"I hope this critter knows what in tarnashun he's doing. This sure seems like a waste of time," Jules complained.

Kathryn reached down and patted Buckshot on the neck. "I don't know. Surely he isn't trying to lead us to Ben. There's nowhere out here for him to *be*. Do you suppose he has a mate out here? If they've had pups I doubt they'd survive the coyotes for long."

Jules took a long look at the dog. "Well, he's young, but I s'pose it's possible. Might need food and water. If so, I take back the names I called him—clever rascal to get help."

They continued around the end of the butte. Then Jules said, "Hey, looks like he's leading us to the cave."

"Oh, then he must have a family in there!" Kathryn urged her horse forward.

Jules shook his head. "No way a dog could get down there—the mouth is a fifty-foot drop straight down."

But that was indeed where Jip was leading them—straight to the big round opening into a system of lava tunnels that ran no one knew for certain how far back under the earth. Kathryn felt her throat closing at the mere thought of it.

"Well, what now, boy?" Jules looked at the dog who sat, panting, by the hole, looking up at them.

"Benji couldn't possibly have gotten down there. Could he?"

Jules was the one who saw the rope tied to sagebrush near the cave. "There's somebody in the cave."

"It must be Benji, then. He and Jip were never apart. He even brought the dog to Sunday school—but I made him wait outside."

Jules was off his horse, examining the rope. "Kathryn, there's flakes of something on this rope that could be dried blood."

"Well, if Benji went down there, his hands probably are bleeding—remember how blistered they were from digging ditches?"

"But why would Benji be down there? It's a fool place for a kid to go—especially one with blistered hands."

Kathryn was filled with compassion for the terrified child. She gazed toward the black pit and tried to imagine what fear could have driven him down that rope with bleeding hands.

What had he done? What had he seen? What had someone done or said to him? Bill Young said Benji had gone off to confront Heston with his blisters to get some help rebuilding the ditches. What could Heston have said to frighten him? With a shudder she remembered that Benji had had his jackrabbit gun with him. It wasn't possible that Benji shot Heston, was it? *Please, Lord, no.*

Maybe no one saw Benji or said *anything* to him—and he was hiding in the cave to keep it that way. Could Benji have seen the murder? And now be shivering in terror that the murderer would come after *him*?

Kathryn jumped off Buckshot and ran to the mouth of the cave. "Ben! Ben! We're here. Don't be frightened!" Her voice didn't even make an echo. She drew back. "Jules, it's dead quiet in there. Like a tomb. You don't think—"

"I think the rascal's scared and hungry. I'll get him out."

Jules set to work, and Kathryn watched in a kind of frozen daze as he examined the rope and knot, decided they weren't strong enough to support him, brought a sturdy lasso from his saddle, tied it expertly to the largest bush around, tore his undershirt into strips and wrapped it tightly around a sagebrush branch to make a torch, and prepared to descend over the lip of the cave.

At last she came to life. "Jules, wait!" She couldn't think about the black network of narrow tunnels he was

175

descending into. That was a horror too awful to contemplate. "Jules! Be careful." She couldn't put her fears into words.

He grinned at her. "I'll go careful, Kathryn. You pray." And then he was over the side.

She gathered her courage and peeped over the edge after him. He was about halfway down now, lowering himself hand under hand, pushing his feet against the lava walls to keep from scraping against them. In a few minutes he landed on the loose dirt at the bottom with a soft thud.

"Are you all right?" She could see he was standing in a large chamber. Light from the entrance lit a wide circle about him, then all was black beyond.

He looked up, and the light fell on his kind, gentle face. "I'm fine. You just keep praying." He looked around. "It 'pears to go both directions."

"See anything?"

He lit the torch. "Yep. Set of fresh footprints heading that way. Not very big boots." He took a few steps. "Um— Kathryn, I'll be fine. But if anything should happen—you know, anything unexpected—tell Marie—well—tell Marie I thought of her."

"Oh. Oh, yes, I will." Her throat closed again at the thought.

Then he was gone into the blackness.

Kathryn sat down by the mouth of the cave to wait. Behind her their horses tethered to a sage bush made gentle noises, and Jip sidled over to lay his head in her lap. The ground was cold, though the overhead sun bore down warm on her hair. She tried to pray, but as always was frustrated by her inability to form words at a time like this. No matter how she tried to keep them out, fearful images filled her mind: long dark tunnels winding endlessly, sharp lava reaching out to tear and cut, sudden drops to . . .

No! She wouldn't let herself do that. She forced her mind to something else. Merrick. She would think of Merrick. But the laughing eyes and merry smile she loved to remember twisted in her memory, and she saw hollow, pleading eyes, a grim-set mouth. The setting was just as bad—not lava caves but a cold, stone prison cell. Merrick sitting, hands together, head down, on a narrow bench in a tiny, dark room. The walls moved closer together and the ceiling lowered. And it wasn't Merrick; it was Jules—the walls of the tunnel were closing in on him.

Then the worst horror of all came to her. What if Jules got stuck? What would she do? It would do no good for her to go down, even if she could. If Jules were wedged in a crevice too narrow for him, there was no way she could pull him out. If he had hit his head on a low ceiling and was lying there bloody and unconscious, she didn't see how she could help him. Even if she could drag him to the entrance, she could never get him up.

No, the only sensible thing would be to go for help. But where? Where was the closest homestead? Years ago it had been the Robinsons, but their place was long abandoned.

She tried to think. What had they ridden past? Just where was the Sullivan place? Would she have to go clear to the Sperlins'? If Jules were in trouble, could he last that long? Would he panic if wedged in? Would he struggle and break a rib—or worse?

She flung both arms over her head in an effort to block out the thoughts. How long should she wait before going for help?

"Jules! Jules! Jules!" She yelled his name down into the hole, each time her voice becoming more insistent, the panic rising. At last she stopped. She had to gain control. Hysteria was the last thing anyone needed.

Pray! she commanded herself. She sat back and forced herself to breathe more slowly. *Pray,* she repeated.

At last words came to mind, "Yea, though I walk through the valley of the shadow of death. . . . Be of good courage. . . . I am with you always." And comfort came as well. The comfort that had always been there—when she was still enough to listen.

177

17

Now she sat calmly, praying. It seemed she had been there for hours, but in truth it was probably no more than fifteen or twenty minutes before at last she saw the flicker of a torch emerge from the tunnel.

"Jules! Did you find him?"

He stood in the circle of light fifty feet below her, looking up and blinking. "Wait. I'm coming up." He snuffed his torch in the dust, grabbed the rope with hands and feet, and began his laborious climb.

When she could, Kathryn grabbed the back of his shirt and pulled, more in moral support than for anything her small strength could add, and he was over the top.

He sat a moment, breathing heavily. Then he shook his head. "There's someone down there all right. I saw fresh footprints. But I couldn't get to him. Shoulders too broad to get through the tunnels."

"Did you try calling out?"

"A few times. No good. It's strange, but sounds don't carry down there. It's like the air's de—"

Kathryn was glad he stopped. She didn't want to hear that word.

"We'll have to go for help." Jules turned toward his horse.

"No, wait!" Kathryn grabbed his arm. "That'll take an hour—maybe two. If Benji's down there frightened or hurt it'll be a lifetime to him." Then she had another thought. "Jules, what if we're right that he's running from the murderer? What if *he* finds the cave while we've gone for help?"

"All right. You ride for help. I'll stay here and watch."

Kathryn took a deep breath. She couldn't let Benji suffer a minute longer than necessary or let Jules face a murderer alone. "No. I'm small enough to get through any tunnel the smallest man could. I'll go down."

"Kathryn, you can't."

Kathryn laughed, finding a strange confidence in the very audacity of what she had proposed. "Yes, I can. Like you said a while ago—I'll be careful. You pray. Can you lower me down?"

"Sure, I could, but I don't think it's a good idea. What if you lost your way in the tunnels?"

That made Kathryn consider again. The thing she had hated and feared the most all her life were dark narrow tunnels, closing in on her. Then she thought of Merrick with a dark narrow cell closing in on him. What if Benji could identify the murderer but they didn't get him out in time—what if he was too frightened or sick to talk when they got to him and they hanged Merrick for a murder he didn't commit? That thought made her choke far worse than any attack of claustrophobia. She knew she would feel a failure the rest of her life if she did not do anything she could to save Merrick.

Jip whined at her feet, and suddenly she had an idea. "It'll be all right, Jules. I won't be alone."

He took her hand. "Kathryn, I know. God will be with you, but—"

"Oh yes, He will. But I meant something else. I'll take Jip with me. If I lose my sense of direction, he won't."

"I don't like it, but I can see there's no use arguing." Jules pulled up the lasso and tied the end into a seat for her to sit in.

Kathryn gathered her skirt and petticoat and fit the rope around her. Then she stopped, surveying Jules's trousers. She had never desired anything masculine, always reveling in whatever femininity she could achieve in her hard life, but now she wished for trousers. Then she smiled, knowing what she could do.

Going over the edge was the hardest, but Jules talked to her every step, telling her just where to put her feet and hands.

"Lean against the rope. All your weight. I want you to see that I can hold you."

"I never doubted it." Kathryn committed her weight to the rope.

"Now, just walk backwards. Keep the rope tight. You can stop whenever you want to. You don't have to do this."

"Yes, I do." Her right foot sought the side of the cave inside the mouth. Then her whole weight was in the seat. Now she was glad for the padding of her skirts as the rope cut.

"Keep your feet out so you won't hit the wall. Lean back for balance." She followed Jules's directions.

When she reached it, The cave floor was comfortingly solid under her feet. As soon as she was out of the seat Jules began lowering Jip in a more complicated harness than Kathryn had used, one to hold each leg so that he couldn't slip out. Then Jules tossed down the sulfur matches for her to light the torch.

At first walking was easy. The ceiling of the tunnel was high over her head, the floor soft dirt. The torch pushed the darkness back at every step, and Jip trotted at her feet.

The air smelled oddly smokey, perhaps from the torch, she thought. Yet it was an older smell, as if the dirt were composed of ancient leaf mold, though there could be no leaves down here. She wouldn't describe it as stale. A fresh current of cold air made the torch waver. Did that mean there was an undiscovered opening somewhere?

Some people thought so. Perhaps their quarry had found another way out, and she was searching an empty cave.

She walked quickly in the wide passage, then it began to narrow. Before she was conscious of the shrinking space she recognized her increased heart rate and uneven breathing. Already she had to watch not to bang her head on the sharp lava above her. Soon she would be crawling. This was as good a time as any.

She wedged the torch into a crack so that she could work with both hands, loosened the band on her skirt, and stepped out of skirt and petticoat. Her heavy cotton pantalets came well below her knees, and her modesty was protected by the darkness of the cave, yet she felt as exposed as if she'd disrobed on Main Street. But the freedom of movement was wonderful.

"All right, Jip. Let's go." She picked up the torch. The sound of her own voice was reassuring, as was Jip's tail-wagging. She forced herself to breathe slowly. She would *not* give in to claustrophobia.

It was not claustrophobia that almost defeated her, however, but a new thought—a terrifying possibility so obvious she couldn't believe they hadn't thought of it before. What if it wasn't Benji down here at all? What if it was the murderer himself? Were these long dark tunnels leading her to a desperado's hideout? Would the next curve she crawled around put her face to face with a killer?

She backed up a few paces until she bumped into Jip. He whimpered. She stopped. No. Jip thought they were going to Benji, didn't he?

She moved forward, then stopped again. What if they were both right? What if Benji *was* down here—with the murderer? Held hostage. Perhaps they were right—Benji saw the murder, and the murderer saw Benji. Now he would see her.

She stepped backward again and bumped painfully against a rock. For a moment that seemed like the last straw. Really it was the answer, for as she rubbed her foot, the Scripture came to her: *There shall no evil befall thee. . . . for he shall give his angels charge over thee. . . . lest thou dash thy foot against a stone.*

Her panic barely under control, Kathryn went forward. She had gone some distance when the corner of her eye caught a wavering shadow on the wall, and a new fear gripped her. Were there animals down here? Bats? Spiders? Snakes? Jules hadn't mentioned any, but he might have thought nothing of it. The thought of a rattler coiled on an overhanging ledge immobilized her. What if she stepped on one?

"Oh, God, help," she prayed out loud. *Listen for the answer. God always answers. I don't always hear.* Her memory of the Scripture was inexact, but it was enough: *Thou shalt tread upon the lion and adder . . . there shall no evil befall thee.* Peace flooded her as if she were in the middle of an open field. The beauty she had always sought, but that had eluded her in physical surroundings, she found now in the depths of a cave. The internal peace of God was the greatest beauty of all.

"All right, boy. Let's go." In a few yards she was crawling on hands and knees, pushing the torch ahead of her. Here the floor was no longer dust but layers of sharp lava fragments. She put her hands and knees down as carefully as possible but still felt the cuts and scrapes. She had to keep her head ever lower and lower. Once she forgot and received a nasty bruise on her forehead.

Now she knew she was in new territory. Jules could not have come this far, so whatever there was to discover waited ahead.

The rag around the torch appeared to be more than half burned. How much farther must she go? No one really knew how far the tunnels went. *Keep it burning, Lord. I've got to go* on. Then she smiled and amended, *We've got to go on.*

Now that she was no longer gripped by fear, Kathryn could reason. That was a mixed blessing, for the first question she had to face was: Was she saving Merrick for Marie? She couldn't answer that, and she knew it didn't matter. No matter what the outcome, she had to save Merrick for himself. For the love she bore for him, no matter what his feelings for her.

For a moment she stopped crawling. *That* was how God felt about her. About Merrick. About the whole world. Christ died for us because of His love for us—no matter what we did with His love.

That insight gave her more courage than any understanding she'd ever had. Her love for Merrick, great and all-encompassing as it seemed to her, was but a pale reflection of God's love for the worst of sinners. God would understand in the most personal way if Merrick turned his back on her love. And God would comfort her.

She crawled only a few more yards before finding herself in a spacious chamber. Surely if someone were hiding in the cave this would be a comfortable space. But there was no sign of anything. On the far side of the chamber the passage narrowed again, then branched in three directions. Without knowing it, this was what she had brought Jip for.

"Which way, boy?"

For the first time he moved ahead of her, trotting down the left tunnel. Kathryn's mind told her she should be afraid. She should fear the narrowing, dark spaces she was following deeper and deeper into the earth. She should cower from the thought of walking into the very den of a murderer around the next curve of the passage. But thoughts of terror now made her smile. She was certain that the unshakable calm she had found in the presence of God would never leave her.

Suddenly she needed all her new-found assurance, for Jip, a few paces ahead, gave a low rumble in his throat.

"What is it, boy?" she whispered.

For an answer he barked. Any thought she might have had of taking her quarry by surprise fled.

Kathryn, however, was the one taken by surprise. A shadowy form leaped out at her with a cry, accompanied by wild barking from Jip. She staggered backward, almost dropping the torch. She cried out as a stone cut into her shoulder, then moved forward as she realized that the form at her feet was sobbing, and Jip was licking its face.

"Benji! What are you doing down here?" She stuck the torch between two rocks and gathered boy and dog into her arms. Was the boy a hostage? Was a killer lurking in another passage?

It took some time before she could quiet them enough to understand what Benji was saying. "Don't let them hang me, Miss Kathryn. I didn't mean to do it!"

"Of course no one's going to hang you, Benji. Are you alone? Tell me what happened."

Between sobs the child recounted his terrors of the last two days. "I saw Mr. Heston and a man go into the blacksmith's. I thought he should know about our ditch collapsing. Pa and I'd gone to town to get help. I thought Heston should help—after all, he built it. But he was real mean. He said some awful things and tried to kick me. I had my gun—Davey and I were going shooting. I held it out and yelled at him to stop. He reached for a piece of iron. I jumped back. I guess my gun went off—I don't know—I don't exactly remember. I just know he was lying there with blood coming out of his head. I killed him! I didn't mean to—please believe me, Miss Kathryn, I didn't mean to!"

Kathryn hugged him tightly to her and rocked back and forth, making soothing sounds. Sobs racked his sturdy young body. It was several minutes until he was calm enough to talk again.

"And so you ran," Kathryn prompted.

"I—I guess so. There's a loose board at the back of the shop. I dived out there. I ran until I got tired. Then I ducked down under some sagebrush. I don't know how long I was there, but a wagon came by. They didn't see me jump on back—it was all full of stuff. First I thought I'd go to Silver City or wherever they were goin', but when I peeked out and saw the butte I had another idea."

"The cave."

"Yeah. I—uh—sorta borrowed a rope and jumped off the wagon. It was pretty dark by then anyway."

"Weren't you afraid to go into the cave in the dark?"

Benji shrugged. "'S all the same—don't know whether it's day or night down here. But I sure got hungry. And my hands hurt awful." He held them up to the wavering light. "Is it tomorrow yet?"

It took Kathryn a moment to understand his question. "Oh yes, it's tomorrow. Early afternoon, I guess. You must have been down here close to eighteen hours. You *must* be starved." She hugged him tighter. "But Benji—if you just wanted to hide, why ever did you crawl in so far? You'd have been hidden around just two bends of the cave."

She felt his small body tremble.

"I was tryin' to get out. I knew I could never crawl back up that rope, not with my hands so sore. I've heard people say there's probably another entrance to the cave, even if they haven't found it yet." He tried to stifle a sob. "But they must be wrong. It just goes on forever. Do you think it goes to hell, Miss Kathryn?"

"Don't be silly." Kathryn assumed a brisk, business-like voice to steady the child. "Come on." She boosted him off her lap. "Let's go get you some food and bandages. Jules is waiting for us."

Benji turned back and clung to her. "No! They'll hang me! I don't wanta swing."

"Don't be silly, Benji. They don't hang children. Besides, it was an accident. You made that very clear. But you must be brave and tell the sheriff everything you've told me. He thinks Mr. Allen did it. He put him in jail."

"Why'd he think a stupid thing like that? Mr. Allen wasn't anywhere around."

"It wasn't Mr. Allen you saw go into the shop with Heston?"

"Nah, it was somebody I never seen before."

"Was he in there when you talked to Heston?"

Benji considered. "I don't think so. I didn't notice."

"Well, come on. We've got to get you home. Your parents must be worried out of their minds."

"No. They think I'm with Davey. I was gonna stay over."

"Well, Jip knew you were missing. He's the one that brought us here."

"Good boy!" Ben buried his face in the long white hair at Jip's throat and took his hand from his back only when he had to crawl on all fours.

Jules's concerned face peering over the rim of the opening told Kathryn he had gone through the same agonies of waiting she had earlier.

"We're fine!" she cried quickly.

His face split in a relieved grin.

"Take Ben up first, but throw your gloves down—his hands are too sore to hold the rope."

In a little over an hour Hazel Young was soothing a pungent ointment on Benji's hands and wrapping them in soft white bandages, while alternating between telling him how much she loved him and scolding him for the terrible scare he had given everyone.

Shortly afterward Bill came in from his fruitless search, and the family was reunited.

By noon the next day Merrick Allen was a free man.

18

Merrick sat before her, much as on the night of his arrest, drinking coffee with Jules and Marie. It seemed a lifetime ago, and Kathryn knew that the changes that had taken place in both of them in those two days might well have taken a lifetime to accomplish in more normal circumstances. Kathryn knew too that she had found an assurance, a center of calm, a well of courage she had been searching for all her life. It had been accomplished at terrible expense to Benji and Merrick, and, of course, A. J. Heston, but she would ever be grateful. Her life from now on would be different.

And Merrick. One look at him told her he was different. He was paler, more subdued, as one might expect of a man who had served a long prison sentence rather than merely two nights in the county jail. He, too, was calmer, more assured, stronger. The undercurrent of reckless wildness she had always sensed in him, that current that had attracted yet frightened her, was gone.

"Was Benji able to describe the man he saw with Heston?" Marie asked.

"Not really," Jules answered. "Guess it doesn't matter much anyway. We seem to have a pretty clear picture of what happened."

"But did anyone see the man come out?" she persisted.

"No. Benji said maybe the man knew about the loose board at the back of the shop too. That made the sheriff laugh. I expect he just didn't notice him come out."

"What about the gun? Did they ever find it?"

"No. Benji thinks he must have dropped it in the desert—or maybe left it on the wagon he hitched a ride on. Says he doesn't think he'll want to hunt much now anyway."

"Strange that nobody heard the gunshot."

Here Merrick answered. "Not really. Earlier Heston and I had been sitting on the bench beside the smithy, trying to settle our business. One reason we gave it up was the ruckus those kids were making setting off firecrackers. Still celebrating the sale. Anyway, that would have covered a firing squad."

They were all quiet for a time, reconstructing the picture of what had happened.

"It's terrible for Benji," Marie said at last. "He'll have nightmares the rest of his life."

"It is tough," Jules agreed. "But everyone's convinced it was an accident. He'll be all right. Hope it doesn't sound too callous of me to mention that now Myron can have his livery stable."

"Oh—speaking of stable—" Kathryn jumped to her feet "—I forgot to water Buckshot."

But Jules was before her. "You rest those sore muscles. Your scrapes healing all right?"

She nodded. "Hazel Young's ointment is really good."

"That's fine. I'll see to the stock. Marie, would you care to get some fresh air?"

Kathryn and Merrick were alone.

After several moments of silence Merrick spoke. "I owe you my life, Kathryn."

"No, no. The truth would have come out. Bill Young was looking for Ben when we took him home. He would have found him."

"Probably, yes. I meant more than that. Starting back when you made me welcome here—gave me the home I thought I'd have to live without the rest of my life. And then your father showed me the way back to God. I don't just mean I owe you my physical life because you kept me from being executed—I mean you've shown me a life worth living."

Kathryn caught her breath. She looked toward the door Marie had gone out. Why was he saying this to her? Was he preparing her for something? Something she didn't want to hear?

"That time I spent sitting in jail—I faced myself in a new way. Really looked at what I'd done and what I wanted to do. I've sure made more than my share of mistakes. But one mistake I'm not going to make is heading off to San Francisco. My life is here."

Kathryn bit her lip and felt her eyes grow large. She held her breath. Whatever he had to say was coming now.

"Kathryn, I don't want to leave you. Not ever."

"Me? You want to stay with me?"

"If you'll have me. I know there's lots of things left to work out, but I think we can do it—if you want to."

"Have you? Want to?" She knew the briefest instant of conflict—she had been so long schooled against such behavior—but suddenly all the shyness and ladylike inhibitions that had been drilled into her were flung aside. She all but knocked over her chair throwing herself into his arms. "Oh, yes! Please."

His kiss was long and tender, and she lost herself in the joy of the moment. Afterward she sat with her arms around his neck, her head on his shoulder. She'd never been so comfortable or felt so safe in her life. "It's so *right*," she murmured.

"That's what I've been trying to find words to tell you. My deciding to stay here—if you'd take me—wasn't the big decision I made in jail. The big one was giving myself to God."

She lifted her head. "I thought you did that—before Papa died."

"I said I was having trouble figuring out how to explain this. I did. When I prayed with your father I told God I was sorry for all my orneriness, and He forgave me. And life has been different—better—since then. But sitting there in that cell, I saw all the mistakes I still make, all the trouble I still get into, all the messes in my life I still haven't cleared up. So I asked God to take charge of all that and show me what to do. I guess if I was a preacher I'd say I gave God the reins to my buckboard."

"And the first thing you did was ask me to marry you!"

"God knew how long I'd been wanting to do that. But He and I both knew I couldn't until I was ready to straighten out everything else."

"Like?"

"Well, the business mess with Heston, for example. That'll still take a bit to sort out. I saw my lawyer in Boise soon's I got out of jail. He's working on it all. I want to do what we can to rebuild weak ditches for people like the Youngs—although, to be fair, sandy soil and jackrabbits can't be blamed on Heston. Anyway, if I come out of it all with any profits I want to invest in something solid—railroads or mining—then start building this farm. If that's what you'd like."

She almost choked on a little bubble of laughter. "Oh yes, I'd love it—but are you sure? The last thing I'd ever guessed you'd do was settle down as a farmer."

"Settle down is the key, isn't it? It's about time I did that. Farming has always been in my blood—generations of Allens and Fletchers have been farmers in Scotland."

"Fletchers?" she interrupted.

"My mother's family. All this time I was rebelling against that—all of my heritage—but I didn't realize it. When I told God He could be boss, He just sort of held a mirror up to me in that cell, and I really saw myself inside—understood what was going on."

190

Kathryn gave a small gasp of laughter. "Oh, if only I could have seen this yesterday when I was sitting out there in the desert so filled with fear and darkness. I didn't know life could be as bright as this."

"There's just one more thing." The somber look on Merrick's face sobered her.

"What?"

"My family. I think I mentioned that Bo McLeod was a kind of distant cousin. I'd put all the family troubles pretty much out of my mind, but some things he said brought the whole thing back. I see now why your father was so insistent that I clear it up. A man can't move forward with something like that dragging him back."

Kathryn nodded. "So what are you going to do?"

"*We* do, I hope. I've not had any luck trying to communicate with them by letter. So I propose that we get married as soon as it's decent and go to Scotland for our honeymoon."

She was so overwhelmed she could only nod. Then when Marie and Jules came in holding hands and looking star-struck, Kathryn knew that truly her cup was running over.

19

Kathryn's journal had never filled so quickly as it did that April. The approach of three weddings in the tiny community seemed to spark even the most mundane activity. Marie went about the house singing when she couldn't be sitting at the organ playing Mendelssohn. Vina hardly let more than three days pass without thinking of an excuse to ride over and show Kathryn a new pattern card or piece of lace—she even brought a whole length of yellow silk purchased at the newly opened Kuna Mercantile. And Kathryn, feeding the chickens, caring for her sheep, or milking Buttercup could do little but try to imagine over and over again what Scotland would be like.

The only tiny blight on her excitement in planning for her wedding and a trip that would mean being gone for so many months was her worry over what his family would think of her. She wished she could be beautiful for him. It never ceased to seem a miracle that he found her pretty—that his "pretty miss" had not been a jest. The fact that she knew she wasn't pretty made it all the more pleasing to hear. But it was unlikely his family would look at her with such favor.

Then she always felt ashamed, for the far more serious concern was what they would think of *him*. It was so important to Merrick's future happiness—and therefore to hers—that this old wound be healed. Sometimes she felt certain there could be no problem—after all, who could resist Merrick when they heard the truth from his own lips, bolstered by the fact that he had traveled seven thousand miles for the reconciliation.

But she would remember how long the breach had existed, how stubborn the Scots were reported to be, how convinced his family seemed that he was guilty—on top of the fact that they had refused to be softened by his letter—and her confidence would evaporate.

Yet it was impossible to stay long in the doldrums, for Merrick, although much occupied in Boise getting his business matters settled as well as making arrangements for the trip, came to Kuna regularly. One thing they always did when he came was to drive into the townsite and view the progress on the new church building. A fine wooden structure with a square tower and elegant gothic-arched windows made steady progress toward completion, in spite of the fact that all its volunteer builders were much occupied planting crops on their newly irrigated land.

Indeed, driving through the desert and seeing fields sprouting green shoots of alfalfa, beans, sugar beets, and other crops was an adventure that brought endless amazement. "If you could have seen Uncle Isaiah's poor wilted beans the summer I arrived." Kathryn shook her head.

On one visit Merrick arrived bearing a grand black steamer trunk with shiny brass fittings.

"Oh! It's beautiful! I've heard of such things, but I've never seen one. I thought only actresses and presidents' wives would have anything so grand." Kathryn ran her hand over the smooth surface, then opened it.

Merrick showed her how to stand it on its end so that she could pull out each of the three drawers that filled half of one side. Then her delight dimmed. "But whatever will I put in it? I'll have my wedding dress, of course, but even if I took my work clothes they wouldn't fill this. Oh, but of course, there'll be your things too." The thought made her blush.

"Not at all. I have my own trunk. Don't you worry. You'll be able to fill this and a carpetbag and a valise or two. I've been asking around. Tomorrow we're going to the best dressmaker in Boise."

Kathryn started to protest at the cost of such a project, but Merrick went on. "Miss Jamison makes all the clothes for Governor Gooding's wife—and he's famous for his excellent taste."

That argument silenced her. Kathryn didn't need to be told that Frank Gooding had come to Idaho from England. The implication was clear—if Miss Jamison could please Governor Gooding's English tastes, she should be able to please his family.

So, feeling like Cinderella, Kathryn was fitted out with traveling suit, morning dress, afternoon dress, tea dress, and even a riding habit with a high black hat. All this on top of her French silk wedding dress, which would serve as a ball gown. All were in the new, slimmer silhouette that Miss Jamison assured Kathryn was the style in New York.

Kathryn pored over the copies of *Petersen's Ladies Magazine* in Miss Jamison's parlor and agreed to the revolutionary change in her wardrobe: dresses with slim sleeves rather than a mutton chop shape, skirts that fell smooth over her hips and flared only in a deep flounce around the hem.

The thing Kathryn loved most was the hats from the milliner's. With such confections as flowers, ribbons, and feathers adorning elegant broad brims atop her head, she need not worry about the stringy hair that had ever been the bane of her life. She even rather felt that, with their highly adorned crowns, the new hats flattered her nose and square jaw. She could almost persuade herself that she deserved Merrick's pet phrase "pretty miss," although she would no longer be "miss."

The day she went for the final fitting, Merrick produced another gift. Kathryn gasped when she removed the silver paper, opened the velvet case, and saw an aquamarine brooch set in delicate silver filagree with matching drop earrings. "Merrick, they're lovely. I've never seen anything like them!"

"They were my Grandmother Phyllida's. She gave them to me for just this moment—long before I fell into disgrace. Thank goodness, or I probably wouldn't have them to give you now. Although I always did feel she was the one family member who might stand behind me."

On a beautiful Sunday in mid-May, Kathryn Esther Jayne and Merrick Clarence Allen were married in the newly completed Methodist-Episcopal church by Rev. Arthur Hays. Marie played the organ for them, as Kathryn had for her just two weeks earlier, and the four-weeks'-married Vina was matron of honor.

For sentiment's sake Kathryn chose not to have her reception on the sage-cleared, but yet ungrassed, church lawn. Instead, she asked her guests to walk the three blocks to the banks of Indian Creek and partake of punch and wedding cake on the very site where Adam Jayne had held the first brush arbor meetings in Kuna seven years earlier.

In a quiet moment after greeting all her guests, Kathryn paused to reflect over those years, the painful and the joyful: Aunt Thelma's funeral, Ned Brewington's death, losing her papa, then Nelly and Isaiah's wedding, Merrick's baptism, the coming of water. They still fueled their stoves with sagebrush. Jackrabbits and coyotes still infested the desert. Only yesterday she had been surrounded by flying ants just as she finished icing her wedding cake and had to scrape off all the icing and start over again after she swept out the piles of little sooty carcasses.

Yet it seemed a different world than the one she had come to. She turned to Merrick, handsome in swallowtail coat, striped cravat, and tall silk hat. Here was her new world. And the first thing they would do was visit the old world to make way for the new.

She turned to hug Marie. "God bless you, Marie. You and Jules are the dearest people on earth to keep our homestead for us while we're gone."

Marie returned her embrace. "It's perfect for us too. It'll give us a place to live while Jules is developing our own land. And I'll keep your organ from getting rusty."

The shiny black carriage and matched pair Merrick had hired from a Boise livery drew up, covered with fluttering white ribbons. Myron waved from the driver's seat.

"Time to go, Mrs. Allen," Merrick said with his mouth close to her cheek.

From the carriage seat Kathryn turned to throw her bouquet of white lilies. Lila Young caught it, and Kathryn couldn't miss the blush that spread over her cheeks when she looked at Davey Brewington across the top of the sweet-smelling flowers.

But they're just children was Kathryn's first thought. Then she realized how much they had grown up. What changes would she find in Kuna when they returned months from now?

Then Merrick clucked to his high-stepping team, and all worries about the past and the future fled in the joy of the moment. Friends called good wishes and waved to them until they were out of sight.

Kathryn and Merrick spent the first night of their marriage in a six-room suite with bath in the Dewey Palace Hotel. Lying in her husband's arms late that night after he had drifted off to sleep, Kathryn knew that all her life she would cherish those special hours together. His loving had been tender and beautiful—a gift to her—but far more precious was the memory of kneeling, hand-in-hand beside the massive, carved, black oak bed and praying together.

She closed her eyes and felt the warmth of the moment flood her body from the top of her head downward. They had been physically close in the moments afterward, but far more precious was the spiritual closeness they had shared in praying together. She knew that was the moment when they had truly become one flesh. No matter what the years ahead held they would never be parted in spirit.

Late the next afternoon they boarded the Oregon Short Line train to take them to New York. Just as Merrick had predicted, Kathryn's steamer trunk, bag, and valises were indeed jammed. The Pullman car was near the back of the train, a huge car, almost half again as long as the second class carriages. Inside, the high-backed, green plush seats and polished wood walls, rising to a clerestory ceiling with rows of tiny upper windows running the length of the car, far out-stripped all Kathryn's visions of comfort in transportation.

They took their meals on white linen, eating from heavy white china with smooth, perfectly polished silverware. Of even more delight to Kathryn than the exquisite food were the fresh pink carnations gracing the center of every table. Having fresh flowers on the table for every meal was a dream she had cherished since she was a tearful five-year-old heartbroken over a bowl of closed up dandelions.

"Can we afford this, Merrick? It's wonderful, but it must be terribly expensive." She had accepted his gift of the new wardrobe without protest, realizing it was important for meeting his family, but surely they should be economizing now—eating sandwiches purchased at depots during train stops as she had observed many passengers in the other cars doing.

Merrick smiled and briefly squeezed her hand on the table. "My business affairs concluded most satisfactorily. I can't promise you a lifetime of luxury, but I can afford a first-class honeymoon. Besides, the train tickets are a wedding present from Bo McLeod."

She thought for a second. "Oh, your friend from San Francisco—the one you almost went to work for."

"That's right. I told you he had a position with the railroad."

She looked around at the elegantly appointed car. "That's terribly generous of him."

"Yes, it is. I think I mentioned he's some sort of distant relative—never really figured it out exactly. Guess he thought it was his duty to the family."

Kathryn chuckled. "I have a feeling the Scottish may not live up to their reputation for being tight-fisted."

Merrick raised his eyebrows. "Well, *some* of them don't."

When they returned from dinner the first night she stood in stunned amazement. "This is the wrong car." She started to turn around, but Merrick stopped her.

"No, no, little goose. The porters pulled out the sleeping berths while we were at dinner."

"But where do they come from?" She looked at the long rows of green curtains on either side of the aisle, some of them pulled open to reveal white-sheeted bunks.

"All hidden away behind the paneling in the daytime. No wonder Pullman's design revolutionized train travel, huh?"

"Which one is ours?"

He led her to the bunks that now filled the space where their seats had been. "But they're so narrow," she protested, then blushed again.

Merrick's eyes twinkled at her. "I know, my love. Do you want the upper berth or lower? I promise you, in England we'll have a private train compartment—no changing in the lavatory and no bunks." He handed her her night case and escorted her to the lavatory at the end of the car.

There was still enough light in the evening sky that lying in her bunk she could look out the window and see the big black locomotive with smoke rolling out of its smokestack as it pulled the train around a wide curve. The sense of power and speed were thrilling, as the rhythm of the wheels clacking over the tracks and the sway of the car were lulling. She closed her curtains.

Some time later she was roused from a half-doze by the long, shrill sound of the train whistle, musical, yet mournful. For a moment she thought of the coyotes her first night in Kuna. "Merrick?" she murmured and reached her arm over the side of the bunk.

"Yes, love." He took her hand.

More than half asleep she murmured the psalm Adam had read to her that long-ago night, "Thou anointest my head with oil; my cup runneth over . . ."

Through the greening corn and wheat fields of the Great Plains—with a nostalgic tug at seeing her native Nebraska again—across the wide, muddy, Mississippi River, and on to the more rolling, wooded terrain of the East, Kathryn seldom took her eyes from the window, except to gaze at her husband. Both scenes held equal fascination for her.

One week after their wedding they boarded the Cunard liner *Carpathia*. With brass bands playing, flags flying, and passengers throwing confetti and serpentine to those on the dock, they set sail for England. A vibration ran down the deck as the great steam engines fired up, and they pulled away from the cheering crowds below.

"This side, now." Merrick took her arm and led her around the deck to where she would have the best view of the Statue of Liberty as they slipped by the feet of the great green lady holding her torch aloft.

The band played "My Country, 'Tis of Thee," and her eyes filled with tears. She felt she should say something in response to such a momentous occasion, but all she could do was put her hand to her throat and say, "Oh!"

The ship was a new world to Kathryn. Merrick took her below deck to their stateroom with its little round porthole, and Kathryn, who had worried much over the thought of having to set sail without her luggage should there have been some mix-up between train, hotel, taxi, and ship, was much relieved to see it standing shiny and unscathed in the middle of the floor.

New York City had overwhelmed her: the tall buildings—some fourteen stories—the streets choked with people, streetcars, carriages, and automobiles. The relative quiet of the ship was a welcome retreat to her.

"I'll give our steward the keys so he can unpack while we go up to secure deck chairs. Or would you rather rest?" Merrick asked.

"Rest? When there's so much to see?"

Her first night at sea Kathryn wore her wedding dress with the aquamarine brooch and earrings to dinner. "I love wearing them," she said when she saw Merrick's appreciative smile. "They make me feel a part of your family."

He came across the room and kissed her neck. "You are my family."

Before they went into the palm-decked dining salon, Merrick draped her cashmere stole around her shoulders and suggested they take a stroll on deck. They stood long leaning against the railing at the stern, watching the sun sink into the Atlantic. At first it flared red and orange, a firey blaze along the horizon, then suddenly turned to a tiny green ball and fell from sight.

Walking slowly, as if in a dream, Merrick led her down to their seven-course, orchestra-accompanied dinner.

That night they lay in bed, feeling the swell and lowering of the waves. "I hope the motion of the sea won't bother you. It does some people," Merrick said.

"Oh, no." Kathryn snuggled closer to him. "I just tell myself it's God rocking me to sleep."

He kissed her forehead. "A lovely thought from a lovely lady."

"We are quite safe, aren't we?" It had never occurred to her to worry before, but she had heard of accidents at sea, of ships sinking.

"Quite safe, my love. And soon such travel will get even safer. I read in a newspaper in the hotel, the White Star Line has announced they're building an unsinkable ship. Maybe next time we go to Scotland we'll sail on the *Titanic.*" He kissed her again. "Sleep well."

And she did.

Kathryn found the dining schedule the most amazing and most delightful part of ocean travel. She, who since the time she could hold a spoon to stir a pot, had been responsible to cook for others, now had exotic food at her fingertips six times a day. It seemed she had to hurry through one meal to be ready for the next: breakfast, mid-morning consommé, luncheon, afternoon tea, dinner, and midnight buffet for those who stayed up so late.

"And if you get peckish between times, just ring for Charles. He'll bring you anything you ask for," Merrick teased when she commented on the schedule.

It was the third, or maybe fourth, day at sea that Kathryn began to feel the slightest uneasiness. She had been drowsing in the afternoon sun in her deck chair when she startled awake with the strong sensation that someone was watching her, observing her closely, about to touch her. She looked around but could see nothing untoward.

A mother with two children was strolling next to the rail, a group was playing shuffleboard up the deck, a gentleman two chairs down from her was sleeping with a newspaper over his face. She must have been dreaming. She put the incident so thoroughly out of her mind that she didn't even mention it to Merrick when he joined her a few minutes later.

But she remembered it the next day when they returned to their stateroom after tea and she found her journal in a different place than she had left it. Merrick, however, was unconcerned.

"Charles has probably been cleaning. We're lucky to have such a good steward. Fellow I met this morning said their steward hasn't run the carpet sweeper once yet."

Kathryn nodded and placed her journal in its usual place. She liked their friendly, Cockney steward, and didn't want to make trouble. But she did hope he hadn't been reading her journal. The thought made her feel exposed. After this she would keep it locked in her trunk, she decided. It would be too inconvenient to take it to the bursar's safe as she had her jewels.

Three days later, however, Merrick didn't take Charles's apparent lapse so calmly. Kathryn and Merrick had started up to tea, when she realized she had forgotten her small beaded bag with her fan and handkerchief in it.

"No, wait here," she told Merrick when he offered to get it for her. "I'll be right back. Just enjoy this wonderful fresh air." She turned and sped down the stairs, running her hand loosely along the handrail.

She was less than halfway down the long, steep flight when her feet flew out from under her. She cried out sharply and clutched at the rail, but she bumped painfully down several steps before she could halt her fall.

Merrick, who had heard her cry, was at her side in an instant. "Are you all right? No, don't move." He pushed her back down. "Summon the ship's doctor!" he ordered a near-by passenger.

"Really, I'm quite all right, Merrick. I just slipped." She sat up on the step, but he would not let her stand until the doctor arrived.

In the meantime Merrick examined the stair she had fallen on. "Soap! This tread is slick with soap! That idiot steward didn't rinse it properly after he scrubbed it. The captain shall hear about this."

Merrick calmed considerably when the doctor assured him that Kathryn was only bruised, but he insisted that she rest in bed with a tea tray. After Charles brought the tray, Merrick took him to task about the soapy step.

"No sir, it's not possible."

"Do you deny you scrubbed those stairs?"

"I swabbed the stairs, yes, early this morning before breakfast. And rinsed them thoroughly. Dozens of people have gone up and down since then—I myself several times. Someone else put that soap there."

"But why? How? That doesn't make sense."

"Oh, surely an accident of some sort. Perhaps someone dropped a piece of soap without realizing it, then others going up and down ground it into the edge of the tread?" Charles paused hopefully.

Merrick turned away with a growl. He was far from satisfied with the answer. "I'll be watching you, Charles. Let's not have any more accidents."

Perhaps it was Merrick's vigilance, or the warning was enough to put the steward on his best behavior, for the rest of the two weeks' voyage was smooth sailing, without doubt the most restful time in Kathryn's life. Even the sensation of being watched, which she experienced twice again, wasn't enough to ruffle her wonderful relaxation.

It wasn't until she was dressing for the captain's gala dinner the last night that she discovered the loss. Apparently even Merrick's vigilance hadn't been enough, for when she opened the black velvet box containing Merrick's wedding gift to her, she gasped. It was empty.

"Oh, Merrick! Your grandmother's beautiful jewels!"

"Are you sure you put them in the case after you wore them the first night?"

"Of course I am. I had Charles put them in the bursar's safe the next morning. I only had him bring them down after luncheon today so I could wear them tonight."

"And they were in the case when he brought it to you?"

"Yes. I looked at them for a long time because they're so beautiful. Oh, Merrick—" Her eyes filled with tears.

"I'm getting the captain."

A few minutes later Captain Bainbridge stood before them in the full splendor of his white dress uniform with gold epaulets. "I can't imagine. Steward Charles Nelson has been with me on every voyage since I took command of the *Carpathia* three years ago. We've never had any trouble."

"I want him thoroughly questioned and his quarters searched," Merrick demanded. "And the rest of the crew."

"Yes, of course. The bursar has a security staff. He'll see to it while we're at dinner. I am so sorry about this, Mrs. Allen. How long were the jewels unattended in your room today?"

"Just while I was at tea."

"And your door was locked?"

"Yes, man. I locked it myself!"

Kathryn hadn't seen Merrick's temper flare for years. It frightened her.

The captain smoothed over the moment with an invitation that they join him at his table at dinner, and Merrick accepted the singular honor.

But the next day at noon Kathryn had to disembark at Southampton with her jewel case still empty. The bursar assured them that his well-trained officers had questioned and thoroughly searched the quarters of every crew member with access to first class quarters. Charles himself had an excellent alibi. He had been assisting the ship's doctor attend to a patient in the next cabin who had cut his hand deeply on a broken whiskey bottle. Patient and doctor both gave assurances that the cleaning, stitching, and bandaging from which Charles was never absent lasted from well before four o'clock until long after teatime.

Captain Bainbridge offered his condolences and left them alone.

Merrick looked as though he could swear, but he controlled himself. "We come all this way for a reconciliation, and the one thing happens that's sure to antagonize the only family member likely to support me."

Kathryn put her hand on his arm. "I'll tell your grandmother it's my fault—that I was careless. I'll tell her how much you cared for them because they were hers."

Merrick shook his head. "Thanks, but it'll take Rowena two sarcastic sentences to convince everyone that the black sheep hasn't changed at all, that he most likely pawned his family heirloom to pay a gambling debt." He turned away, his eyes hollow, his shoulders stooped. "And the trouble is, until four years ago it would have been true. Anything they want to say about my being wild and worthless is true."

"Was true. You're a new man now, Merrick."

Her words brought light back to his eyes. "You know it, I know it, God knows it. But how I'll ever convince my family only God knows." Then he smiled and kissed her. "What I would do without your faith in me I can't imagine."

She laughed and returned his kiss. "It must be the air. We've barely docked, and your Scots accent is back. When your family hears that you'll have them at your feet."

"I doot it. They'll think I've gone heathen with my American tones."

"And American wife?"

"Nay, they'll love you."

He took her hand and led her up on deck. They walked down the gangplank to a sea of waving Union Jacks and the rousing strains of "Rule Britannia."

20

The boat train sped them from Southampton to London's Waterloo Station, and a hackney cab delivered them to the Ritz. Only two hours later Kathryn Jayne Allen, desert pioneer from Kuna, Idaho, was sitting on a pink gilt chair beneath the frosted glass ceiling of the Ritz's Palm Court, sipping Darjeeling tea from a delicately flowered china cup. She had never been so thankful for her new wardrobe as she was when she observed the exquisite tea gowns ladies wore at nearby tables. Her own lavender lace was far less dashing, but the lines were right. Miss Jamison knew her business.

Kathryn was equally thankful for the inhibiting manners Aunt Thelma and ladies of the Edgar congregation had drilled into their preacher's daughter, teaching her how ladies walked, sat, and drank tea. She had had little opportunity to practice, and the most polished of her teachers would have been far outshone in this setting, but the basics they taught were enough. She smiled and took another strawberry tart from the silver tier tray.

From that first fairy-tale moment, Kathryn loved London. New York had been too crowded, too busy, everything moving too fast. She had been overwhelmed and a little frightened. London gave her the strangest sensation of having come home. She felt safe, relaxed. Here she found the beauty she had sought all her life: the green, flower-filled parks and squares, the architectural magnificence of Westminster Abbey and the Houses of Parliament, the amazing dome of St. Paul's, where Merrick, standing on the other side of the great expanse whispered to her and she heard him plainly. His "I love you" made her blush and look about quickly, but no one else had heard.

They were returning from St. Paul's along The Strand and just turning into The Mall when their driver pulled up sharply.

"What is it?" Merrick asked.

"Looks like Mrs. Pankhurst's at it again, G'vnor."

The driver's answer made no sense to Kathryn, who leaned out of their carriage for a better look.

A group of women, twenty maybe, wearing banners and carrying placards proclaiming "Votes for Women," had blocked all traffic going to Buckingham Palace. Harried bobbies were trying to clear the road while onlookers shouted from the sidewalks—some mocking the women, some agreeing.

"Tryin' to get the attention of King Edward—or Princess Alexandra, more like." The cabbie shook his head. "Don't know what they'll do with the vote if they get it."

Just then one of the suffragettes hit a bobby over the head with her placard, and he dragged her, kicking, off to a waiting paddy wagon.

As the cabby turned his horse and headed the hackney up Regent Street, Kathryn considered. She had heard of suffragettes in New York and other places in eastern United States as well. How did she feel about women taking to the streets in such a harsh, demanding manner?

Women had voted in Idaho since 1896. Papa had been a staunch supporter of President Roosevelt, and if Kathryn had been twenty-one at the time, she would have voted for him too. Last fall she had voted for President Taft, although as busy as she was running things at home she had given little attention to the running of the nation. She had voted as part of her duty, but she held few notions that her vote made much difference to the nation or to herself.

Now she asked herself how she would have felt had she been denied the right to vote. Would she have felt that her rights as a human being were being denied her? Would she have felt personally affronted? The idea probably would not have occurred to her. Yet she had been glad for her vote, glad that her candidate had won. She could understand why these women would want the same privilege. She wondered if it would ever be theirs.

They had only two days in London, but Kathryn would have them in her heart the rest of her life. When she was back in Kuna chopping sagebrush she would be able to close her eyes and picture the graceful gold nymph of the Palm Court bathed in ethereal apricot pink light, and she would chop harder. When she was cooking beans and sowbelly in her homestead shack, she would be able to hear in her head the tail-coated waiter ask, "Would the lady care for another eclair?" and she would reply that *indeed, the lady would,* and turn the sowbelly in the cast iron skillet. And when she had to care for obstreperous lambs, stinking of sulfurous sheep dip, she would in her mind hold to her nose the delicately scented violet nosegay Merrick gave her that last night when they attended a concert in Albert Hall.

Early the next morning Kathryn found herself seated in the private train compartment Merrick had promised her, speeding in a cloud of steam out of Marylebone Station toward Carlisle. As when crossing the vast United States, Kathryn seldom took her eyes from the window.

"It's so green," she said over and over, each time with a fresh tenderness in her voice.

Merrick's eyes crinkled, and he squeezed her hand, "Aye, but the weather's ruddy awful. Ye can't ken how much rain it takes to keep things so green." She smiled, hearing their nearness to Scotland reflected in his speech. "Oh, but it's worth it!"

In the Midlands white sheep dotted green fields banked by masses of trees, with occasional oaks providing shade or shelter in the midst of open spaces. "Oh, I shouldn't have come," Kathryn cried. "I'm homesick already."

"You miss your lambs?"

"No, no. I mean when I'm home with my lambs I'll miss these green fields. Now I really know what the psalm means—'He maketh me to lie down in green pastures.' This is heaven."

"Nay, it's just a very small piece of earth set in the cold North Atlantic." He took her hand again and held onto it this time. After all, it was a private compartment. "It seems odd that you find such a kinship to a place you've never been."

"I know. It's as if I've been here before—no, not been here, but always wanted to be without knowing it. I always loved the English novels Papa read to me, and the stories he told me about our family history. We were Irish and English—along with a lot of other things—perhaps my grandmother or great-grandmother . . . Oh, I don't know—I certainly don't believe in reincarnation or anything like that—but I guess we're just born with certain things inside us."

"Like your love of flowers and music."

"Yes—and green things." She sighed. "Oh, never mind. I'm being fanciful. How far is it to Carlisle?"

"Almost three hundred miles from London to Carlisle. I expect we're about halfway there."

Then the porter walked down the aisle outside their compartment ringing a chime to announce that luncheon was served.

Kathryn ordered a delicate poached whitefish served in lemon sauce with tiny white boiled potatoes rolled in butter and parsley. She savored every bite but regretted the times she had to take her eyes from the scenery to look at her plate.

They were back in their compartment when they came to the Lake District: rolling hills covered with leafy trees, shimmering lakes blue through the branches, and tiny, stone-walled farms tucked in every draw.

Merrick sat silent beside her for miles. When he spoke his voice sounded perplexed. "I thought ye'd like this best of all. But ye've said naething. Don't . . ."

She turned a tear-streaked face to him, lips smiling and eyes shining. "God must love this country very much to make it so beautiful."

"Aye, He does. As He loves all the world in all its different beauty."

She nodded. "I was thinking about a Scripture Papa loved. In Isaiah, I think, about what it will be like when the whole world is filled with knowledge of the Lord as the sea is with water. It's so wonderful now, even with all the sin and evil in the world—just think . . ." She couldn't find words to finish.

They arrived at Carlisle after dark. Merrick had them taken to a big pink stone hotel with rich stained-glass windows, but Kathryn was too tired to appreciate anything except the crisp white sheets.

In the morning Merrick hired a team and carriage at the livery stable to complete their journey.

"Don't the trains go into Scotland?" Kathryn asked when she was settled on the well-padded black leather seat.

"Yes. To Glasgow and Edinburgh, even up to Inverness, but Selkirk is a mite out of the way."

"How far is it?"

"Fifty miles. Less. A pleasant enough drive if it doesn't rain on us." He cocked an eye at a bank of clouds to the northwest.

A short distance out of Carlisle, Merrick pointed to the remains of a massive stone and earthwork wall stretching as far as she could see to the east. "Hadrian's Wall. The Romans built it to keep out the heathen Scots. We were one of the few places on earth the Romans never con-quered."

"Or civilized?" Kathryn laughed.

"There's many a folk who'd say we've never been civi-lized." He laughed too and snapped the team to a faster pace.

Now the roads were narrower, the hills steeper, the curves sharper, and at the bottom of every draw a rapid stream ran across the road. The ground was rockier, the farms smaller, and the flocks of sheep larger than in the south. The narrow stone bridges and sharp curves de-manded more attention from the driver, so it was some time before Kathryn spoke again.

"Did you let your family know you're—we're—coming?"

"Why? So they could send me a telegram saying to stay home?"

"Oh, Merrick, don't sound so bitter. I'm sure they'll welcome you."

"Well, we'll see. It's a long way to come for a slap in the face."

"Have you any plan how you'll approach them?"

He shrugged. "Joost tell the truth and shame the dev-il, I suppose. I'll tell them that even though I can't prove it, I'm certain I couldn't have shot my brother, and even if I did I've come to beg their forgiveness. I don't know any-thing else to do." He was quiet for a moment.

The clopping of the horses' feet blended with the soughing of a rising wind in the dark fir trees on the hill above them and the gurgling of a rushing stream, which he had taught Kathryn to call a burn.

Merrick shook his head. "It sounds a fool plan after traveling seven thousand miles."

She tucked her hand in the crook of his elbow. "The truth's never a 'fool plan.' Besides, I'm praying for you."

"Your prayers are my only hope."

Then the rain started.

211

21

Many miles later they came around a bend in the road, the wind blowing sharply in their faces, and started down a long hill. Through thick mist and evening dimness Kathryn saw the gray stone village of Selkirk tucked in its circle of heather-clad hills. Spires, towers, and trees thrust upward above curving streets, snug shops, and cottages with tiny gardens.

They passed through the deserted streets quickly and proceeded up a thickly forested hill. In the growing dark Merrick almost missed the turn, but at the last minute he guided the team onto a narrow path leading upward between thick-needled trees.

Around another bend Woodburn was before them. It stood in a clearing on the top of a rise. Acres of natural lawn tumbled down the hill in front of it. Here it was lighter, and the curtains had not yet been drawn at the lamplit windows.

Kathryn's first impression of the two-story white house with its turreted round tower and gingerbread eaves was that it looked like a small French or German castle, not at all what she had expected in Scotland. Then she wondered what she based such an impression on, for she had grown up with few picture books. Papa's storytelling had filled her childhood imagination.

Kathryn wished she could have arrived at her in-laws' doorstep less windblown and rain-soaked, but nothing was to be done about it. Merrick hitched the team to a post and led her to the door.

An ancient woman in a black dress, with gray hair pulled back in a severe bun, opened the door, frowning.

"Agnes! Is that you?" Merrick stepped forward into the light of the doorway.

The old servant blinked, then threw out her hands. "As I live and breathe, it's Mr. Merrick! Come away in, then." She drew them both into the entry and slammed the door against the storm. "It's no night for a Christian to be out. Mr. Merrick, you're a sight these old eyes never thought to see again."

Merrick hugged her and introduced Kathryn.

"Aye, your bonnie lassie. The master nae told me aboot yer wedding, but I saw the letter. And I was happy for ye." She took the hand Kathryn held out to her. "Now sit you down—both of you—there's a fire in the parlor." She ushered them into a cozy room. "I'll just tell the master ye've arrived." Agnes bustled off.

"I thought we weren't expected," Kathryn said, "but Agnes sounded like she knew you were coming."

"I don't think so. That's just her way. But it is odd to have so many lights on and a fire in the parlor if company isn't expected."

They didn't have long to ponder, however, before Egan Millard Allen flung open the double doors of the parlor and strode forward, his forehead furrowed, his eyes hard above his gray-streaked old-fashioned muttonchop beard.

"So, ye've come home to face the music, have ye?"

"Father." Merrick stood and offered his hand, which was ignored. "May I present my wife, Kathryn Esther Allen?"

Kathryn stood, unsure what to do. A lady offered her hand first, except to much older or higher-ranking gentle-

men, she recalled. She dipped her head in acknowledgement, her hands at her side.

"Indeed, ye may present the lass." Egan Allen grasped
her cold hand in his lion's paw. "Whatever the lad's done
is no blot on ye. Ye'll be a daughter in this house."

Kathryn was grateful but felt she should say something to defend her husband. She would have if she could
have thought what to say.

"Ye've missed dinner, but the tea tray is just about to
go into yer grandmother's sitting room. Ye may join her
there. No doubt *she'll* be glad to see ye."

No matter how dismayed Kathryn was at Egan's un-
cordial greeting to his son and at the news that there
would be no dinner for them, she couldn't help smiling.
She had been charmed by the musical English voices in
London, often losing the sense of the words in the joy of
listening to the accent, but here was a new enchantment.
Now she knew why Merrick had said his family would
think he spoke like a barbarian. What she had thought a
heavy Scots accent in his voice was nothing compared to
the broad brogue his father spoke with every o pronounced *oo* and all a's like long i's. Their sound so en-
tranced her it brought a stinging tickle to the back of her
eyes.

Kathryn's strange mixture of emotions, however, all
turned to fear when they entered the sitting room. The
room was dark with heavy, mid-nineteenth-century furniture and fringed, maroon velvet hangings. The fire on the
hearth flickered light over the swirled greens, browns, and
ochres of the carpet. At the far end of the room, like the
Old Queen on her throne, sat Grandmother Phyllida, her
white hair shining high above the stiff neckline of her
black taffeta gown.

She raised her lorgnette and stared at them as if a
large hairy bug had just entered the room. At last she
lowered her glasses. A garnet ring flashed on her finger as
she thumped the arms of her chair.

"And about time too. I always said ye'd come back. It isn't like an Allen to run off with his tail between his legs —at least not one of *my* descendants."

When Merrick and Kathryn didn't move, she raised her voice. "Well, come here, boy, and give me a kiss. I've been waiting for it these six years. I may not last forever. Although those as hope to inherit my property think I'm trying."

Merrick strode across the room. She stood to meet him, and he made the most of his opportunity to kiss his grandmother.

"Well, come here, gel." Phyllida glared at Kathryn.

Kathryn felt as if she should curtsey when she reached the old woman, but instead Phyllida bent to kiss her on the cheek.

"And so ye took a chance that this graceless grandson of mine would make something of himself yet, did ye?"

Kathryn could think of no proper way to protest at the implications of this speech, but Phyllida gave her little chance. "Well, ye're a fine-looking lass. But then Merrick always did have good taste. My side of the family does." With that she resumed her seat and began pouring tea into the extra cups Agnes had scurried in with.

The next day Merrick's sister Rowena rode over from her nearby farm. In her early thirties, Rowena Buchanan was a handsome woman with the same strong bone structure as her brother but having the red hair one would expect to see in the Scots, rather than the black hair Merrick had inherited from his father.

"Great-grandfather Douglas was known far and wide as the Black Scot," Merrick explained when he introduced his flaming-tressed sister. "Rowena took her coloring from our mother."

The reference to their mother, though, did not make for an auspicious beginning .

"I'm surprised to hear ye remembering our mother, Merrick Allen. You who couldn't be bothered to come back for her funeral."

Rowena, however, approached warmth when she greeted her new sister-in-law. "Aye, and have this husband of yours bring you to Ashe Garth for tea one day."

Then she turned back to Merrick. "But don't you be expecting a loan from Robert."

Kathyrn was amazed to see Merrick grin as Rowena went in to greet Phyllida. "Well, that's far better than I expected from her, considering that her son Robbie Bruce will remain the heir to Woodburn only so long as Father keeps me out of his will."

In the coming days the sound of the voices never lost their charm, although the words often stung as deeply as if they had been uttered in harsh, flat tones. Merrick's grandmother, Phyllida, had been more welcoming than her son, but it soon became apparent to Kathryn that if Merrick was to stay until the family warmed to him they would be there a long time indeed.

Had it not been for their coldness to Merrick, however, the thought of an extended stay would have been most welcome to Kathryn. Everyone was unfailingly polite to her, and some, such as Agnes, Phyllida, and Rowena, approached warmth.

It was perhaps meeting Rowena that made Kathryn regret most sharply the rift in the family. One look at this statuesque woman with her wild red hair and blue eyes, and Kathryn felt instantly that they could have been friends. As it was, she felt admiration.

Whatever the family attitudes, much of Kathryn and Merrick's time was spent away from Woodburn exploring the countryside, which never failed to surprise and delight her. The first day they had gone to the gray stone church just beyond the marketplace, where Merrick's mother and twin brother lay in the churchyard.

Kathryn stood a long time before his mother's grave, reading the carving on the gray stone:

The Lord is my Shepherd
Rachel Ellen Allen
nee Fletcher
Wife and Mother
1853-1902

"My favorite psalm. I wish I could have known her."
Kathryn tucked her hand in his arm.

"I tell myself things would be different if she were
here. But if I'm not going to get this solved maybe it's a
mercy she's spared going through it again. It almost broke
her heart the first time. I'm not sure she ever really recovered. That may be part of the problem—Father may blame
me for her death too, although that's one accusation he's
spared me."

Kathryn edged closer to him offering unspoken comfort. "Nineteen two. That's the year I first saw you."

He nodded. "Yes. She was dead then, but I didn't
know it yet. Bo didn't give me the letter until we got to San
Francisco."

"But why? You were traveling together."

"Said he didn't want to upset me until we were settled—there was nothing I could do anyway. I don't know
that he was right—I might have come home then if I'd
known sooner—who knows?"

"But why did Bo have the letter at all? Is he from
around here?"

"No, the McLeods live in Edinburgh. His mother was
my father's aunt, so his family wrote."

"Why didn't yours?"

"Didn't know where I was."

Then they moved a few paces to the left, where a
smaller stone read simply:

Raynor Abel Allen
1879-1897
Beloved Son

"Only nineteen." Kathryn shook her head.

"Eighteen, actually. I suppose in the circumstances they didn't feel they could have 'The angels took him' put on the stone, and 'Murdered by his brother' wouldn't do."

Then Kathryn gasped at the name. "Abel. His name was Abel."

"At least mine isn't Cain." The bitterness in his voice stung her. "But I was sent out to wander the earth."

After a few more moments Merrick took her arm and turned away. They left the Auld Kirk and walked down the steep Kirk Wynd.

They wandered on up the road, Kathryn reveling in the sound of birdsong from the woods, until Merrick stopped and pointed to a large, grassy mound.

"Ye have afore ye Selkirk Castle. Center of Scottish resistance to Edward the First's brutal invasion of 1296, and much fought over in the long Wars of Independence."

Kathryn laughed. "What long memories you have here."

"Aye. And in the next century there were two Selkirks: King's Selkirk here at the castle and Abbott's Selkirk at the Abbey to the east. When the Abbey moved up the road to Kelso, David the first created Ettrick Forest a private hunting reserve." He stopped and grinned. "Sorry. I'm boring ye. I didn't realize I carried all that in my head—or that it was wanting to get out."

She touched his arm. "You've missed it all terribly, haven't you? Besides, I'm fascinated. History was my favorite subject in school, but we certainly didn't study about this."

"Good then. If ye can take more, there's plenty to show." Merrick led her back to the marketplace. He stopped before an impressive stone building with clocks on each side of its massive square tower. "Ye've not seen Selkirk until you've seen Sir Walter's Courtroom."

"Sir Walter?"

"Aye. Sir Walter Scott was sheriff of Selkirk for thirty-three years. Many around here still call him the 'Shirra.'"

Kathryn stood amazed. "So this is Scott's home? *The Heart of Midlothian* was Papa's favorite novel. Maybe that's why I've felt so at home here. I was only seven or eight when Papa read it to me the first time."

Merrick led her inside to view the very bench and chair on which Scott presided as judge. She looked up at a glowing red, green, and gold stained-glass window. "Aye, that's the Flodden memorial," he said.

"Flodden?"

"Aye, where Warrior Fletcher fought." When she didn't respond, he went on. "Have I not told you the story of Fletcher the Warrior from whom my mother was descended?"

"No. Please do!"

"Aye, ye'll need to know, for the Common Riding's approaching. I've looked forward to seeing the casting of the colours again—if my father's hospitality will last so long."

"I'm completely lost," she protested.

"Well, it was September of 1513 when King James the Fourth called for men to fight the troops of that scoundrel Henry the Eighth. When the appeal came, the men of Selkirk were ready, as they always were. They marched off eighty strong."

He paused to clear his throat. "Only one returned. Wounded and weary, Fletcher rode in bearing a flag captured from the English—the only remnant of honor to survive the bloody battle. Even King James had fallen to the English archers. Fletcher dismounted and faced the men, women, and bairns of Selkirk in the Market Place. Too overcome with grief to tell the terrible tale in words, he held the tattered pennon aloft in both arms and whirled it around his head, then cast it to the cobbles of the street, declaring the dire tidings."

Kathryn, identifying with the women of that time, wiped a tear from her eye.

"Here," Merrick pointed to a glass case. "The Flodden Flag."

It was hard to make out just what the green silk banner, bordered in gold braid with two of its corners rounded, had once signified to the English baron who had borne it into battle against the Scots, but there was no denying the pride the flag now represented to Selkirk—and to Merrick, who was descended from the valiant warrior who had snatched it from the disgrace of defeat.

They spent the rest of the day strolling the gentle streets and wynds of Selkirk. In the West Port Merrick showed her an ancient inn where Robert Burns sat to write poetry and letters over a tankard of local ale. On up High Street they leaned against a stone wall surrounding the green to watch a game of bowls. Behind them stood the golden stone arches and mullioned windows of Victoria Hall.

A boy with a black Labrador on a leash walked toward them from the bowling green. "And would ye be liking to contribute to the statue?" he asked.

Kathryn blinked, then saw that the dog had a collecting box attached to its halter. The dog shook, and coins rattled inside. "Statue?" she asked.

"Aye, the game's in aid of it today. Lord Rosebury's heading a drive to erect a statue of Warrior Fletcher in front of Victoria Hall. A fine, big bronze one it'll be, holding the flag proud."

Merrick folded a five pound note and slipped it into the box.

"Thank *you*, sir!" The boy saluted and moved off toward other observers.

"Maybe you can come back when the statue's unveiled." Kathryn turned to Merrick.

But he looked grim. Grim and sad. "I doubt I'll ever be back. If I can't make it up now I never will."

The rest of the day seemed dimmed by the weight of failure Merrick carried with him. The longer they stayed, the more Kathryn realized how much the breach with his family had cost him. It was not the material cost of losing the inheritance of the estate—she doubted that he wanted to come back here to live. One who had grown used to the freedom of the American West couldn't settle easily again in a village where they counted it sin to whistle on Sunday. But it was clear that he hated being severed from his background.

She heard the longing in his voice the night they walked far out on the lawn of Woodburn so that she might hear the ringing of the curfew.

"That bell has been rung continuously in the burgh since ancient times. Fletcher heard it. Scott heard it. Burns heard it. At least some things don't change."

She squeezed his arm. "You'll hear it again, Merrick. I pray you will."

Kathryn was true to her promise to pray for Merrick, for his family, for the whole situation. Her prayers were all she had to cling to, for every time Merrick tried to approach the subject of reconciliation, struggled to make them understand what had happened the tragic day that all the trouble started, he could find no one to listen to him. Even Grandmother Phyllida with her cloud of white hair and steady pale eyes would only look at him hurt and disappointed, then change the subject.

On Merrick's third attempt, Egan strode from the dinner table rather than reply to his son. So Rowena, who was a guest with her husband and son from their nearby estate, spoke out.

"Merrick, forget about Raynor's death. It was a terrible, tragic accident from which this family will never recover, but it was long ago. All ye do is bring back all the anguish when ye try to talk of it."

"But how can I make up with father—with everyone—if we can't talk?"

"Merrick, it's not Raynor. It's you. It's the life ye've lived all these years in America. To Father gambling is worse than murder. And drunken brawls. And ye've been accused of killings in America. Ye can't expect Father to open his arms to such as that."

"But I've explained all that—tried to. I did drink and gamble, yes. But not anymore. God has forgiven me. Why can't Father? Why can't you?"

The question hung in the air. Kathryn tried to argue the answer down, because she felt it was unworthy, but it stayed in her mind. *Rowena doesn't want Merrick forgiven. She wants Robbie to inherit.*

Then a new idea occurred to her. It was so revolutionary, so alarming she had to put her napkin over her mouth to suppress a cry. Rowena wasn't the only one who would benefit if Robbie inherited. What about her husband, Robert Bruce, Sr.?

She struggled to remember what Merrick had said about the day Raynor was shot. Rowena was in childbed with Robbie. But what about Robert? What about the man who then suddenly knew he had a son to whom the entailment could go? Where was Robert Bruce that day? She longed to turn to him and ask but stifled the impulse in a bite of hard, sour cheese.

Kathryn loved every minute of their sight-seeing excursions into the country around Selkirk, even though she suspected part of Merrick's motivation was to get away from Woodburn. One day they visited the tweed mills tucked away in the valley.

"In medieval times shoemaking was the trade of Selkirk—and natives still call themselves 'souters,' the ancient Scottish name for shoemakers. But since 1600 when cloth was made on hand looms here, woolens have been our major industry." Merrick led Kathryn into a showroom stacked floor to ceiling with bolts of fabric.

"Would the lady fancy a length o' tweed?" a shopgirl asked.

Kathryn started to explain she was just seeing the sights, but Merrick insisted she choose enough to make a new suit. It didn't take her long to settle on a soft heather and ivory tweed. "So the fabric is named for your river?" she asked as the girl measured the fine wool.

"Most likely," Merrick agreed. "But there are some as say it's from a London merchant who misread 'tweel'—our local dialect for 'twill,' which the woolen cloth was once called—as tweed, and the name stuck."

"Well, either way, it's lovely," Kathryn ran her hand over the soft cloth.

Merrick insisted she choose a tartan as well. Kathryn had noted fashionable ladies in New York wearing suits of lovely plaid fabric, so she was happy to agree to a length of dark blue and green plaid with a fine red line crossing it—the Fletcher plaid.

The next day was one she especially enjoyed as they spent it going over Abbotsford, Sir Walter Scott's home, just four miles up the road from Selkirk.

"Scott planted all these trees himself." Merrick indicated a wide expanse of thickly wooded hillside surrounding the extensive assemblage of architecture that constituted Scott's home.

"It looks like a whole village built together." Kathryn tried to make sense out of the series of turrets and chimneys topping the connected buildings that Scott had constructed during his lifetime there.

They crossed the drawbridgelike structure leading to the end of the building where it resembled a castle. It was when she was crossing the mosaic floor of Herbrides marble that Kathryn felt her neck prickle. She paused, trying to recall where she had felt that before. Where and why? She turned to see if someone were following her, then laughed with relief when she almost bumped into an enormous suit of armor. "Oh, I guess I thought it was alive."

They walked on, admiring the carved oak panels, the shields of various Border families, then Scott's writing desk, table, and armchair.

In the small corner turret room called "Speak-a-bit" the uneasy feeling returned. She froze, certain she was being watched. Then she recalled where she had known that sensation before—aboard the *Carpathia*.

"Nonsense," she whispered to herself and followed Merrick into the library, where he was pointing out a drinking cup that had once belonged to Bonnie Prince Charlie.

Two days later Merrick proposed a fishing expedition.

"Oh, I haven't gone fishing since I caught carp and trout in the Little Blue in Edgar."

Rowena was delighted to loan them tackle, and they set out. They walked through a splendid stretch of valley with the green and heathery Hills of Ettrick rising beside them and the Ettrick Water flowing over a wide, rough bed of gray stones at their feet until they came to its junction with the River Tweed. Here the sight of leaping salmon gave Kathryn all the invitation she needed to slip on Rowena's rubber boots.

Merrick attacked a fly to her pole. "Do ye ken how to cast?"

"Nae," she answered as broadly as she could and laughed at the face he made at her. After an extensive lesson she still hadn't mastered the secret of flipping her wrist so that the line would settle gracefully just where the last salmon had jumped, but she felt Merrick should be freed to his own fishing. "Thank you. I think I just need to practice now. You go ahead."

"Are you sure?" He sounded skeptical.

"Yes. I'll just stay here by the bank and practice. You go on and catch us one of those lovely salmon. That might just be the key to softening up Grandmother Phyllida." Then she was sorry she had referred to the trouble, for his eyes clouded.

But he moved downstream and after only a few expert casts drew in a beautiful silver salmon. He plopped it in the creel around his waist, then observed the current and the direction of the sun. "I think I'll move just a mite downstream if ye don't mind."

Kathryn had abandoned her pole and was sitting in idle comfort, leaning against a boulder and running her hand over the velvety grass of the riverbank. "No, I don't mind." She heard a few splashes that might have been Merrick wading around the bend in the river, then all was swallowed up in the gentle rush of the water, the buzz of a bee, and the warmth of the sun through her straw hat.

She wasn't sure how long she had dozed, and she wasn't sure she had heard Merrick cry out, but something jolted her awake. "Merrick!" She leaped to her feet and ran in the direction she had seen him go.

When she crossed the point of land that had blocked him from view she stopped. He was nowhere. "Merrick!" she cried again, this time her voice rising in alarm.

22

The wide, shallow river rushed rapidly over its rocky bed, breaking into white foam over the larger lichen-covered stones. Sun danced on the surface, fish jumped, sticks floated by—all adding to Kathryn's confusion.

Where was Merrick? Had he slipped on a stone and hit his head? Was he lying now under the rapids, his lungs filling with water? "Merrick!" she shouted again and ran downstream, her eyes raking the river.

Then she saw him, almost entirely submerged, only his brown tweed coattail and wicker creel floating on the surface. She lifted his head above the stream, but the water dragged at his limbs and clothes, pulling him backward. Once she lost her grip on his wet wrist. She cried out as she felt it slip through her fingers.

At last she spotted a sturdy tree branch on the bank, dragged it into the flow, wedged it under his shoulders, and was able to lever him to the bank. There, free from the pull of the water, she rolled him over on his stomach and pressed on his back until he vomited the water he had swallowed.

"Oh, God, thank you!" She took him in her arms and rocked back and forth, crying.

At last Merrick sat up on his own strength.

"What happened?" she asked.

He shook his head. "I don't really know. Something hit me behind the knees—a log floating down the river, I suppose." He rubbed a spot on his forehead that was already red and swollen. "I think I yelled, then hit my head on a rock in the river. Er—" he managed a weak grin "—thank you. Seems you're always rescuing me."

"I'm just so very thankful I was here." She gave him her hand to stand up. "Do you think you can walk home?"

They walked slowly through the long, afternoon shadows falling across the valley, Merrick holding her arm for balance.

At Woodburn, Agnes and even Phyllida fussed over him enough to give Kathryn hopes for a congenial dinner—maybe the beginning of the reconciliation they still hoped for. It had to come soon because Merrick had sent a telegram to London booking their return passage for next week. She was sure they would have returned days ago—after the last blow-up with his father—had not Merrick so wanted to attend the Common Riding.

Merrick must have been thinking similar thoughts, for after a restoring rest he chose his best dress suit for dinner.

"I think I like that patch on your forehead. It adds a certain rakishness that suits you," she said.

"Rakishness was not the image I wanted to portray. I think I've blotted my copybook beyond repair. They'll never believe I'm anything but a good-for-nothing. Not worthy to bear the Allen name."

"Merrick—" She paused mid-thought to tuck a small aqua feather fan in her up-swept hair. This was the night she would have worn her aquamarines if she had them. "Merrick, have you ever wondered how they seem to know so much about your life in America? Surely you didn't write to them about all your misadventures?"

"Of course not. I just accept it as a fact of life that bad news travels—even across the Atlantic. And I can't deny anything I've been accused of—except shooting my brother on purpose."

"Do you think someone—like Robert—could have spies or something?"

"Unlikely. Rob's always been very decent to me."

She thought that could be a cover-up, but a few minutes later when Merrick offered his arm to lead her to the oak-paneled dining room where a bright fire crackled on the hearth, she didn't argue.

Egan sat in solid black and white respectability at the head of the table and Grandmother in high-necked, heather-colored lace at the foot. Agnes served from a heavily carved, Jacobean sideboard. Things got off to such a good start that Kathryn thought this might indeed be the night that would see the answer to her prayers. Phyllida was genuinely glad Merrick was so well recovered, and Egan was full of talk about the Common Riding, which was to start the next night.

"Please tell me more about this," Kathryn said. "Everyone talks about it, but I don't really understand."

It was obvious that if she had calculated her question to soften up Egan she could have done no better. He stroked his thick sideburns, puffed up his chest, and cleared his throat. "The royal heritage of Selkirk is in our Common Lands granted to our burgh by the Crown in recognition of the valiant and sacrificial services our people rendered in the ancient wars against the Auld Enemy."

Kathryn didn't ask, but she was pretty sure the "Auld Enemy" was England.

"To preserve these lands," Egan continued, "it has been since old necessary that the men of the burgh ride around them. Aye, and a grand sight it is. Many a time in ancient days there was loyal blood spilled among the heather in defense of the Common Lands."

"Will you all ride?" Kathryn asked, not wanting to think of blood in the heather.

"Oh, aye. All the men o' the burgh. Even Robbie, for he's auld enou' this year."

Merrick agreed. "Aye, I made my first riding the year I was twelve."

Kathryn wanted to ask if Merrick would be allowed to ride again. Were outcasts considered part of the burgh? Probably not—although she knew he carried great loyalty to his heritage in his heart.

Merrick's father continued to warm to his topic, talking of the banners of the guilds, the pipes, fifes and drums, the singing, the speeches, when he was interrupted by Agnes bearing a platter of fine poached salmon surrounded by sprigs of fennel and a light sauce.

"A fine specimen, indeed." Phyllida put her lorgnette to her eyes and observed the platter. Then she looked at Merrick. "Not worth yer getting bashed in the head for, my boy, but angling worthy of an Allen."

Merrick glowed like a little boy under her praise. *Now,* Kathryn silently urged him. *This is the right time. Try again, Merrick.*

Merrick seemed to catch her message, for he leaned forward and opened his mouth as if to address his father.

But it was his Grandmother who spoke—to Kathryn. "My dear, why hasn't that grandson of mine given my aquamarines to ye? They were my grandmother's afore me and would exactly suit your eyes." She turned to Merrick. "I want her to have them, Merrick. To wear with that dress. They would be perfect."

It hung in the air like a heavy, black cloud about to unleash a thunderstorm. At last they spoke—at the same time. "I did, Grandmother." "He did, Mrs. Allen."

They looked at each other and tried again. "They were lost." "Stolen."

"Let me, Merrick," Kathryn said. "Mrs. Allen, Merrick gave me your beautiful jewels as a wedding present. He told me how much they meant to him, and I wore them for

229

our wedding. But they were stolen on the voyage over here."

"What? Stolen? Merrick, I distinctly heard you say *lost*. Am I to understand that jewels have been in our family for almost two hundred years have been lost by your carelessness or perfidy?" Phyllida's pale eyes were not gentle now.

"What's this? Got into a card game aboard ship and lost the jewels, did ye?" Egan Allen slapped his white linen napkin down on the polished mahogany table. "It's a good thing that was the only piece of your heritage ever entrusted to ye. It'll be the last." He strode from the room.

"Mrs. Allen, it wasn't Merrick. He hasn't gambled since he became a Christian. Please believe us." But Kathryn knew her words were falling on deaf ears.

The ceremonies started Thursday evening, "The Nicht Afore the Morn," as they all called it. Kathryn wished she had her length of tartan made into a skirt and jacket to wear but, since she didn't, wore the simple gray suit she had traveled in.

Egan had barely spoken to Merrick since dinner the night before, but he did not object to their going together in the family carriage. All the streets of Selkirk that ran out from the Market Place—High Street, Ettrick Terrace, West Port, Kirk Wynd—were filled with people. Egan left the carriage in Back Fues behind Victoria Hall, and they proceeded on foot. Everywhere people were dancing, waving flags, calling to one another, and singing.

Suddenly from ahead of them there came a terrible, piercing wail.

"Oh, Merrick—" Kathryn grabbed his arm "—what is that awful noise?" She started to put her hands over her ears as the screech increased in intensity, but Merrick stopped her.

"That's the pipes. Don't let my father know you don't like them—that would be a sin far worse than any I've committed."

230

"That's *bagpipes?* I thought pipes were a soft, gentle sound like a flute." She resisted the urge to duck her head as she walked forward.

A large, square platform, extending high above the heads of the throng, had been erected in the open area in front of the Town Hall. From that building a fife and drum corps, all clad in traditional kilts proclaiming their clans, led the way through the crowd. Everyone moved to make way at their approach. Behind the fifes, clad in breeks and plaid, attire that predated the wearing of kilts, strode the Officer of the Burgh.

As they made their way across the Market Square, Kathryn strained to catch the words of the song everyone was singing with the pipes. In the confusion of crowds and noise, they were impossible to distinguish. But she joined those around her in cheering for the Provost when he mounted the platform and began reading out the traditional proclamation.

"Notice! Magistrates and counselors of the Royal Burgh of Selkirk, having fixed tomorrow, Friday, the fourteenth day of June 1909 for the riding of the marches of the common land, having hereby summoned the council they have hereby appointed the following . . ."

There followed a list of those who would be carrying guild flags in the riding tomorrow, but Kathryn's attention strayed. The sight of a remarkable red beard in the crowd to her left made her chill. Of course it wasn't Merrick's old companion from San Francisco. There were red beards enough around here, and if it had been there would be no particular harm in it, she told herself. There was little he could do here to lead Merrick astray—even if Merrick would be led, which she knew he wouldn't.

There was no reason for her head to feel cold and her forehead clammy. It must be her old claustrophobia returning. She had been blessedly free of it since she conquered Kuna Cave, but this throng was a severe test.

The Officer continued his list of names, the crowd cheering after the name and address of each leader, standard-bearer, and attendant. No cheering was greater than that for the bearer of the standard of the Burgh of Selkirk—the flag that must be ridden around the common lands, returned in safety, and then cast in the ancient tradition of Fletcher the Warrior.

"Bearing great honor and responsibility of carrying the flag of our royal and ancient burgh—Robert Bruce Buchanan."

Kathryn held her applause to check first how Merrick responded to the announcement. When she saw him cheering with gusto, she joined in as well.

Then the Provost continued. "There will be all these, and a great many more, and all to make ready to start to ride at the sound of the second drum."

Another great cheer rose from the crowd, followed by a roll on the drums and singing to the fifes. Kathryn longed to know the ballad. She wanted to join in the singing, to be a part of these people from whom her husband had sprung.

Then followed a great playing of a bagpipe band for the bussing of the flags of the ancient Incorporations, or guilds, of Selkirk and of various military units. The fervor of the crowd rose with the passing of each swirling flag and marching unit. At last the band began a new song—one that Kathryn could join in: "Should auld acquaintance be forgot, and never brought to mind, should auld acquaintance be forgot and days of auld lang syne."

The words of Burns's poem sprang to her lips as readily as to any native-born singing of the long ago times, although the pictures she held in her heart were of barren, flat, sage-covered lands, of small, lonely gravestones on the edge of the desert, of hands and faces brown and wrinkled from heat and dryness. Those fields, those graves, those faces were incredibly dear to her, dearer than she had realized in many weeks of absorbing new experiences

232

and dealing with new problems. Now she knew how truly she missed her home and family. "We'll take a cup o' kindness yet for auld lang syne."

Her heart full, she turned to Merrick. "Oh, Merrick, this can't be the end. You can't let it all go. Try again. Try once more to make your father listen."

He didn't answer, but when they returned to Woodburn he requested, and was granted, one last interview with his father. They went into Egan's study and closed the doors.

Kathryn went upstairs with a hopeful heart, but it was not long before even in her upstairs room she heard angry voices rising from below.

So it was over. More truly over than their mere return to Carlisle on Saturday and the subsequent boarding of the train to London, then the ship to America. For Kathryn it was the end of a wonderful trip, the experience of a lifetime, which she would always carry in her heart. For Merrick it was the end of all his hopes—the end of his family ties as surely as if they had all succumbed to the plague. She knew he would not attempt to build a bridge again, nor would it be reasonable to try. He had done all he could; she had prayed all she could. And they had failed.

With a cramp at her heart she realized what that knowledge must cost Merrick. She was saddened for herself; she would love to have a family in Scotland, to write to Phyllida and Rowena, to exchange Christmas parcels. She was losing a great pleasure. Merrick was suffering a bereavement.

She jumped at the slam of their bedroom door. "Merrick, I—" She halted and stepped backward at the look on his face.

"Well, I hope you're happy. I groveled. I pled with him. It made him angrier than when I argued and shouted. Now he's more convinced than ever that I'm doing it all to gain the inheritance—that I shot Raynor for the inheritance —that I'm a no-good schemer, a would-be supplanter."

His face was far harder than the granite of the Sawtooth Mountains at home. "So you lost, my dear. From the

233

first your father urged this course upon me, then you took up his plea. Was it to get the inheritance? Is that what you wanted? Did you marry me thinking you'd be a Scottish heiress if you played your cards right?"

She was too stunned to reply. All she could see was the terrible mistake they had made—*she* had made. They were wrong to have come. She had been wrong to urge him. She realized that now. The old wounds, while not healed, were endurable. Merrick had borne them long and could have gone on so. But now, with all the conflict renewed, the lacerations were fresh—raw and bleeding, torn anew, ragged over old scar tissue that would never heal.

And he blamed her.

He picked up his nightshirt and walked to the door. "You should have let me stay in jail." The door slammed.

Alone in the empty bed in the dark room she prayed. "Oh God, what's happened? Is our marriage over? What did I do wrong? Did I rush ahead and step outside of Your will? What of Merrick? He's your man. Speak to him. Make him call on You. Oh God, please, please. This can't be. You must do something, God."

Always joy had come in the morning—but would it this time? Could even God bring good out of this? She had spent many bad nights in her life, but this was the worst. "Does Your promise hold, God? What are You doing?" Even in the silence she heard her prayers shrieking. She was calling on God with the same desperation she had shouted for Jules by the cave and Merrick by the river. She had allowed her prayers to be overwhelmed by panic.

She forced her mind to still, her breathing to slow, her cramped face and hands to relax. Then she could hear God's voice. Always, when she quit screaming inside she could hear the voice that had been there all the time. *Be of good courage, and he shall strengthen your heart.*

She spoke His promise aloud, "I will keep him in perfect peace whose mind is stayed on thee."

23

"The Bright Morn" of the Common Riding began at sunrise, and Kathryn was up with the first singing of the birds, determined that this, her last day in Selkirk, would be a bright one. Merrick, who looked as if he hadn't closed his eyes all night, seemed determined not to spoil it, for he was polite. Stiff and cold, but polite.

A rousing skirl of bagpipes greeted them at the thronging Market Place. The band struck up a new song, and several hundred voices sang, "Hail, smiling morn, smiling morn, that tips the hills with gold—the rosy fingers of the tilt of day . . . darkness flies away, flies away, darkness flies away. . . . Hail, hail, hail, hail, hail."

In spite of the corner of heaviness in her heart that even her most determined efforts couldn't chase away, Kathryn joined in on the last set of "hails."

Suddenly she was singing with them with no groping for the words as they rejoiced with a familiar hymn: "Lead, kindly light, amid th'encircling gloom; lead Thou me on!"

Kathryn caught her breath at the appropriateness of the words: "The night is dark, and I am far from home; lead Thou me on! Keep Thou my feet; I do not ask to see the distant scene; one step enough for me."

Yes, Lord, her mind cried, as the singers returned to "Hail, smiling morn that tips the hills with gold, darkness flies away . . ."

Then the burgh Officer took the stand with Rowena's Robert behind him. "I now declare the flag of the royal and ancient burgh of Selkirk to be well and truly bussed for the year 1909 and with the handin' of the flag over to the standard-bearer wish him every success in the execution of his duties."

There was a great cheer, none louder than from where the Allens stood, as Robert Bruce Buchanan stepped forward. Her sandy-haired, freckled brother-in-law, with his great bush of eyebrows, seemed to Kathryn to be sturdy as a tree. She smiled at the thought. It was probably just the similarity of *Bruce* and *spruce*—but whatever it was, the name suited him just as it had the Medieval Scottish king who had first borne it.

The Officer continued, "Standard-bearer Buchanan, on this glorious June morning, your flag has been well and truly bussed. As officer of this royal and ancient burgh of Selkirk I charge you to carry this flag aloft around the marches of our burgh lands. Let it be known throughout the world—the souters of Selkirk this morning are celebrating their rights, their privileges, and their heritage.

"Robert, take this flag from me. Return it to me in the Market Square later today unsullied and untarnished."

Cheers rose again as Robert grasped the blue flag with its white cross of Saint Andrews, bearing the gold seal of Selkirk in a white medallion in the center, and brandished it aloft. The wide gold fringe rippled around the border of the banner, and above, bravest of all, fluttered a smaller, green silk pennon, representative of Warrior Fletcher's Flodden Field flag.

The riders took horse. To the beating of drums and the skirl of pipes they were off—two hundred strong. Everyone cheered to the clatter of iron-shod hooves on cobbles. And then they fell silent. As the last of the riders

236

disappeared up the road leading to the hills and fields of the Common Lands the band resumed playing, but the atmosphere seemed dispirited to Kathryn.

She looked at Rowena and thought the excitement had dulled for her too. Perhaps her look was tinged with just a bit of concern for the safety of her twelve-year-old son on his first ride and for the task her husband was charged with. It was no small matter, galloping at the head of two hundred riders, carrying a heavy flag over miles and miles of rugged terrain, and watching out for the safety of a child at the same time.

Kathryn's concerns for Merrick were no less heavy. She knew his spiritual and emotional burdens and hoped he wouldn't take them out in unnecessarily rough riding. "Many's the year there's been blood among the heather," Egan had said.

"Rowena—" she turned to her sister-in-law "—couldn't we follow them? I don't mean the whole way, of course, but aren't there points where we could ride out to see that they're all right—er—that is, to follow their progress, I mean."

Rowena smiled. She knew what Kathryn meant. "Yes! Come. Robert keeps horses at the livery. I even have a saddle there, and we can rent one for you."

They turned to Phyllida for permission, but they didn't even have to ask. "I'd ha done the same thing at your age. Agnes and I'll take a nice cup o' tea at the inn. Off with you."

To Kathryn who grew up on prairie and desert riding astride like a man, the proper ladies' sidesaddle was a new and inhibiting experience, but she soon became accustomed to it.

Although most of Selkirk had chosen to remain in the village, singing with the band and taking refreshment, a few other riders had chosen the same course as Kathryn and Rowena, so there were several on-lookers waiting to cheer the riders when they crossed the top of the first farm of the Common Lands.

The wait wasn't long, but even in that time Kathryn felt her excitement mount. Her horse pricked his ears forward, then she felt a rumbling of the earth. Over the far right rise the first riders appeared with a shout. The leading group galloped down the slope toward the Ettrick Water and clattered across the stone bridge, with other clusters of riders following.

"What's wrong?" Kathryn scanned the riders, her eyes narrowed against the sun. "Where's Robert? Why isn't he in the lead?"

But Rowena explained, "His duty is to bring the flag in unsullied, not necessarily ahead of all riders. Some of the young bloods make it a race, but it's not."

No sooner had she spoken than Kathryn spotted the silken banner, then saw Robert on his cream white horse coming through the heather at the head of a cluster of riders. They were making good time, but not racing. Kathryn searched until she found what she sought. "Oh, there he is." She pointed to Merrick, riding proud and tall on Egan's best chestnut stallion.

"Yes. Oh, I'm so happy he's with his uncle. He'll be fine then."

At Rowena's words Kathryn realized that Robbie was the rider her sister-in-law had been searching for. She was pleased that Rowena trusted Merrick to be her son's companion. Then a dark thought made her shiver. Was that because she knew someone else had caused Raynor's death?

Another sight also disturbed her. "Rowena—" she grabbed her arm and pointed— "who's that—in the gray hat with the red beard?"

Rowena looked, then shrugged. "There must be fifty or more red beards in the field today. How can I know one from another?"

But Kathryn felt a familiar prickle of fear. It was more than the beard, although she couldn't say what. A manner of bearing? The scowl she felt even though she was too far distant to see? The harshness with which the rider whipped his horse?

"Come, let's to the next farm." The other observers were staying until more of the riders passed, but Kathryn and Rowena had seen those they cared most about, although Egan was in a later group.

Instead of going back by the road, Rowena suggested they ride across the hills, following the riders. Kathryn was more than happy to agree. She had always considered riding along roads to be boringly tame fare, and especially now that she was feeling at home on her sidesaddle.

After the many days of rain that had preceded this one, the sky was a clear, gentle blue with the sun smiling on the sweet-scented heather and the birds singing. There could have been no finer day to ride through the hills of the Scottish borderlands.

They came over a rise and paused, admiring the sight of the riders below them and the fine land spread out at their feet with forested hills beyond. Rowena was the first to notice. "Something's amiss. Robbie's not there."

"Perhaps he sped ahead to be with his father?" Kathryn suggested. Then she noticed that Merrick also was absent from the group.

"Nae." Rowena pointed. "Robert's far ahead. Alone."

So he was. The cold prickling Kathryn had felt so often at the back of her neck was with her again. "Perhaps they pulled aside to rest—over that hillock or in that thicket. Let's go see." Kathryn didn't wait for Rowena's reply to turn her horse in the direction she had indicated.

There were, indeed, riders taking a slow pace behind the rise that Rowena called a hummock, but not those they sought. They hurried on toward the trees. These offered welcome shade as the day was nearing noon, so they dismounted, tied their horses to nearby saplings, and walked into the cool, quiet copse.

Kathryn's first impression was that she heard a small animal cry, perhaps one caught in a trap. She clutched Rowena's hand, and they stood listening.

At the next cry they knew the sound was human. Instinctively Kathryn put her hand over Rowena's mouth and shook her head. Something was very wrong indeed. She didn't want Rowena to reveal their whereabouts by crying out until they knew what was going on. Stepping carefully, so as to avoid snapping twigs, they moved toward the sound of the cry.

Then the land leveled, and they saw. Robbie, bound and gagged, his back to a boulder, was valiantly rubbing his fetters across the rough granite surface, although with little effect to the harsh hemp ropes.

A few paces farther on Merrick stood with hands raised, looking steadily at the small, gray steel gun a red-bearded man pointed at him. "So it was you all along, Bo. I should have guessed, I suppose, but all your protests of friendship fooled me. And did ye really shoot Raynor so I'd be blamed and you'd come into your own as residual legatee?" Merrick's laugh was harsh. "It must have been a terrible blow to your plans when ye heard Rowena'd had a son at the very moment you went to so much work to get Woodburn."

"Shut up," Bo growled.

"But I don't see how the authorities are supposed to think I killed Robbie when they find my body here too."

"Robbie will look like a riding accident—poor wee lad and on his first Common Ridin' too. *You* they'll never find."

24

Kathryn drew in her breath silently. She must do something, but what? If she and Rowena rushed the gunman, he'd shoot at least one, if not both of them. She looked at the thicket floor. Branches, fir cones, stones everywhere—but she knew her aim was not nearly good enough to deflect the arm of a killer. *Lord? Help.* For a moment she was quiet. Then she knew.

If she and Rowena rode in from opposite sides they would easily sound like a whole group of riders in the thicket. But they must hurry. Before Bo McLeod pulled that trigger. Her finger to her lips, she pointed back toward the edge of the copse and moved swiftly.

Her fingers fumbled hopelessly as she tried to unknot her reins, and her foot slipped from the stirrup twice in her attempt to mount quickly. From the corner of her eye she saw Rowena in the saddle, spurring her horse to the far side of the trees to carry out the plan Kathryn had whispered to her in a rush.

Once inside the thicket Kathryn began singing at the top of her lungs, "Hail, smiling morn, smiling morn . . ." and beating a stick on the branches to sound like several riders making their way through the trees.

From the other side she heard Rowena call, "Robbie?" then, as if shouting back to others, "Come along this way—I think he's in here. Don't worry, Father, we'll have him soon." Rowena threw several hastily gathered stones to sound like riders approaching from a broad expanse.

Bo McLeod hesitated for the space of a heartbeat. It was enough.

Just as Kathryn broke through into the clearing, Merrick sprang, full-length, arms extended. She stifled her impulse to scream for fear of distracting him. This time there must be no opportunity for a bullet to go astray, perhaps hitting Robbie, nor for a prolonged struggle that would end in a shot, as had his conflict with Hank.

The surprise of Merrick's lunge and his greater strength, combined with confusion over the sound of approaching horses, was enough to buckle McLeod's knees. He went over backward like an uprooted sapling.

Merrick flung the gun beyond reach and pinned Bo securely to the ground.

Rowena jumped from her still moving horse and ran to her son.

"He threw my dirk in the brush," Robbie cried in outrage as soon as Rowena removed his gag. It was clear the youngster was confident he would have made quick work of his assailant had he not been disarmed of the small, sharp dagger Scotsmen traditionally carry. Rowena began searching for it to cut Robbie's ropes.

Merrick flicked his gaze from Bo to Kathryn, then back again. "He shot Raynor."

"I heard." But instead of the great relief and gladness Kathryn thought such news would bring, she felt instead a vast, empty sadness. "What a waste. What a terrible, terrible, evil waste. A young life for your greed—and but for the grace of God there'd have been two more."

She looked at Bo writhing on the thicket floor, saw the beady sharpness of his eyes, and could think of nothing but the rattlesnake that had struck Ned Brewington.

Suddenly it all poured out of her. Without any thought to what she was saying the words came. "It was you all along, wasn't it? You soaped the stairs on the ship, you stole my jewels, you almost drowned Merrick—all evil, greedy, selfishness. There's no end to the evil men will do when they sell their souls for a mess of pottage." She would have gone on, but she stopped to gasp for air.

Merrick nodded toward the gun. "Take that. Watch him while I tie him up." When Kathryn held the weapon steadily in both hands, he turned to pick up the rope Rowena had cut from Robbie's feet.

Not until McLeod's hands were securely tied behind his back did Kathryn shift her eyes from him to the gun in her hand. She would have thought she was incapable of further amazement, but she gasped and stared at the object she held. "I know this gun! I've held it before. Benji Young brought it to Sunday school. I took it away from him. I noticed this odd little mark on the side. What are you doing with Benji's gun?"

Even as she asked, she knew. "Heston. You shot Heston, knowing Merrick would be blamed for it, didn't you?"

McLeod's only answer was a snarl.

"He was only stunned when Benji's gun fired. Benji dropped the gun, and you finished it, didn't you? What did you do—bash him against the anvil?" Kathryn spoke with insight beyond conscious thought.

McLeod snarled again.

They were just emerging from the trees when two riders thundered toward them, one of them carrying the burgh flag.

"Father! Robert!" Rowena cried.

"Are ye all right?" Robert shouted. "Egan caught up to me and said Robbie was nowhere about. Another rider said he saw Robbie knocked from his horse." He looked at the group in front of him. "What's happened?"

Rowena started to answer, but Robbie interrupted her. "Uncle Merrick saved me, Father. This man—" he pointed to Bo "—ran his horse into mine to make it look like an accident. He was going to kill me for Woodburn, but Uncle Merrick stopped him. Then he was going to kill Uncle Merrick, but Mama and Auntie Kathryn stopped him."

"Is this true?" Egan Allen commanded the attention of his family.

"True, Father," Rowena answered. "I heard with my own ears—Bo shot Raynor, knowing Merrick would be blamed—all for the inheritance."

One last item clicked in Kathryn's mind. "Rowena, who told you about all of Merrick's misadventures in America? Was it Bo?"

Rowena considered for a moment. "No, but his mother, and other grapevine sources from Edinburgh way—it must have all come from him."

Robert Bruce stood with his arm around his son. "We owe ye a great deal, Merrick. I don't know that we can ever repay, but . . ." He looked from the flag to Merrick, then at his father-in-law.

Egan nodded. "Aye, 'tis fittin'."

Robert thrust the burgh flag into Merrick's hand. "The honor should have been yours long ago. Carry it for all to see ye've been reinstated in your heritage."

Merrick didn't move. His face showed only amazement. He bowed his head for an instant, whether praying or fighting to control his emotions, Kathryn never knew, but when he raised his face she could see he was fully restored. "Aye, thank you, Robert. I'll carry it with pride, Father."

Merrick mounted and galloped off at tremendous speed, the flag whipping behind him. He had much time to make up.

Egan and Robert turned to deal with the bound McLeod. "We've quite a tale to tell the shirra," Egan said as he hoisted his captive onto his horse.

Kathryn, Rowena, and Robbie, the latter much protesting at not being allowed to complete the Common Riding, but obedient to his father's instructions that he escort the ladies, turned back to town.

Kathryn heard the pipes from the other side of the hill even before she saw the spires and towers of Selkirk. From the cheers she could tell that riders were arriving. Even with having taken a shortcut they arrived back just in time to find Phyllida and Agnes before Merrick thundered in with the flag.

Phyllida dug in her reticule and drew out her lorgnette to make certain her eyes didn't deceive her. "Will someone kindly tell me what's going on?"

Rowena and Kathryn both tried, but Robbie won out. A slow look of satisfied pride spread over Phyllida's face as his story tumbled out. She snapped her lorgnette closed. "Doesn't surprise me a bit. I always thought he was the best of the lot. The most like me."

Merrick mounted the platform then and proclaimed in ringing tones, "Mr. Provost, my attendants and I have been round the burgh marches and found these intact and in good order. And it gives me great pleasure to bring back to you the flag o' the burgh of Selkirk unsullied and untarnished."

A great cheer rose to this proclamation. Kathryn gathered from the look on the Provost's face that he had been apprised of the change of standard-bearers and the reason for it. Apparently Robert and Egan had already reached the sheriff and his men.

"Standard-bearer *Allen*," the Provost pronounced his name with careful clarity, "it gives me particular pleasure to receive back the flag of this ancient and royal burgh unsullied and untarnished. As you have done, so have your forebears. They have ridden our marches and reported to the Provost that all was in good order. To all you folk here at the end of Market Square, let it be a certain sign —changes will come but Common Riding will go on!

"Three cheers for the royal and ancient burgh of Selkirk: Hip, hip, hooray!"

The crowd shouted with him. "Hip, hip,hurray! Hip, hip, hooray!"

Then Merrick was alone on the platform. The drum roll started low and distant-sounding, and Merrick raised ⁺he flag aloft with both arms over his head. As the drums increased they were joined by the fifes, calling forth pictures of men in ancient costume marching bravely into battle. Merrick began swirling the great flag above his head, slowly on the first round, then faster and faster as the drum and fifes built to a crescendo.

Finally, as in a mighty lament, Merrick cast the flag to the ground, his head and shoulders slumping over it, just as his ancestor had on that long ago sad day. A lone piper sounded the note of mourning.

Kathryn saw before her eyes the fallen of Flodden Field, as she saw the fallen of all wars where men had died for freedom and justice. She knew that just so must other men live for freedom and justice under God.

That evening Kathryn wore the heirloom aquamarines. The sheriff had recovered them from Bo's boarding-house room where he'd been staying to work his mischief.

Phyllida peered at them through her lorgnette, then nodded with a satisfied air. "Just as I predicted. They're perfect."

Kathryn smiled at her and turned to Merrick. "But I don't understand how he could have been on the *Carpathia* all that time and we not know it."

Robert answered for Merrick. "I was there when he bragged to the sheriff about how clever he'd been. Seems he had the stateroom across the hall from yours so he could watch your every move."

"But the soap on the stairs—what was he trying to accomplish?" Kathryn shuddered. "Kill me?"

"You or me—or injure one of us. I don't expect he cared much either way. I think he just wanted to do anything he could to spoil things. He must have been getting pretty desperate by then, knowing that if we actually got here the chances of our making up the quarrel were fairly good."

Merrick looked long and deep into Kathryn's eyes. "I can tell you one thing. If he'd hurt you, it would have been the end of everything for me. I'm sure he knew that."

Kathryn shivered, remembering all the chilling times she'd felt she was being watched. "But why would he do all that? Woodburn is a lovely place—but to *kill* for it . . ."

Egan's eyes were hard as he answered her. "His family's poor. His father was a gambler—a no-good who lost heavily and died young in a brawl."

Kathryn suddenly understood why Egan had been so upset by Merrick's wild behavior—thinking he was following a similar lifestyle. Bo must have understood that, too, for he made the most of it. "So Bo reported all of Merrick's misadventures in America to you?"

Rowena answered. "He was a little more clever than that, but that's what it amounted to."

Kathryn shook her head. "What a shame he chose that route to try to restore his family fortunes. He could have done it by spending half the effort on honest labor that he spent scheming and working evil."

"I think it was more than money," Merrick said. "He made good money working for the railroad. I think it was jealousy. Jealousy and covetousness. We were much the same age—he was about three years older, I think. I had been born with every advantage, he with none. I think he wanted to destroy me. And he didn't want just any estate; he wanted Woodburn."

Kathryn shuddered. "But why did he come all the way to Scotland to try to kill you? Why didn't he just kill you off in the States? He must have had lots of opportunities— didn't you travel alone together sometimes?"

Merrick looked thoughtful. "No reason to kill me then. As long as he could keep me estranged from my family with his tales of my misbehavior, that was all he need ed. But when he saw me taking my place in the family at the Common Riding, he must have read into it more than actually existed He had no way of knowing that I'd be leaving unreconciled the next day."

Kathryn was trying to sort it all out. There was so much to understand.

"He was still awfully young to plot Raynor's murder." Kathryn shook her head. "And then he spent the rest of his life scheming. What a waste. His victims' lives weren't the only ones ruined."

"He told the sheriff his shooting Raynor was an accident," Robert said. "I don't know that I believe him. But since he didn't make the accident known, it comes to the same thing as murder."

"Do you think he shot Hank?" Kathryn asked.

"No," Merrick replied. "The gun went off by accident when we were struggling. But I'll bet Bo dealt the cards to make it appear I'd cheated."

"And there's no doubt Heston's killing was cold-blooded." Then Kathryn had a happier thought. "Benji and his family will be so happy to know the cloud has been lifted from them. I can't wait to tell them!"

"So are ye going back then, Son? Can ye no forgive us for misjudging ye so?"

"Of course I can forgive you, Father." Merrick turned to Egan in open-faced amazement. "It was your forgiveness I wanted."

"Well, ye have it. And more." Egan reached down the table and clasped his son's hand. I'll call my solicitor tomorrow and have ye reinstated."

Merrick bowed his head for a moment, when he raised it Kathryn had never seen his smile brighter. "Thank you, Father." Then he hesitated. "But everyone is so tired tonight. Let's discuss it in the morning."

Kathryn and Merrick sat long in their room, talking. Then Merrick was silent, awaiting her answer. What should she say? What did she want? It was so beautiful here—the greenness, the flowers, the sparkling water—wouldn't she be even unhappier with the ugliness and hardship of the desert after seeing this? Here was the beauty she had sought all her life, and she was being offered an opportunity to stay—to stay in the elegance and comfort of Woodburn rather than returning to her barren homestead shack.

It was not an easy choice. She held out her hand. "Let's pray together, Merrick." Side by side they knelt at the edge of the massive, four-poster bed and sought God's direction for their lives.

When they had both prayed Kathryn looked up, her face shining. She got to her feet, walked around the bed, and picked up her Bible from the nightstand. The Lord had answered, as He so often did, with Scripture. It took her only a moment to find the passage in Isaiah: "And the ransomed of the Lord shall return, and come to Zion with songs and everlasting joy upon their heads: they shall obtain joy and gladness, and sorrow and sighing shall flee away."

Then, lest there should be any doubt whether Kuna or Selkirk was to be their Zion, she turned back to the Psalms. "Therefore his people return hither; and waters of a full cup are wrung out to them. So often the Lord prepared a table before me in the desert; so often I found my cup running over."

Merrick took her in his arms. "Aye. That was what I was hoping ye'd say. Robbie will make a fine heir. Already he has a feel for the land." He surprised her with his own quotation, "Yea, the Lord shall give that which is good; and our land shall yield her increase."

Kathryn looked down shyly. "It's not only the land that will yield an increase." She placed a hand on her stomach. "I want our child to be born in America—on our own land."

Epilogue

Kathryn was never more certain of the rightness of her choice than on the July afternoon that the train pulled into Kuna and their friends and neighbors welcomed them home.

"Yes, it is home!" She held out her arms to all of them.

Already, in less than three months, the changes were remarkable. Main Street was lined with finished and half-finished buildings, not the least of which was Myron's livery stable. Kathryn smiled at the quickly built wooden structures. They looked so insubstantial after the stone buildings of Selkirk that had stood for hundreds of years. Yet she knew the same spirit had built them: love of freedom, fierce civic pride, a love of the land. That spirit would carry them through any hard times that might lie ahead.

Jules and Marie drove them out to the little brown homestead shack in the desert.

"We moved into our own place last week," Marie told her, "but I cleaned everything and stocked the cupboards when we got your telegram that you were coming."

"The fields! They're green!" Kathryn gazed around her. Any land not irrigated lay brown and thirsty as always, but where touched by the miracle of water it was producing new life. Kathryn lay her hand on her stomach and repeated the psalm she had quoted at Woodburn, "The waters of a full cup are wrung out to them."

Then she gazed beyond the fields to the rugged blue Sawtooths and the gentler Owyhees in the other direction. There was beauty here—strength and rugged beauty in this raw land. "I will lift up mine eyes unto the hills from whence cometh my help," she murmured.

That night when they sat in the open doorway of their house, Kathryn heard yet another miracle come to the desert. "Crickets!" she cried. "Frogs and crickets! The water brought singing creatures. Someday we'll even have songbirds."

"Aye, and we'll plant roses—a whole bed of red, pink, yellow, everything you want."

Kathryn laughed at his extravagance. "Aren't you the dreamer? I'll settle for sunflowers and daisies—but roses *would* be nice.

Author's Note

Kathryn and Merrick are based loosely on my grand-parents, Esther and Clarence Fletcher, although they did not go to Kuna until after the water came. The actual events of my story are fictionalized, but they are based on pioneer manuscripts by Lucy and Hazel Teed and a descendant of D. R. Hubbard.

Hubbard is one of the few actual names I have used, because his promotion was central to the development of Kuna. Carlson was the first blacksmith. The first postmaster was F. H. Teed, and he did earn $3.27 for his first year of services. The flying ants, coyotes, jackrabbits, and sagebrush are not fictionalized.

The shooting of Heston is based on an actual event that occurred in Kuna a few years later than I have staged it.

My appreciation to Karen Bassford at the Kuna Library and to the librarians at the Boise Public Library, Northwest Collection, and Idaho State Library, Historical Archives.

And to my son, John, who played Jules for me when I rappelled into Kuna Cave one week after my fiftieth birthday.

Moody Press, a ministry of the Moody Bible Institute,
is designed for education, evangelization, and edification.
If we may assist you in knowing more about Christ
and the Christian life, please write us without obligation:
Moody Press, c/o MLM, Chicago, Illinois 60610.